SOCIAL AND INTELLECTUAL NETWORKING
IN THE EARLY MIDDLE AGES

Fig. 1. Detail from Hieronymus Bosch, *Ship of Fools* (1490–1500)

First published in 2023 by Gracchi Books, Binghamton, NY, an imprint of punctum books, Earth, Milky Way.
https://punctumbooks.com

ISBN-13: 978-1-68571-054-5 (print)
ISBN-13: 978-1-68571-055-2 (ePDF)

DOI: 10.53288/0374.1.00

LCCN: 2023935929
Library of Congress Cataloging Data is available from the Library of Congress

Book design: Vincent W.J. van Gerven Oei
Cover image: Alexander Sánchez, The Archeological Park of Reccopolis, The Visigothic Palace

punctumbooks
spontaneous acts of scholarly combustion

GRACCHI

"Too many echoes, not enough voices."
— Cornel West

Michael J. Kelly &
K. Patrick Fazioli (eds.)

Social and Intellectual Networking in the Early Middle Ages

Contents

Editors' Acknowledgments

A single spacE With parallel images; universal representation actualized in time. —Michael J. Kelly

The Visigothic Idea:
Are the Visigoths Still Networking?

Michael J. Kelly

In the opening scene of the *Gilmore Girls* episode "A Deep-Fried Korean Thanksgiving," the mother-daughter, Vladimir-and-Estragon-type duo fire rapid responses at one another about the Kennedys, namely, their family intrigues, history of odd, unfortunate and even bizarre occurrences, and yet also their inherent chic, charm, beauty, independence, happiness, and memorability… they are memorable.[1] It is something in their — in the words of *Crazy Ex*'s Rebecca Bunch — "sexy French depression," the mysterious Catholic Irish-French otherness, Kennedy and Jackie, in contrast to the suburban Connecticut background of our mother–daughter Lorelai and Rory.[2] Who is this wrong-Christian political network challenging the proper-Protestant hegemony? Who are these outsider-insiders? Who are these dis-

---

1   *Gilmore Girls,* "A Deep-Fried Korean Thanksgiving," Season 3, Episode 9, dir. Kenny Ortega, writ. Amy Sherman-Palladino and Daniel Palladino, first aired November 26, 2002, and Samuel Beckett, *Waiting for Godot: A Tragicomedy in Two Acts* (New York: Grove Press, 2011).

2   *Crazy Ex-Girlfriend,* "I'm So Happy That Josh Is Happy," Season 1, Episode 7, dir. Lawrence Trilling, writ. Rachel Bloom and Aline Brosh McKenna, first aired November 23, 2015.

turbers of the status quo who have reached the highest offices in the land, these modern-day Ardaburii? Or, Visigoths?[3]

The Beckettian-form dialogue ends as immediately as it proceeded, and the scene moves to the opening credits, allowing a few moments for audience reflection, or transcending us into another time via space. We reactualize now in another location, the kitchen of Lorelai's "Independence Inn," at a point in which her chef Sookie is mid-food-prep and virtually shouting out orders: "[R]un it through the sieve again, I want it smooth as glass. Don't cut corners, people!"[4] Reminiscent of my own time as a sous-chef in a proper Harrogate establishment, and for anyone else who's worked in a professional kitchen, this is reflective simply of the intensity of the moment mixed with the drive for perfection. Yet, Sookie's opening line is met by Lorelai's sarcastic aside to her ever-sarcastic-sardonic, clichéd French inn manager, Michel, "Is she melting?" to which he responds, "Like butter on a skillet."[5] Lorelai turns then to Sookie for a classic Lorelai–Rory repartee, the show's style, but Sookie disrupts her with a couple of critical remarks to her sous-chefs, insulting them with innuendos related to their lack of sex lives and frustration taken out on the food, their inabilities to (have the opportunity) to perform, take control of their desires, and so aggressively acting out, not unlike Isidore's critique of the Visigothic sexual violence (*rapio*) against Hispania in the *De Origine Gothorum* (or, for that matter, apropos Michel's retort, Sidonius Apollinaris's disgust of the Burgundians spreading smelly butter through their hair).[6]

---

3 On the Ardaburii, see Aleksander Paradziński, "Inclusion and Exclusion of 'Barbarians' in the Roman Elites of the Fifth Century: The Case of Aspar's Family," in *Inclusion and Exclusion in Mediterranean Christianities, 400–800,* ed. Erica Buchberger and Yaniv Fox (Turnhout: Brepols, 2019), 259–78.

4 *Gilmore Girls,* "A Deep-Fried Korean Thanksgiving," at 2'.

5 Ibid.

6 On this reading of Isidore's *De Origine Gothorum* (*Historia Gothorum*), see Michael J. Kelly, *Isidore of Seville and the "Liber Iudiciorum": The Struggle for the Past in the Visigothic Kingdom,* The Medieval and Early Modern Iberian World 80 (Boston and Leiden: Brill, 2021), 114–17. For his expressed distaste of the Burgundians, see Sidonius Apollinaris, *Letters and Poems,*

But what sign is there really of early medieval figures, beyond the manifestations of my own gaze? What is actually happening in the kitchen? "Chaos" Sookie tells us, and, she says, "a travesty," a space now contaminated by the likes of "Bob" the souschef. But there is hope because Bob is trained in the master's (Sookie's) image, not a mere simulacrum but *ex Patre Filioque procedit,* or *Matre* in this case. But what to do when the other nature of the Son is imperfect while (the) Creation is still associated with the Mother/Father? Does that make the Mother/Father less perfect? The imperfections manifest in the creation, in the meal, and so there must be a symbolic meal, beyond imperfection, which can (be) serve(d) as perpetual perfection consumed. An everlasting bread. Lorelai tells Sookie she's (self-)tortured, submitting herself willingly to suffering for her creation (in contrast to the "silent sufferer" Lorelai). At this point, in walks the more-than-emulative savior, the elegant Mother of the mother, Emily, Amalasuintha, offspring of the Great Amal, who will sustain the master's (culturary culinary) ways, Amelia connecting the Valley to the Sea, whose partner will conquer Hannibal and deliver a truly saving meal. Lorelai, in rhetorical monologue, asks the resurrected commander, Emily, "Back from the dead, J…?"[7]

Suddenly revealing herself, the Mother of mothers devours whole the imperfect/perfect, eternal/ephemeral mother, as the latter relates, and as the Mother and the Father, it is announced, will not be in their hometown for the birth of Christ, we are told. As such, the Feast of Family must be at the Thanks-Giving. At the behest of the Four, Lorelai–Rory are now committed to an apocalyptic ("our finest," nay, "final hour," they quip) — or Evangelical? — Feast Day: of canonical Luke, of whom they cannot disappoint; of the Mother Emily, preserving the salvation of the Empire; of Lane, *lana,* the innocent covering and product of the Lord's Sheep, the Christian figure; and Of Sookie, Shoshana

---

ed. and trans. W.B. Anderson, Loeb Classical Library 296 (Cambridge: Harvard University Press, 1963), 212, *Carm.* 12, ls. 1–8.

7   *Gilmore Girls,* "A Deep-Fried Korean Thanksgiving," at 3'30".

molested in oil, saved from the elders by the young Righteous, from the old judges by the new yet Everlasting. Covered in oil. Hosanna in the Highest, 118, Sukkot, the feast of the autumn, the bringing together of the family, the clan, the Kennedys, the community, Stars Hollow.[8] The Eve over, Lorelai–Rory in the morning gather, compile the cornucopia. The arrival at Shoshana's, and her response, "Thank God, civilization has arrived."[9] Look at all that oil, she demands, a vat of oil, being prepared to de-civilize the cooking of a "beautiful, expensive, organically grown turkey," a symbol of upper-middle-class guilt satiated by the prevailing ideology's primary act, consumption, more expense is more morality, the how over the what of food preparation, remarkably akin to thinking inside a different ideological dimension, the Sidonius admiring the Visigothic Theoderic in Toulouse and admonishing generic Burgundians as well as the Vandal Geiseric, the early medieval culinary world and its relation to culture, and ultimately to a (Romano-)Christianity and the latter parts food-feast-divinity trinity.[10] The oil of anointing, the oil of salvation, the Shoshana preserving civilization and all that is good. What is the oil at Shoshana's for? Lorelai: it's "For pouring on Visigoths."[11]

The Visigoths here represent an eclectic knowledge tied to religious imagery and the Dark Ages, versus civilization. As it was for Sidonius, "Visigoth" as an identifier was purified or rather nullified by Theoderic's attention to proper, civilized banqueting, whereas identities like Burgundian were amplified by distasteful, uncivilized dining. As Sidonius would agree, Sookie is right to equate a poorly prepared meal with chaos, early in the episode, and then later, directly with the collapse of civilization.

---

8   See Daniel 13.
9   *Gilmore Girls,* "A Deep-Fried Korean Thanksgiving," at 19′.
10 For discussion on Sidonius and culinary culture in the period, see Emmanuelle Raga, "Romans and Barbarians at the Table: Banquets and Food as Tools of Distinction according to Sidonius Apollinaris (Fifth-Century Gaul)," in *Inclusion and Exclusion in Mediterranean Christianities,* ed. Buchberger and Fox, 239–58.
11 *Gilmore Girls,* "A Deep-Fried Korean Thanksgiving," at 19′.

And this early medieval connection or association is evident, it would appear, to the writers, who, in the latter scene, equate the Visigoths to uncivilized dining — deep-fried turkey — to the eating of the plebs or barbarians or *rustici* — I mean, same thing, after all. The oil not only typifies this, but it is also said to be poured on the Visigoths, an anointing of the Visigoths, as the subsequent Catholic political leaders, with a vulgar version of the classical world, a Bob-simulacrum, not an Emily–Lorelai reproduction, Emily with her — we'd go on to see — perfectly prepared, civilized meal. But this false anointing horrifies Sookie, the oil being salvific, leading to suffering that ultimately ends with encountering the prophetic and the very hand of God. This is not the role played by the Visigoths in the narrative.

More than a nostalgic flashback to an annjoyable show, what this reading of the Visigoths in *Gilmore Girls* reveals is what I call the "Visigothic Idea," a universal truth with unlimited networking capacity, engendering infinitely the signifier "Visigoth," which oscillates between immanence and transcendence, which can serve as, as in the case of the *Gilmore Girls* episode, a non-actualized object of the Real, which, as the sublimated fabric of that present world (situation), appears momentarily as a confirmation of actually existing truths, just as "communist" tends to appear in Western discourse today not as a rebirth of the Communist Idea but as a confirmation of the capitalist truth, that is, as the foil that confirms the "obvious" righteousness of capitalist ideology, i.e., the present world. In this case, "Visigothic" confirms the barbaric nature of deep-frying a "beautiful, expensive, organically grown turkey," that is, of using popular, "low-culture" working-class food-preparation techniques to prepare what is a quintessentially mainstream middle-class food item. In order words, Lorelai and Sookie do not reveal the Visigothic (or medieval or barbarian, etc.) idea but rather promote, using both a functioning trope (barbaric), and a comedy that appeals to their middle-class (or middle-class admiring) audience, something that is awful within the prevailing logic, the capitalist truth, that is, the breaking through the walls of the traditional, elite customs by alternative, barbarian, ways of life.

This presents, then, not only an analysis of the meaning of Visigoth in the present, but also, more importantly I think, serves as an example of the universal truth "Visigoth(ic)" as unactualized or transcendent. This specific actualization, or historical realization, of the Visigothic Idea stands in stark contrast to the Visigothic Idea as it was actualized in, for instance, seventh-century Hispania, when "Visigoth" represented a prevailing logic and appeared as an immanent truth. When Goth or Visigoth was used, whether by Isidore or in the Councils or in the formularies or inscriptions, it represented Visigoth as in itself an object of ideology, as opposed to a sublimated *unter*-trope.

Thus, what we see presented to us in the *Gilmore Girls* episode is a popular (middle-class) American vision of the Visigoths, not a representation of a once-and-only-once-been historical subjectivity now only imaginable as an object out of time, nor simply of inauthentic and authentic Daseins coexisting in and over space-time, but rather a continuous network of Visigoths from Liuvigild to Lorelai, from Recciberga to Rory, from Floresinda to Sookie, from Isidore sitting down to compose the *Etymologies,* to anonymous editors in 655 redacting its book VI computistics, to the Longleat House fragment, to Paris BnF lat. 5543, to Vat. Reg. Lat. 1024, to the scribe of Paris BnF lat. 1557, who added Isidore to Sisebut's reign, to the scribe Sisebut of the *Codex Aemelianensis,* to the first "Isidorian Renaissance" discussions, to Jean-Luc Picard's wondering if "Honorius watching the Visigoths coming over the seventh hill truly realized the Roman Empire was about to fall,"[12] to Americans' thoughts on the Visigoths as their own Senate was overrun, to "Quicumque igitur a nobis vel totius Spaniae populis qualibet coniuratione vel studio sacramentum fidei suae, quod pro patriae gentisque Gothorum statu vel observatione regiae salutis pollicitus est, temeraverit aut regem nece attractaverit aut potestate regni exue-

---

12 *Star Trek: The Next Generation,* "The Best of Both Worlds, Part 1," Season 3, Episode 26, dir. Cliff Bole, writ. Gene Roddenberry, first aired June 16, 1990, at 20'.

rit, aut praesumtione tyrannica regni fastigium usurpaverit"[13]
to "Insigni merito et Geticae de stirpe senatus,"[14] to "Eius in-
terventu quidam vir nobilis ex Visegothorum propagine, clarus
genere, Agapius nomine,"[15] to "La loi des Wisigoths voulait que,[16]
to exactly right now as I write this in 2021, the scenes of Isidore
completing the *De Origine Gothorum* or Reccared II fatefully
ascending the throne are being received as the present on the
exoplanet Kepler-452b (warping our notion of time and space
into space as time).

What unites all of these "Visigoths" is the Visigothic Idea.[17]
Through it, the Visigoths in *Gilmore Girls,* as all of these Visigoths, are part of a living network, with its materialist-dialecti-
cal origins in some evental "Visigoth" or "Visigothic" moment,
and, as such, the Visigoths in Fontaine are effectively the same as
those sitting in Seville in 619, or Toledo in 672, or at Covadonga
in 722, or even those in the undelivered graduation speech of
New York University's late professor of communication arts,
Neil Postman:

13 IV Toledo's canon 75, ed. Gonzalo Martínez Díez and Félix Rodríguez, *La
    Colección Canónica Hispana* 5 (Madrid: Consejo Superior de Investigacio-
    nes Científicas, 1992), 252: "From this point on, whoever, of us or anyone
    from the whole of Spain, by any conspiracy or other means, violates the
    oath made for the security of the king and the prosperity of the Gothic state
    and people, or recklessly endangers the king, undermines the authority of
    the monarchy, or tyrannically attempts to usurp the throne."

14 Form. Wis. 20, ed. Edorta Córcoles Olaitz, *Las "Formulae Wisigothicae":
    Aproximación a la práctica jurídica visigoda* (Lecce: Edizioni Grifo, 2010),
    105–12: "Distinguished by merit and Gothic of senatorial lineage."

15 Inventionis Zoili, 4, ls. 8–10, ed. Ángel Fábrega Grau, *Pasionario Hispánico
    (Siglos VII–XII)* (Madrid: Consejo Superior de Investigaciones Científicas,
    1953), 380: "At his intervention, an aristocrat by the name of Agapius, illus-
    trious by birth and of Visigothic heritage."

16 Montesquieu, *De l'Esprit des Lois,* 16, ch. 25: "The laws of the Visigoths
    wanted that."

17 For a theoretical grounding of the Kantian "Idea," see Alain Badiou, "The
    Communist Hypothesis," *New Left Review* 49 (2008), https://newleftreview.
    org/issues/ii49/articles/alain-badiou-the-communist-hypothesis, and, of
    course, Immanuel Kant, *Critique of Pure Reason,* trans. Max Müller and
    Marcus Weigelt (New York: Penguin, 2008), esp. on the transcendental aes-
    thetic, 59–84.

The second group of people lived in the place we now call Germany, and flourished about 1,700 years ago. We call them the Visigoths, and you may remember that your sixth or seventh-grade teacher mentioned them. They were spectacularly good horsemen, which is about the only pleasant thing history can say of them. They were marauders—ruthless and brutal. Their language lacked subtlety and depth. Their art was crude and even grotesque. They swept down through Europe destroying everything in their path, and they overran the Roman Empire. There was nothing a Visigoth liked better than to burn a book, desecrate a building, or smash a work of art. From the Visigoths, we have no poetry, no theater, no logic, no science, no humane politics.[18]

When in the episode (or, logical set) "Kill-Switch," Dana Scully asks "InVisigoth?" about an electronic address and Fox Mulder inquires to a character standing nearby, "Are you InVisigoth?" they establish another node "Visigoth" in a continuous and universal network, they splice rhizomatically the sprawling plateau of the Visigothic Idea's ontological infinity.[19] The success of this splicing, this reterritorialization of the Visigothic Idea, depends on the capital that an actor has within a network. When *Gilmore Girls,* for instance, rebirths Visigoth and presents the idea in a certain way, that brings or sustains an actualization of Visigoth in a more concrete way across a wide chain of actors (viewers) inside of a specific, historical, popular network, as opposed to a historian eliciting the Visigoths, as the historian typically has less networking capital in our society than a Hollywood actor. Yet, the historian holds the power of radicality.

Historiography is effective by revealing hidden knowledge and meaning in the present by way of the past broken through into it, while language and scenes in the narrative operate as

---

18 Neil Postman, "My Graduation Speech," *Yearbook of the National Society for the Study of Education* 107, no. 2 (2008): 161–64, at 162.

19 *The X-Files,* "Kill Switch," Season 5, Episode 11, dir. Rob Bowman, writ. Chris Carter, William Gibson, and Tom Maddox, first aired February 15, 1998, at 12'.

nodes for alternative historical paths, as ways for the historian to expose the logics, or defining features, of the present situation. As a category, then, history should preserve fidelity to this event, the Event. The evental as historical category reflects a fidelity to an alternative truth, but also serves as a reminder that genuine fidelity to it — to the evental truth, e.g., the Visigothic Idea — should never reach completion (hence Isidore's theological commitments to historiography as form and the open process of conversion[20]). The event of radical change engendered by the historian is a perpetual, universal process that is never completed: full conversion would equal the end of the Idea's presence. If and when it is forced and becomes a declared meaning — when the historian

---

20 Conversion is the continual process of preparing for Judgment Day: Revelations 20. On Isidore's views of conversion, including as a gradual process of learning, see his *Sententiae,* 2.8 and *De Viris Illustribus,* 28. In the secondary literature, see Henriette-Rika Benveniste, "On the Language of Conversion, Visigothic Spain Revisited," *Historein* 6 (2006): 72–87, and Wolfram Drews, *The Unknown Neighbour: The Jew in the Thought of Isidore of Seville* (Boston and Leiden: Brill, 2006), 224, n. 134, who argues that Isidore "regards the daily conversion of a Christian as a voluntary act. Every Christian is called upon to convert, which is understood as an active process […]. The conversion is brought about and made by God's grace." Also, Jacques Fontaine, "Conversion et culture chez les Wisigoths d'Espagne," *Settimane di Studio* 14 (1967): 87–147, at 132, calls the Isidorian Renaissance Isidore's "continuous conversion" of the Visigoths. Isidore's theological position is mediated through Pope Gregory the Great who said in a 591 letter to the bishops in Arles and Marseilles, "The Word is therefore to be used for those who ought to overcome in themselves the thorns of error and preaching to enlighten those it clouds" ("adhibendus ergo illis est sermo, qui et errorum in ipsis spinas urere debeat et praedicando quod in his tenebrascit inluminet"). (Paul Ewald and Ludovic M. Hartmann, eds., *Gregorii I Papae Registrum Epistolarum, Libri I-VII,* Monumenta Germaniae Historica [Berlin: Weidmann, 1891], I, 45, 71–72). There were multiple occasions on which Pope Gregory demanded the kind treatment of Jews, about which see Solomon Grayzel, "The Papal Bull *Sicut Judeis,*" in *Studies in Essays in Honor of Abraham A. Neuman,* ed. Meir Ben-Horin, Bernard D. Weinryb, and Solomon Zeitlin (Boston and Leiden: Brill, 1962), 243–80. For Isidore's *Sententiae,* see Pierre Cazier, *Isidorus Hispalensis Sententiae,* Corpus Christianorum Series Latina 111 (Turnhout: Brepols, 1998), and for his *DVI,* see Carmen Codoñer Merino, *El "De Viris Illustribus" de Isidoro de Sevilla: Estudio y Edición crítica* (Salamanca: Consejo Superior de Investigaciones Científicas, 1964).

performs as the actors in our series do, confirming the ideology of the present by reaching into the Visigothic network — it retreats as a truth. This reduction of the universal to a particular situation transcends the referent Idea without diminishing its universality or, as such, its networking capacities. The Visigothic Idea, like the Communist Idea or the Trinitarian Truth, as a universal can never be permanently reduced to the singular, whether it is the seventh-century Hispanian or the 21st-century American or the chronologically independent Kepler-452b.

And yet, each of these historical events — like the conversion process, hence the early medieval Christian anxiety — opens up the present to alternative existence and meaning: Lorelai's Visigoths are a potential caesura, a true historical event resulting from of a logic within a situation (here American capitalist ideology) reaching an event horizon followed by the indeterminate announcement of the excess (that knowledge which does not fit into the logic of the present, i.e., the Visigoths as both monstrous to the logic of the present and *that* as being their admirable quality). The emergence of the excess, what I call the "antihistorical" act, historically awakens the political subject and ties history formally to the pre-political and the political.[21] The subject is an exception to the situation, in a relationship to something in its world as also to something outside of it, an alternative truth, and it is at this level that history is interesting, relevant, and progressive regardless of whether it is premodern or modern, Eurocentric or not, because it is here that the subject can touch the infinite and elicit alterity. Political solutions emerge from beyond history, yet history is fundamental to their creation. Historiography is a perpetual dialectic — between history and politics — and this is why it is entangled with politics and necessary for alterity: History is radical potential; the historical is, as Lorelai shows, the confirmative.

---

21 For more on my notion of "Antihistory," see Michael J. Kelly, "Approaching a Non-Modern Historical Theory: Catholic Theology, Alain Badiou, and Antihistory," in *Understanding Badiou, Understanding Modernism,* ed. Arka Chattopadhyay and Arthur Rose (London: Bloomsbury, forthcoming).

In closing, network theory craves datasets from which to draw conclusions. How is a historian dedicated to the field as a humanities discipline, and who thinks rhizomatically and dialectically, supposed to engage such social-scientific conceptualizing? The answer is that the Continental approach to the question of Visigothic networking proposed here not only complements the largely Analytical argument that is to follow in this volume, it also opens up the possibility of collecting a massive data set on historical actualizations of the Visigothic Idea that transcends disciplinary categorizations, conventional ideas of fiction/nonfiction, and even space-time itself, allowing historians to analyze the assemblage "Visigoth(ic)" without any single actualization of the idea — whether of Recciberga or Rory — any more inherently legitimate as Visigothic than the other, just as no individual territorialization of the Communist Idea is any more authentic than the next; no actualization, no historical "eventing" ever negates the universality of the Visigothic Idea, or negates its radical potential.

As Sven Meeder will show in the following Introduction, the rest of the chapters in this volume are, I am sure happily for the reader, less Kantian-Badiouan, although K. Patrick Fazioli's contribution has its philosophical moments. I say philosophical because my co-editor's chapter properly develops the theoretical modeling of the network theory that fueled this volume and was the basis of the conference that led to it. That international research event was held in September 2017 in Nijmegen and at Radboud University, led by me and Sven Meeder, a joint conference of the respective networks, Networks and Neighbours and Networks of Knowledge. I would like to thank Sven, Radboud, and their European funding agencies, my own Binghamton University for its support for making that event happen, Richard Broome for connecting me to Sven Meeder and his Networks of Knowledge, and the blind peer-reviewers for this volume. One of the most rewarding aspects of running OA research activities is getting to experience how many colleagues are truly dedicated to the research over and above the logics, determinations, and false essentialities of capitalism.

Bibliography

Manuscripts
Codex Aemelianensis. Madrid. Real Biblioteca del Monasterio de San Lorenzo de El Escorial d.I.1.
Paris. Bibliothèque nationale de France, lat. 1557. https://gallica.bnf.fr/ark:/12148/btv1b100324392.
Paris. Bibliothèque nationale de France, lat. 5543. https://archivesetmanuscrits.bnf.fr/ark:/12148/cc64506m.
Vatican City. Biblioteca Apostolica Vaticana, Reg. lat. 1024. https://digi.vatlib.it/view/MSS_Reg.lat.1024.

Primary & Reference
Beckett, Samuel. *Waiting for Godot: A Tragicomedy in Two Acts.* New York: Grove Press, 2011.
Crazy Ex-Girlfriend. "I'm So Happy That Josh Is Happy." Season 1, Episode 7. Directed by Lawrence Trilling. Written by Rachel Bloom and Aline Brosh McKenna. First aired November 23, 2015.
Córcoles Olaitz, Edorta, ed. *Las "Formulae Wisigothicae": Aproximación a la práctica jurídica visigoda.* Lecce: Edizioni Grifo, 2010.
Gilmore Girls. "A Deep-Fried Korean Thanksgiving," Season 3, Episode 9. Directed by Kenny Ortega. Written by Amy Sherman-Palladino and Daniel Palladino. First aired November 26, 2002.
Inventionis Zoili. In *Pasionario Hispánico (Siglos VII–XII),* edited by Ángel Fábrega Grau, 379–81. Madrid: Consejo Superior de Investigaciones Científicas, 1953.
Isidore of Seville. *De Viris Illustribus.* Edited by Carmen Codoñer Merino. *El "De Viris Illustribus" de Isidoro de Sevilla: Estudio y Edición crítica.* Salamanca: Consejo Superior de Investigaciones Científicas, 1964.
———. *Sententiae.* Edited by Pierre Cazier. *Isidorus Hispalensis Sententiae.* Corpus Christianorum Series Latina 111. Turnhout: Brepols, 1998.

Martínez Díez, Gonzalo, and Félix Rodríguez, eds. *La Colección Canónica Hispana* 5. Madrid: Consejo Superior de Investigaciones Científicas, 1992.

Montesquieu. *De l'Esprit des Lois.* Paris, 1748.

Pope Gregory I. *Gregorii I papae Registrum Epistolarum, Libri I–VII.* Edited by Paul Ewald and Ludovic M. Hartmann. Monumenta Germaniae Historica. Berlin: Weidmann, 1891.

Sidonius Apollinaris. *Letters and Poems.* Edited and translated by W.B. Anderson. Loeb Classical Library 296. Cambridge: Harvard University Press, 1963.

Star Trek: The Next Generation. "The Best of Both Worlds, Part 1." Season 3, Episode 26. Directed by Cliff Bole. Written by Gene Roddenberry. First aired June 16, 1990.

The X-Files. "Kill Switch." Season 5, Episode 11. Directed by Rob Bowman. Written by Chris Carter, William Gibson, and Tom Maddox. First aired February 15, 1998.

Secondary

Badiou, Alain. "The Communist Hypothesis." *New Left Review* 49 (2008). https://newleftreview.org/issues/ii49/articles/alain-badiou-the-communist-hypothesis.

Benveniste, Henriette-Rika. "On the Language of Conversion, Visigothic Spain Revisited." *Historein* 6 (2006): 72–87. DOI: 10.12681/historein.61.

Drews, Wolfram. *The Unknown Neighbour: The Jew in the Thought of Isidore of Seville.* Boston and Leiden: Brill, 2006. DOI: 10.1163/9789047408925.

Fontaine, Jacques. "Conversion et culture chez les Wisigoths d'Espagne." *Settimane di Studio* 14 (1967): 87–147.

Grayzel, Solomon. "The Papal Bull *Sicut Judeis.*" In *Studies in Essays in Honor of Abraham A. Neuman,* edited by Meir Ben-Horin, Bernard D. Weinryb, and Solomon Zeitlin, 243–80. Boston and Leiden: Brill, 1962.

Kant, Immanuel. *Critique of Pure Reason.* Translated by Max Müller and Marcus Weigelt. New York: Penguin, 2008.

Kelly, Michael J. *Alain Badiou: A Graphic Guide.* London: Icon Books, 2014.

————. "Approaching a Non-Modern Historical Theory: Catholic Theology, Alain Badiou, and Antihistory." In *Understanding Badiou, Understanding Modernism,* edited by Arka Chattopadhyay and Arthur Rose. London: Bloomsbury, forthcoming.

————. *Isidore of Seville and the "Liber Iudiciorum": The Struggle for the Past in the Visigothic Kingdom.* The Medieval and Early Modern Iberian World 80. Boston and Leiden: Brill, 2021.

Paradziński, Aleksander. "Inclusion and Exclusion of 'Barbarians' in the Roman Elites of the Fifth Century: The Case of Aspar's Family." In *Inclusion and Exclusion in Mediterranean Christianities, 400–800,* edited by Erica Buchberger and Yaniv Fax, 259–78. Turnhout: Brepols, 2019. DOI: 10.1484/M.CELAMA-EB.5.116688.

Postman, Neil. "My Graduation Speech." *Yearbook of the National Society for the Study of Education* 107, no. 2 (2008): 161–64. DOI: 10.1111/j.1744-7984.2008.00190.x.

Raga, Emmanuelle. "Romans and Barbarians at the Table: Banquets and Food as Tools of Distinction according to Sidonius Apollinaris (Fifth-Century Gaul)." In *Inclusion and Exclusion in Mediterranean Christianities, 400–800,* edited by Erica Buchberger and Yaniv Fax, 239–58. Turnhout: Brepols, 2019. DOI: 10.1484/M.CELAMA-EB.5.116687.

Introduction

Sven Meeder

When, sometime in the early nineteenth century, scholars at the library of the abbey of St. Gall found in a medieval book binding a small snippet of parchment measuring only about 2.5 by 2.5 inches, they had very little to go on in order to determine its significance. These scholars, who may have been the celebrated librarians Johann Nepomuk Hauntinger and Ildefons von Arx, must have recognized the timeworn parchment and the ancient insular letters, but the surviving words were too scanty to identify the original text. Assessing the value of this scrap of parchment revealed that there were just too few dots to connect it. As a result, the fragment did not find its way into one of the famous *fragmentaria* compiled by Hauntinger and Von Arx, but instead it got lost between the pages of a seventeenth-century catalogue of early prints and remained out of sight for over a century.

A large cleaning operation of the historic reading room of St. Gall's library in January 1955 resulted in the rediscovery of this parchment strip. By that time scholars had unearthed additional dots with which to connect our fragment. It became clear that this was a companion to three strips of parchment reclaimed from medieval codices since the 1930s by none other than Alban Dold and a young Bernard Bischoff. Together the four pieces form one of the oldest known fragments of Isidore of Seville's *Etymologiae,* the sad remains of what appears to have been a glorious copy in Irish script, which we can date to the middle of the seventh century.[1]

The presence of these snippets at the St. Gall Stiftsbibliothek (now known as MS 1399a, Nr. 1) and their discovery represents the culmination of a long series of intellectual contacts and dissemination of learning. The fragments testify to an early spread of the writings of Isidore (d. 636) from Visigothic Spain to readers and scribes trained in Irish script, probably in Ireland itself.[2] This demonstrates not only the speed of early medieval intellectual exchange, but also the potential for Latin scholarship to be received with interest and enthusiasm by scholars thousands of miles away from its original author. Further philological study offers a glimpse of the (subsequent) routes taken by the text and suggests that MS 1399a, Nr. 1 has textual relationships not only with another seventh-century fragment in Irish script[3] but also with the version of the *Etymologiae* in the manuscript now in Leiden's University Library under the signature MS Voss. F.74.

---

1   St Gallen, Stiftsbibliothek MS 1399a, Nr. 1. See Alban Dold and Johannes Duft, *Die älteste irische Handschriften-Reliquie der Stiftsbibliothek St. Gallen mit Texten aus Isidors Etymologien* (Beuron in Hohenzollern: Beuroner Kunstverlag, 1955); Marina Smyth, "Isidorian Texts in Seventh-Century Ireland," in *Isidore of Seville and His Reception in the Early Middle Ages*, ed. Andrew Fear and Jamie Wood (Amsterdam: Amsterdam University Press, 2016), 111–30, at 118–22.

2   See Bernhard Bischoff, "Die Europäische Verbreitung der Werke Isidors von Sevilla," in *Isidoriana: Colección de Estudios Sobre Isidoro de Sevilla*, ed. Manuel C. Diaz y Diaz (Leon: Centro de Estudios "San Isidoro", 1961), 317–44, repr. Bernhard Bischoff, *Mittelalterliche Studien: Ausgewählte Aufsätze zur Schriftkunde und Literaturgeschichte* (Stuttgart: Anton Hiersemann, 1966), 171–94, at 180; Johannes Duft and Peter Meyer, *Die irischen Miniaturen der Stiftsbibliothek St. Gallen* (Olten: Urs Graf Verlag, 1953), 82; but compare Johannes Duft, "Die Irische Handschriften der Stiftsbibliothek St. Gall," in *Die Iren und Europa im früheren Mittelalter*, ed. Heinz Löwe (Stuttgart: Klett-Cotta, 1982), 916–37, at 931, and Claudia Di Sciacca, *Finding the Right Words: Isidore's "Synonyma" in Anglo-Saxon England* (Toronto: University of Toronto Press, 2008), 59.

3   The so-called Longleat fragments are described by James P. Carley and Ann Dooley, "An Early Irish Fragment of Isidore of Seville's *Etymologiae*," in *The Archaeology and History of Glastonbury Abbey*, ed. Lesley Abrams and James P. Carley (Woodbridge: Boydell Press, 1991), 135–61.

This ninth-century book which itself is testimony to the scholar Lupus's personal connections with Ferrières and the intellectual powerhouse Fulda. On a more material level, the lively exchange of books of the early medieval West brought the seventh-century Irish copy of the *Etymologiae* to St. Gall, home to a bustling interest in Isidorian work, as Evina Steinová describes in this volume. Despite this fact (or maybe because of it), the copy that predated the foundation of St. Gall Abbey was cut up sometime in the tenth century (probably), and its leaves were used to reinforce the bindings of other books. This enterprise now connects a number of composite manuscripts to each other and is testament to a tenth-century intellectual intervention. When the various dots are thus connected, it underscores the fact that the St. Gall fragment moved (and continues to move) in a network of intellectual connections that traverse both space and time.

Historians of intellectual history have shifted their focus in recent decades from eminent institutions or "great men" to the connections between historical actors and the communities of learning they formed. Inspired by the social sciences, the term "network" has been adopted to describe the myriad of textual, personal, cultural, and institutional relations and interconnections of historical artifacts, people, and even ideas. The "network" not only provides historians with a theoretical framework and a host of novel methodological approaches (carefully outlined by K. Patrick Fazioli in this volume), it is also a powerful metaphor, evoking a clear image of "an arrangement or structure with intersecting lines and interstices" (quoting the *Oxford English Dictionary*). This sharp mental picture is helpful in an age that favors the image over text, and funding bodies that prefer scientific-looking "data" over narratives. In fact, with the help of sophisticated, yet freely available software, it has become ever easier to present networks in the form of graphs. Though not all equally articulate or clear-cut, network graphs have become increasingly prevalent in historical publications, including those concerned with networks in the Middle Ages.

The study of historical networks is characterized by diverse approaches, multifarious subject matters, and vast differences in scale and nature. Every study, however, subscribes to the intrinsic truth that human interaction is behind every creative act. For every historian studying medieval scholarship, this seems self-evident: manuscripts were not compiled in splendid isolation, but were the products of communities of collaborating scholars, scribes, teachers, and even the herdsman tending to the livestock whose skins became parchment. Texts, equally, were not written, read, or copied in a vacuum, and scholarship did not (and does not) survive perfect disconnection. Even when ignited by a spark of individual genius, new thoughts are always built on previous ideas. The transmission of ideas is essential for any intellectual dynamism, and in the early Middle Ages this depended on networks of communication that took the form of instruction and discussion among scholars, as well as the physical transport of books, booklets, and letters, and the actual travel of learned men and women.

Notwithstanding the pellucidity of the role of networks of connections in medieval intellectual life, the study of medieval social and intellectual networks is not necessarily straightforward. The nature of the lines (or edges) in the metaphorical network graphs is never completely known to us, and neither is the precise behavior of the dots (or nodes). The chapters in this volume describe a range of applications of the study of social and intellectual networks in the early medieval West and address some of the pertinent questions to which this historical study gives rise. The papers are the result of a lively exchange of ideas and fruitful discussions held during the international conference "Intellectual and Social Networks" in Nijmegen in August and September 2017 under the auspices of the project "Networks of Knowledge: The Spread of Scholarship in the Carolingian Era," funded by the Dutch Research Council (Nederlandse Organisatie voor Wetenschappelijk Onderzoek, NWO), and in collaboration with the international project based in Binghamton, NY, Networks and Neighbours. The conference mostly took place in a side chapel of Nijmegen's historic St. Stephen's Church, a central node in the city's network since its thirteenth-century dedication by Saint Albertus Magnus himself. The meeting was the reflection and expansion of our own intellectual networks, and in keeping with the theme of the conference, the speakers were invited to continue their conversations with their papers' respondents well after the conference. The studies in this volume represent the fruit of these interactions during and after our social and intellectual networking in Nijmegen. They are diverse in their approaches, themes, and subject matter and provide a valuable overview of case studies of intellectual and social networks in the early medieval West.

A first and obvious question would be to scrutinize the title of this book: what exactly is a social network? And what are we to understand an intellectual network to be? And how does it work? Here, imagining the visual representation of a network as a graph is actually helpful, with nodes connected by edges, visualizing a set of relational data, in particular the connections, relationships, and dependencies between human or nonhuman entities. A *social* network foregrounds the relationships between individuals or communities of people, which may be (re)constructed by data on family links, correspondence between people, relationships in "real life," or connections on social media online platforms. As Patrick Fazioli reminds us in his chapter, social network analysis was long thought to be particularly relevant to connections shaped by modern social media.

Academics have demonstrated, however, that networks can be shaped by more than mouse clicks and "likes" and that social networks are not the only flavor. *Intellectual* networks can be seen as a subset of social networks, where information exchange is the primary function of the connections. We find the traces of intellectual exchange in the different text recensions of medieval works in extant manuscripts, the influence of scholarly works and learned ideas in new compositions, the surviving letters of correspondence between intellectuals, and the narratives of travels and interactions between scholars, educators, and men of learning. But in essence, the network graph aims to sketch the contours of the continuous flow of inspiration and influence between minds.

The capacity of network analysis to work with large and complex databases, as well as its flexibility, offers promising applications for studying the circumstances and development of learning in the Middle Ages. In his very welcome overview of the history of network analysis for studying the medieval past, Fazioli addresses the methodology's strengths, risks, and limitations, as well as its theoretical underpinnings. Network theory's flexibility allows us to use sources such as manuscripts, texts, and artifacts as proxy evidence for human movement and communication.

Manuscripts can be said to be in relationship with one another by virtue of containing the same text(s). Similarly, texts are connected by virtue of being copied in the same manuscript, as a product of a scribe's or scholar's vision of the most useful combination of learned works. Elizabeth Archibald's paper employs the tools of network analysis in her study of grammatical miscellanies from the age of Charlemagne and Louis the Pious. While these didactic *florilegia* were compiled according to the often very individual choices of schoolmasters, they function in a network of learning in which curricular content was spread and shared among schoolmasters. Network analysis has the potential to show us the contours of the core texts of elementary grammar curriculum, drawing us closer to the early medieval "mindset" on grammatical education. Especially when analyzing large data sets, this research method can present unexpected results, which help us to formulate new questions with which to return to the manuscripts or the learned texts.

Adapting a phrase from Archibald's essay: no self-contained intellectual universes exist. Every element in a graph of intellectual networks represents an active deed of dissemination and reception: letters are written and read; texts are copied, rephrased, and adapted; books are lent out, borrowed, transported, composed, or pulled apart. Intellectual networks are thereby responsible not simply for transporting learning; they increase and propagate the products of intellectual activity. Intellectual networks thus differ fundamentally from economic and trade networks, or even networks of political power. The transportation of goods along trade routes does not increase the number or volume of those goods, and, other than aging and possible decay, the products will be identical on either end of the journey. Not so with the primary commodities of intellectual networks: ideas and insights.

Networks of learning amplify intellectual products, be they ideas or texts. A successful idea is very often a well-connected idea, as Steinová demonstrates in her paper on the innovations made by early medieval scholars in their reception, glossing, and adaptation of the first book of the *Etymologies*. Steinová demonstrates that, while the decision to separate the first book of Isidore's *Etymologies* from the rest of the text in order to teach grammar was probably not a Carolingian idea, it nevertheless took flight because it fitted extremely well with the educational, societal, and political ideals of their *renovatio*. The success of an innovation is thus not (entirely) dependent on the place of origin of the innovation, but rather on its connectedness to an active network that is willing to receive the innovation with interest. Meanwhile, this willingness is governed by more than intellectual preferences only: political, cultural, religious, and economic concerns all play a role.

Intellectual networks are never wholly insulated from social relationships of a different character or developments in the outside world. In Ksenia Bonch Reeves's essay on the rhetoric employed in a key episode in the ninth-century Iberian *Chronicle of Alfonso III,* she demonstrates how intellectual networks can be disrupted or, in this case, coagulate through migration. Her study sheds light on the cultural and intellectual connections of the scholars of Asturias with the Christian authors of Al-Andalus. It shows how influences in genre or intangible shifts in narrative styles are rooted in the physical networks of intellectual exchange, whose medium is texts in material books and learning in teachers of flesh and blood. Bonch Reeves explores the literary effects of the large-scale movement north by the *dhimmī* community living under Islamic rule, which brought the Andalusi intellectuals physically closer to their Asturian counterparts.

In the background of the network graph in our mind's eye, there are thus political, social and cultural developments at play that influence the shape of the network. Moreover, the edges in intellectual network graphs represent contacts that are not solely of a learned nature. Along the routes taken by learned ideas, fellow travelers are to be found, such as emotions of friendship or antipathy, and impressions of political and economic power. Edward Schoolman's chapter in this volume shows how the history of Novalesa's political and economic relationships, as mediated through its rich charter collection (forged or genuine), is also a semblance of the monastery's cultural and intellectual affinities. He reflects on the networks of the monastery of St. Peter at Novalesa in two distinct phases of its history. The Carolingian phase of Novalesa lasted for 180 years, from its foundation in 726 to its destruction by "Saracens" in 906. A new phase began around 1000 CE when Abbot Gezo re-established the monastery at Novalesa. Schoolman demonstrates the reciprocal relationship between the monastery's networks of both phases. The orientation of Novalesa to Carolingian Gaul is gratefully recounted in the eleventh century when Novalesa again turned to the northwest (now Cluny). Our understanding of Novalesa's oldest monastic connections thus comes from its careful reconstruction in the monastery's eleventh-century historiography.

This directs our attention to the element of time in interpreting intellectual networks. Our understanding of historic networks is sometimes entirely dependent on later sources, whose politics of selection may remain unknown to us. Novalesa's chroniclers may have sought to obscure the differences between the monastery's earliest networks and those of the eleventh century by overstating a sense of continuation. Novalesa's eighth-century network is in many ways a product of eleventh-century imaginations, as Edward Schoolman demonstrates.

Similarly, the tangible evidence of the networks formed at Merovingian royal schools consists of letters between former school friends. These were often composed decades after the friends had each left court, attained ecclesiastical offices, and subsequently found themselves geographically separated from each other. The moments during which the relationships were formed are only visible through the glass darkly of later recollection. The genesis of the networks and their development remain shrouded in the mists of time. Yitzhak Hen demonstrates how education relies on human interaction and how the formation of Merovingian intellectual circles and royal schools was the product of the connections between dignitaries and scholars. In fact, part (most?) of the attraction of an education at court for one's children was the flow of talented aristocrats to the same place, laying the ground works for political connections in later years. The connections between peers, at court or later in life, were not confined to the exchange of learned texts or thoughts, but included feelings of friendship, admiration, jealousy, or animosity, as well as calculated considerations of social or political strategy. In other words, every edge in a graph of an intellectual network carries a unique combination of information exchange and social meaning.

The essays in this volume testify to the value of looking at intellectual history as a history of information exchange, networks, and human interaction. They demonstrate how the study of the historical networks raises new questions with which to approach our sources. We are thus offered more insight into the ways in which ideas flourish when shared with others. I am grateful to the authors for sharing their ideas with us.

Bibliography

Manuscripts
Leiden. University Library, MS Voss. F.74.
St. Gallen. Stiftsbibliothek, MS 1399a, Nr. 1.

Secondary
Bischoff, Bernhard. "Die Europäische Verbreitung der Werke Isidors von Sevilla." In *Isidoriana: Colección de Estudios Sobre Isidoro de Sevilla,* edited by Manuel C. Diaz y Diaz, 317–44. Leon: Centro de Estudios "San Isidoro," 1961. Reprinted in "Die Europäische Verbreitung der Werke Isidors von Sevilla." In *Mittelalterliche Studien: Ausgewählte Aufsätze zur Schriftkunde und Literaturgeschichte,* 171–94. Stuttgart: Anton Hiersemann, 1966.

Carley, James P., and Ann Dooley. "An Early Irish Fragment of Isidore of Seville's *Etymologiae.*" In *The Archaeology and History of Glastonbury Abbey,* edited by Lesley Abrams and James P. Carley, 135–61. Woodbridge: Boydell Press, 1991.

Di Sciacca, Claudia. *Finding the Right Words: Isidore's "Synonyma" in Anglo-Saxon England.* Toronto: University of Toronto Press, 2008. DOI: 10.3138/9781442688117.

Dold, Alban, and Johannes Duft. *Die älteste irische Handschriften-Reliquie der Stiftsbibliothek St. Gallen mit Texten aus Isidors Etymologien.* Beuron in Hohenzollern: Beuroner Kunstverlag, 1955.

Duft, Johannes. "Die Irische Handschriften der Stiftsbibliothek St. Gall." In *Die Iren und Europa im früheren Mittelalter,* edited by Heinz Löwe, 916–37. Stuttgart: Klett-Cotta, 1982.

Duft, Johannes, and Peter Meyer. *Die irischen Miniaturen der Stiftsbibliothek St. Gallen.* Olten: Urs Graf Verlag, 1953.

Smyth, Marina. "Isidorian Texts in Seventh-Century Ireland." In *Isidore of Seville and His Reception in the Early Middle Ages,* edited by Andrew Fear and Jamie Wood, 111–30. Amsterdam: Amsterdam University Press, 2016. DOI: 10.1017/9789048526765.007.

1

Modeling the Middle Ages: A Review of Historical Network Research on Medieval Europe and the Mediterranean World

K. Patrick Fazioli

Introduction

In May 2008, a short piece was published in *Nature*'s "News & Comment" section under the headline "Social Networking Gets Medieval: Researchers Give a French Province the 'Facebook' treatment."[1] Although one might have guessed from this odd title a story on medievalists' social media habits, the article in fact covered the work of French mathematicians who had created "the oldest detailed social network ever constructed" by analyzing one thousand notarial contracts stretching back to the thirteenth century in the Castlenau-Montratier seigneury

1   I would like to thank Michael J. Kelly and Sven Meeder for inviting me to participate in the 2017 symposium on "Social and Intellectual Networking in the Early Middle Ages" at Radboud University, from which this paper ultimately derived. This chapter greatly benefited from the comments of two anonymous reviewers.

of southwestern France.[2] This high-profile application of network analysis to the Middle Ages — which revealed a sprawling network of interpersonal relationships across boundaries of space, time, and social class — caught the attention of medieval historians, who quickly realized that the underlying research (published earlier that year in the journal *Neurocomputing*) was more focused on using a massive historical database to test the validity of network algorithms than it was on shedding light on medieval society.[3] The following month, the historian Jonathan Jarrett critiqued the researchers for paying insufficient attention to the historical context of their dataset, noting that "the validity of the results has to be questionable given that a lot of the data that is being mined is of dubious relevance, and a great deal excluded as well as whatever has been missed out in the copying up of the actual manuscripts."[4] To their credit, the French mathematicians responded graciously to historians' criticism, and an ensuing dialogue led to the publication of several articles that paid greater attention to the historical context and implications of their network research.[5]

Although remarkably cordial as academic squabbles go, this episode nicely illustrates the promise and perils of applying network analysis to the study of the medieval past. Specifically, it exemplifies the problems that can arise when such research questions are not given proper interdisciplinary consideration. Not only were some of the network scientists' initial interpretations

---

2   Geoff Brumfiel, "Social Networking Gets Medieval: Researchers Give a French Province the 'Facebook' Treatment," *Nature News*, May 19, 2008.

3   Romain Boulet, Bertrand Jouve, Fabrice Rossi, and Nathalie Villa, "Batch Kernel SOM and Related Laplacian Methods for Social Network Analysis," *Neurocomputing* 71, nos. 7–9 (2008): 1257–73.

4   Jonathan Jarrett, "'Social Networking Gets Medieval,' Does It? A Historian's Take on Some Recent Research on Computing in the Humanities," *A Corner of Tenth-Century Europe*, June 5, 2008, https://tenthmedieval.wordpress.com/2008/06/05/social-networking-gets-medieval-does-it-a-historians-take-on-some-recent-research-on-computing-in-the-humanities/.

5   See Fabrice Rossi, Nathalie Villa-Vialaneix, and Florent Hautefeuille, "Exploration of a Large Database of French Notarial Acts with Social Network Methods," *Digital Medievalist* 9 (2014).

of questionable validity, but their ultimate conclusion — that rural society in late-medieval France comprised a highly localized and fragmented social network with a few densely connected individuals — was hardly a shocking revelation for historians. Despite these shortcomings, this research gestured toward the potential of networks to provide novel information on the medieval past. For the historian wading through troves of agrarian contracts, the archaeologist reconstructing long-distance trade patterns, or the historical geographer modeling the spread of an ancient plague, network analysis offers an invaluable tool for making sense of hundreds or thousands of data points. Despite the recent growth in the application of network perspectives to the study of medieval Europe and the Mediterranean world, the value of this method remains somewhat underappreciated by the broader community of medievalists. With the right kind of dataset and some basic training (or cross-disciplinary collaboration), there are numerous opportunities for network analysis to be more widely applied in medieval history, archaeology, geography, philology, literary studies, and beyond.

The goal of this chapter is to introduce historical network analysis to the interested medievalist by addressing some of the most commonly raised questions about this line of research: how exactly does it work? What are its strengths and limitations? Is it a method, a theoretical perspective, or both? After providing a brief overview of network analysis and its disciplinary origins, the chapter sketches out a taxonomy of network approaches in medieval studies, assesses the relative advantages and drawbacks of this perspective, and briefly discusses its theoretical underpinnings. Although several overviews of medieval network research have been recently published in German, very little is available for a non-specialist English-speaking audience.[6] To be clear, this chapter does not provide an exhaustive

---

6   German language overviews of medieval network research in include Stephan Selzer and Ulf Christian Ewert, "Netzwerke im europäischen Handel des Mittelalters," *Vorträge und Forschungen* 72 (2010): 21–47, and Eva Jullien, "Netzwerkanalyse in der Mediävistik. Probleme und Perspe-

account of the scholarship on medieval networks but rather offers a snapshot of a dynamic and growing subfield that has for too long been hindered by disciplinary, national, linguistic, and thematic boundaries.

Basic Terms and Concepts of Network Analysis

Network analysis is a tool for investigating relationships between entities, consisting of a model built from points called "vertices" (i.e., nodes) that are connected by lines called "edges" (i.e., arcs). While it is possible to examine any set of relational data from this perspective, network analysis has generally been applied to large and complex datasets that are less amenable to traditional qualitative methods. One of the great benefits of this approach is its flexibility: nodes and edges can be defined in myriad ways and at multiple scales, and network analysis has been used to examine everything from Alzheimer's disease and ant colonies to global shipping routes and international relations.[7] Typically, nodes in a network are defined as a single class of data (in order to make computational analysis more straightforward), but bimodal and multimodal networks (which include more than one class of data) can also be illustrative in certain situations. Edges can also be defined in many ways, and depending on the kind of relationship being explored, it is possible to include information on the strength and directionality of the connection.

---

ktiven im Ungang mit mittelalterlichen Quellen," *Vierteljahrschrift für Sozial- und Wirtschaftsgeschichte* 100, no. 2 (2013): 135–53.

7   See, respectively, Danielle P. Mersch, Alessandro Crespi, and Laurent Keller, "Tracking Individuals Shows Spatial Fidelity Is a Key Regulator of Ant Social Organization," *Science* 340, no. 6136 (2013): 1090–93; Kaustubh Supekar, Vinod Menon, Daniel Rubin, Mark Musen, and Michael D. Greicius, "Network Analysis of Intrinsic Functional Brain Connectivity in Alzheimer's Disease," *PLoS Computational Biology* 4, no. 6 (2008): 1–11; César Ducruet and Theo Notteboom, "The Worldwide Maritime Network of Container Shipping: Spatial Structure and Regional Dynamics," *Global Networks* 12, no. 3 (July 2012): 395–423; and Emilie M. Hafner-Burton, Miles Kahler, and Alexander H. Montgomery, "Network Analysis for International Relations," *International Organization* 63, no. 3 (2009): 559–92.

Once nodes and edges have been defined, the information about their relationships (that is to say, *how are nodes connected?*) is arranged into an adjacency matrix and can be visually displayed as a graph as well as analyzed with various algorithms designed to ascertain network properties, such as (1) the types of nodes that tend to be interconnected (e.g., assortativity, transitivity, and clustering); (2) the nodes located in the most important parts of the network (e.g., centrality measurements); and (3) the overall organization of the network (e.g., density, centralization, and the "small world" phenomenon).

Before explaining how network research can be applied to the Middle Ages, a brief review of its disciplinary genesis will clarify how this method became a part of the medievalist's toolkit. Most scholars trace the origins of network thinking to Swiss mathematician Leonard Euler's (1707–1783) solution to the "Seven Bridges of Königsberg" problem, which sought to identify a single continuous route that crossed only once each of seven bridges connecting the mainland and two islands in the Pregl River. Euler demonstrated the impossibility of such a route by constructing what is now known as a network graph and showing that the key variable was determining how many other nodes a given node was connected to (i.e., the degree of the node).

In solving this puzzle, Euler laid the foundations for graph theory, which would become the mathematical basis of network analysis. Over the next several centuries, this branch of discrete mathematics was adopted by a variety of other fields, including physics, linguistics, and geography, thanks to its unique ability to analyze relational data. In the 1930s, Jacob Levy Moreno (1889–1974) was the first to bring a network perspective to the study of human groups. His "sociometry" approach was premised on the idea that human behavior could be explained by the overall structure of network relationships as well as an individual's location within it. He famously used this method to show how the pattern of interpersonal relationships among students at an all-girls boarding school could account for a recent spate of runaways.[8] Building on Moreno's insights, the field of Social Network Analysis would emerge in the second half of the twentieth century, thanks especially to contributions from social anthropologists at the University of Manchester,[9] relational sociologists at Columbia University,[10] and political scientists at the University of Chicago.[11]

Historians, as a general rule, were slower to embrace network approaches than other social scientists, despite the great potential of this perspective for investigating their relational datasets. In the late 1990s, Charles Wetherell attributed his fellow historians' reticence to a declining interest in interdisciplinary collaboration, a dearth of quantitatively focused historical scholarship, and the method's formidable data requirements.[12] However, this trend has significantly reversed over the past twenty years, perhaps due to historians' growing interest in cross-disciplinary and quantitative approaches (e.g., Big History), technological advances in computing power and affordable statistical and GIS software, or even the ubiquity of social media networks as a cultural phenomenon. Not coincidentally, as Tom Brughmans and Matthew Peeples have recently demonstrated, archaeology has

---

8   Jacob Levy Moreno, *Who Shall Survive? A New Approach to the Problem of Human Interrelations* (Washington, DC: Nervous and Mental Disease Publishing Co., 1934).

9   See Elizabeth Bott, *Family and Social Network: Roles, Norms and External Relationships in Ordinary Urban Families* (London: Tavistock Publications, 1957), and John A. Barnes, *Social Networks* (Ann Arbor: Addison-Wesley Publishing Co., 1972).

10 See Harrison White, *Identity and Control: A Structural Theory of Social Action* (Princeton: Princeton University Press, 1992), and Charles Tilly, *Trust and Rule* (Cambridge: Cambridge University Press, 2005).

11 See John F. Padgett and Christopher K. Ansell, "Robust Action and the Rise of the Medici, 1400–1434," *American Journal of Sociology* 98, no. 6 (May 1993): 1259–319, and John F. Padgett and Paul D. McLean, "Organizational Invention and Elite Transformation: The Birth of Partnership Systems in Renaissance Florence," *American Journal of Sociology* 111, no. 5 (March 2006): 1463–1568.

12 Charles Wetherell, "Historical Social Network Analysis," *International Review of Social History* 43, Supplement S6 (1998), 125–44, at 125.

experienced a similar surge in the popularity of network analysis since the turn of the century.[13]

A Taxonomy of Medieval Network Research

The incredible flexibility and analytical power of network research have made it an essential tool across the natural sciences, social sciences, and digital humanities. Yet, in spite of the recent uptick in interest among medievalists, there is still a widespread lack of recognition of the myriad ways in which this method can be used to investigate medieval society. In order to highlight its tremendous promise, this section provides a brief overview of recent research in medieval network analysis, organized by the type of data used to build the model: people (i.e., social networks), places (i.e., spatial networks), things (i.e., artifact networks), and ideas (i.e., conceptual networks).

The most common type of network used in medieval research is the social network, in which nodes represent individuals, groups, or institutions. This category can be further subdivided into *sociocentric approaches,* which seek to investigate the network as a whole, and *egocentric approaches,* which focus on the personal networks of a few individuals.[14] Scale is an important difference between these two kinds of networks. Sociocentric approaches typically produce larger and more complex networks that lend themselves to quantitative analyses. For example, the aforementioned work on medieval notarial contracts generated a bimodal network (with nodes either representing individuals or documents) consisting of more than 10,500 data points.[15] Similarly, the "Peoples of Medieval Scotland" project at Kings College London and the University of Glasgow has developed a database with information on more than 9,000 in-

---

13 Tom Brughmans and Matthew Peeples, "Trends in Archaeological Network Research: A Bibliometric Analysis," *Journal of Historical Network Research* 1 (2017): 1–24, at 7.

14 John Scott, *Social Network Analysis* (London: Sage, 2017), 34.

15 Rossi, Villa-Vialaneix, and Hautefeuille, "Exploration," 5.

dividuals who lived between 1093 and 1314.[16] Other whole-network studies have been used to investigate social hierarchies in Byzantine Egypt,[17] urban oligarchs in late-medieval England,[18] trading networks in the medieval Mediterranean,[19] kinship networks in high medieval France,[20] networks of influence in the Norman kingdom of Sicily,[21] and religious networks across the medieval world.[22]

Egocentric networks are typically smaller (less than a dozen nodes in some cases) and therefore tend to focus on qualitative descriptions or visualizations highlighting the connections among individuals and groups. One common application in medieval research is the epistolary (or correspondence) network, which has been especially popular in Byzantine studies thanks to Margaret Mullet's influential work on Theophylact of Ochrid.[23] Beyond letter writing, egocentric approaches have

---

16 Cornell Jackson, "Using Social Network Analysis to Reveal Unseen Relationships in Medieval Scotland," *Digital Scholarship in the Humanities* 32 (2017): 336–43.

17 Giovanni Ruffini, *Social Networks in Byzantine Egypt* (Cambridge: Cambridge University Press, 2008).

18 Joe Chick, "Urban Oligarchy and Dissolutioned Voters: The End of Monastic Rule in Reading, 1350–1600," *Cultural and Social History* 16, no. 4 (2019): 387–411.

19 Francisco Apellániz, "Venetian Trading Networks in the Medieval Mediterranean," *Journal of Interdisciplinary History* 46, no. 2 (2013): 157–79.

20 Laurent Nabias, "Constellations de Parentés dans la noblesse médiévale d'Île-de-France (1000–1440)," *ARCS — Analyse de réseaux pour les sciences sociales / Network Analysis for Social Sciences* (2018): 1–46.

21 Hervin Fernández-Aceves, "Social Network Analysis and Narrative Structure: Measuring Communication and Influence in a Medieval Source for the Kingdom of Sicily," *Intersticios Sociales* 14 (2017): 125–53.

22 Daniel Bauerfeld and Lukas Clemens, eds., *Gesellschaftliche Umbrüche und religiöse Netzwerke: Analysen von der Antike bis zur Gegenwart* (Bielefeld: Transcript Verlag, 2014). See especially the chapters by Wolfgang Spickermann, Christian Nitschke, Richard Engl, and Yannick Pouivet and Benno Schulz, all of which focus on the medieval era.

23 Margaret Mullett, *Theophylact of Ochrid: Reading the Letters of a Byzantine Archbishop* (New York: Routledge, 1997). Other recent network studies on epistolography in the Eastern Empire include Michael Grünbart, "'Tis love that has warm'd us': Reconstructing networks in 12th Century Byzantium," *Revue belge de philologie et d'histoire* 83, no. 2 (2005): 301–13, and Adam

recently been used to illuminate the rivalry between Byzantine generals Belisarius and Narses during their campaigns against the Goths and Vandals,[24] the role of Templars in the papal curia during the thirteenth century,[25] and the social network of abbot Odo of Cluny.[26]

While historians primarily use written evidence to create their social networks, medieval archaeologists, historical geographers, and paleo-epidemiologists have found creative ways to combine network analysis with GIS data to produce spatial networks. Here, nodes are defined as places in the landscape (e.g., cities, villages, cemeteries, harbors, monuments, etc.) rather than individuals, while edges represent lines of communication, trade, or migration.[27] Recent studies of spatial networks include the investigation of transport routes in early medieval England,[28]

Schor, "Becoming Bishop in the Letters of Basil and Synesius: Tracing Patterns of Social Signaling across Two Full Epistolary Collections," *Journal of Late Antiquity* 7, no. 2 (2014): 298–328. See also contributions in Carmen Angela Cvetković and Peter Gemeinhardt, eds., *Episcopal Networks in Late Antiquity: Connection and Communication across Boundaries* (Berlin and Boston: de Gruyter, 2019). For a recent study in Western Europe, see Bronagh Ann McShane, "Visualising the Reception and Circulation of Early Modern Nuns' Letters," *Journal of Historical Network Research* 2 (2018): 1–25.

24 David Alan Parnell, "The Social Networks of Justinian's Generals," *Journal of Late Antiquity* 8, no. 1 (2015): 114–35.

25 Karl Borchardt, "Die Templer an der Römischen Kurie im 13. Jahrhundert: Ein Netzwerke?," *Ordines Militares: Colloquia Torunensia Historica* 20 (2015): 25–38.

26 Isabelle Rosé, "Reconstrucción, représentacion gráfica análisis de las redes de poder en la alta edad media. Aproximación a las práctices sociales de la aristocracia a partir del ejemplo de Odón de Cluny († 942)," *Redes: Revista hispana para el análisis de redes sociales* 21, no. 5 (2011): 139–272.

27 For a very early attempt to reconstruct medieval spatial networks, see Forrest R. Pitts, "A Graph Theoretic Approach to Historical Geography," *The Professional Geographer* 17, no. 5 (1965): 15–20.

28 Stuart Brookes and Hoai Nguyen Huynh, "Transport Networks and Towns in Roman and Early Medieval England: An Application of PageRank to Archaeological Questions," *Journal of Archaeological Science: Reports* 17 (2018): 477–90.

barbarian pathways near the Main River in Germany,[29] and maritime networks across medieval Europe.[30] Spatial networks have also proven useful in tracing the spread of the bubonic plague during the thirteenth century,[31] exploring area-population relationships of medieval cities,[32] and tracing the spread of monastic reform in the eleventh-century Italian marches.[33]

While most archaeological work on medieval Europe has focused on spatial networks, a few ambitious studies have also investigated distributions of material culture from a network perspective. Of particular note is Søren Sindbæk's research on Viking Age trade and communication, in which he demonstrates a "small world" phenomenon (i.e., where the shortest path between nodes increases slowly as a function of the number of nodes in the network) by creating a database that links archaeological sites sharing three or more artifact styles.[34] Other recent studies applying network perspectives to material culture have illuminated the distribution of marble chancel screen panels in the late-antique Mediterranean and the circulation of Burgundian coins and pottery in early medieval Gaul.[35] Al-

29 Armin Volkmann, "Perspectives for Network Analysis: Roman Roads, Barbarian Paths and Settlement Patterns in the Borderlands at the Limes Germanicus in the Main River Region," *Open Archaeology* 3 (2017): 123–38.

30 Johannes Preiser-Kapeller and Falko Daim, eds., *Harbours and Maritime Networks as Complex Adaptive Systems* (Mainz: Verlag des Römisch-Germanischen Zentralmuseums, 2015).

31 José Gómez and Miguel Verdú, "Network Theory May Explain the Vulnerability of Medieval Human Settlements to the Black Death Pandemic," *Scientific Reports* 7, no. 43467 (2017): 1–7, and Lars Skog and Hans Hauska, "Spatial Modeling of the Black Death in Sweden," *Transactions in GIS* 17, no. 4 (2017): 589–611.

32 Rudolf Cesaretti, José Lobo, Luís M.A. Bettencourt, Scott G. Ortman, and Michael E. Smith, "Population-Area Relationship for Medieval European Cities," *PLoS One* 11, no. 10 (2016): 1–27.

33 Kathryn Lee Jasper, "Peter Damian and the Communication of Local Reform," *The Catholic Historical Review* 104, no. 2 (2018): 197–222.

34 Søren Sindbæk, "The Small World of the Vikings: Networks in Early Medieval Communication and Exchange," *Norwegian Archaeological Review* 40, no. 1 (2007): 59–74.

35 Nicholas W. Dugdale, "Examining Late Antique Trade through Geospatial and Network Analysis: A Case Study Using Marble Chancel Screen Panels"

though "artifact networks" hold great promise for reconstructing the flow of ideas and information, such analyses are faced with additional interpretive challenges related to chronological imprecision, differential preservation, and the fact that objects provide only proxy evidence for past human movement and communication. As Sindbæk himself has acknowledged: "The basic problem is that material affiliations in the archaeological record do not offer a measured network to analyse, nor a foolproof guide to interpret the meaning of any measurable similarity or centrality."[36]

The least common (but arguably most creative) approach to network analysis explores the relationships of ideas or concepts. As with material culture, the spread of ideas offers proxy evidence for past social relationships that can be fraught with interpretive difficulties. One fascinating example is Paul Ormerod and Andrew Roach's study of medieval religious dissent from an epidemiological perspective. They argued the Catholic Church became more effective in snuffing out heretical ideas when it recognized that heresy was a "scale-free" network in which a few well-connected nodes (i.e., individuals) were crucial to the spread of the ideological "disease." They point to a switch in strategy from punishing known heretics by sending them on a pilgrimage (which put them in contact with a greater number of people) to either imprisoning or publicly shaming them through bright yellow crosses on their garments, both of which had the effect of discouraging others from socially interacting with them.[37] Conceptual networks have also been used to reconstruct the theological influences of glosses and commentaries of

---

(PhD diss., University of Southampton, 2017), and Ryan Hayes Wilkinson, "The Last Horizons of Roman Gaul: Communication, Community, and Power at the End of Antiquity" (PhD diss., Harvard University, 2015).

36 Søren Sindbæk, "Broken Links and Black Boxes: Material Affiliations and Contextual Network Synthesis in the Viking World," in *Network Analysis in Archaeology: New Approaches to Regional Interaction,* ed. Carl Knappett (Oxford: Oxford University Press, 2013), 71–94, at 76.

37 Paul Ormerod and Andrew P. Roach, "The Medieval Inquisition: Scale-Free Networks and the Suppression of Heresy," *Physica A* 339, nos. 3–4 (2004): 645–52.

the Wurzburg St. Matthew,[38] explore the transmission of medieval manuscripts and texts,[39] and trace the rise of perspective in optics in late-medieval Italian universities.[40]

Strengths of a Network Perspective: Analyzing Large Datasets

Having established the different types of medieval networks that can be examined, in this section we will explore two key benefits of network analysis: (1) the analysis of large and complex datasets, and (2) the integration of different classes of data. To appreciate how network analysis can reveal hidden patterns within apparent chaos, a more detailed look at the various network algorithms is necessary. While dozens of computational tools have been developed, this section highlights five of the most commonly used in medieval network research: centrality, transitivity, clustering coefficient, network density, and network intensity. Since the focus is on what these algorithms mean and how they can address historical and archaeological questions, we will not be concerned with the underlying mathematical operations.[41]

Centrality describes a node's location within the network, which is essential for understanding its function and importance within the overall network structure. Centrally located nodes may have greater access to information, serve as bridges between different branches of the network, or exert significant influence on other nodes. Network scientists have developed

---

38 Malte Rehbein, "From the Scholarly Edition to Visualization: Re-Using Encoded Data for Historical Research," *International Journal of Humanities and Arts Computing* 8, no. 1 (2014): 81–105.

39 Gustavo Fernández Riva, "Network Analysis of Medieval Manuscript Transmission: Basic Principles and Methods," *Journal of Historical Network Research* 3 (2019): 30–49. See also Elizabeth Archibald's contribution in this volume.

40 Dominique Raynaud, *Optics and the Rise of Perspective: A Study in Network Knowledge Diffusion* (Oxford: Bardwell Press, 2014).

41 Those searching for greater mathematical and methodological detail should consult Katharina A. Zweig, *Network Analysis Literacy: A Practical Approach to the Analysis of Networks* (Vienna: Springer, 2016).

different measures of centrality, including closeness centrality (how often does this node lie on the shortest path from one node to all other nodes?), betweenness centrality (how often does this node lie on the shortest path between all *pairs* of other nodes?), degree centrality (what portion of all nodes is this node connected to?), and eigenvector centrality (how many *other* important nodes is this node connected to?).

A recent study by Stuart Brookes and Hoai Nguyen Huynh on late Roman and early medieval transport routes in England provides a useful illustration of how centrality measures allow us to investigate questions of past patterns and processes. The authors reconstructed a network of past transport routes using extant historical and archaeological data on the Roman and medieval road systems, riverine navigation routes, and the probable location of towns and large villages. Using transport hubs as nodes and probable routes as edges, they ran each of the aforementioned centrality measures to see which produced a network most closely aligned with the existing data. Their results suggested that the eigenvector measure known as Page-Rank (originally developed to order Google search results) was the best fit with the data, meaning that transport nodes with high PageRank scores were generally close to important Roman and medieval towns. The authors therefore conclude that this particular centrality measurement has great potential for reconstructing past infrastructure networks.[42]

Transitivity is a measure of how frequently two connected nodes are connected to a third node (thereby forming a triad). José Gómez and Miguel Verdú used this algorithm to trace the spread of the Black Death across Eurasia and Africa during the thirteenth century. Drawing upon historical evidence to estimate arrival dates and levels of devastation caused by the bubonic plague in 1,311 Old World cities, they sought to understand why certain locales suffered from unusually high mortality rates. Network analysis revealed that mortality rates were correlated with higher centrality and transitivity scores, from which

---

42 Brookes and Huynh, "Transport Networks," 488.

the researchers inferred that highly interconnected nodes were likely infected multiple times by different strains of the plague, significantly worsening its impact on these communities.[43]

Another network tool similar to transitivity is the clustering coefficient; in a highly clustered network, small, interconnected groups of nodes (triads) have relatively few ties to the other parts of the network. Robert Gramsch-Stehfest used this algorithm to examine shifting patterns of political alliances among German nobility during the coregency of Emperor Frederick II and his son, King Henry VII, in the thirteenth century. Drawing on information from written sources, such as testimony in charters, Gramsch-Stehfest and colleagues created a database of personal and political connections (classified as either friendly, hostile, or ambivalent) that consisted of more than 4,400 dyads between 150 important individuals within the German and broader European nobility. An analysis of clustering coefficients of social networks created for each year between 1225 and 1235 revealed a noticeable shift from a bipolar to a multipolar alliance structure. Gramsch-Stehfest interpreted this disintegration from large to small factions as evidence of the success of Henry's political strategy, thus challenging the received wisdom that he was an ineffectual ruler. Ironically, Henry's success ultimately gave Frederick an opportunity to depose his son since the latter was unable to mobilize a powerful princely party to challenge his father.[44]

The final two algorithms discussed here are network density and network intensity. The former divides the total number of connections among nodes into the total number of possible connections, while the latter measures the frequency of interactions between nodes. David Gary Shaw used these network tools to quantify how the social elite ensconced themselves into a town's social web in late-medieval England. Shaw examined court

---

43 Gómez and Verdú, "Network Theory," 4–5.
44 Robert Gramsch-Stehfest, "Entangled Powers: Network Analytical Approaches to the History of the Holy Roman Empire during the Late Staufer Period," *German History* 36, no. 3 (September 2018): 365–80, at 377.

documents from the city of Wells to determine social network density and intensity across different social classes: oligarchs, middling officers, petty officers, and commoners. He found that the elite had, on average, lower network density and intensity, which demonstrated their importance as bridges between different social networks. Shaw concludes that it was these roles as trusted arbitrators that enhanced their power and influence within the community, facilitating the rise of oligarchic rule.[45]

Finally, it is worth noting that network analysis can help alleviate some of the methodological problems that accompany the investigation of large datasets. For example, relational data mining methods can identify transcription and interpretation errors made in prosopographical databases containing a multitude of individuals without surnames when it is not always clear whether the same name on different documents refers to one person or two. Fabrice Rossi and colleagues have shown that network analysis can provide useful contextual information to make such determinations, such as identifying when a single individual had an unrealistically long lifespan or the same name appeared in two distinct sections of the network, both cases suggesting that this one name was two separate persons.[46]

Strengths of a Network Perspective: Interdisciplinarity

The second strength of medieval network research lies in its ability to provide a common framework through which to integrate multiple lines of evidence across disciplinary boundaries. This potential for facilitating interdisciplinary work among historians, archaeologists, historical geographers, and other areas of medieval studies could help to break down long-standing institutional boundaries, differing theoretical perspectives, and distinct lines of evidence. This section provides a few examples of how network analysis has brought subfields into greater con-

---

45 David Gary Shaw, "Social Networks and the Foundations of Oligarchy in Medieval Towns," *Urban History* 32, no. 2 (2005): 200–222, at 218.

46 Rossi, Villa-Vialaneix, and Hautefeuille, "Exploration," 3.

versation, providing a shared language and set of analytical tools that could achieve a more robust and holistic understanding of the medieval world.[47]

One of the most prominent examples of this integration of historical and archaeological lines of evidence is found in the work of Johannes Preiser-Kapeller and colleagues in the "Topographies of Entanglement" group at the Austrian Academy of Sciences. In a recent study of Byzantine Thrace, Preiser-Kapeller championed a "multiplex" network approach that combined a spatial network of land and sea transport routes with state and ecclesiastical administrative hierarchies for the Byzantine and Bulgarian state and Patriarchate. Comparative analyses of these distinctive spatial and social networks (including clustering coefficients, centrality measures, and centralization) revealed the administrate networks to be more highly centralized than transport networks, and also that combining three datasets produced a "small-world" phenomenon with a high density of local ties as well as several central places that had connections across the entire network.[48]

On the other end of Europe, a team of geoscientists and archaeologists led by Rowin van Lanen has been carrying out innovative interdisciplinary network research in the Rhine-Meuse delta. The Dutch researchers have pioneered a "network-friction" model that combines archaeological and historical data with high-resolution paleo-geographical, geomorphological,

---

47 For example, the author has recently argued that network analysis holds the potential to unite various types of data in the study of medieval frontiers. K. Patrick Fazioli, "Social Networks, Complex Systems, and the Medieval Frontier: Towards an Interdisciplinary Approach to the Study of Borderlands" (Keynote Address, "Rethinking the Medieval Frontier" Conference, Leeds, UK, April 10, 2018).

48 Johannes Preiser-Kapeller, "Networks of Border Zones: Multiplex Relations of Power, Religion and Economy in South-Eastern Europe, 1250–1453 AD" (presentation, CAA2011 — Revive the Past: Proceedings of the 39th Conference on Computer Applications and Quantitative Methods in Archaeology, Beijing, China April 12–16, 2011). See also Katerina Ragkou, "The Economic Centrality of Urban Centers in the Medieval Peloponnese: Late 11th-Mid-14th Centuries," *Land* 7, no. 4 (2018): 153–76.

and pedological maps in order to identify past "movement corridors" in lowland areas.[49] The researchers created network-friction models for three points in the first millennium CE (c. 100, 500, and 900) in order to gauge the long-term stability of the network. Their results suggested that the transportation and communication networks exhibited about 80 percent persistence between each time frame, with meander migration and avulsion activity of the rivers as the main factor impacting route changes.[50]

Finally, one of the most creative (and controversial) interdisciplinary applications of medieval networks research has been Pádraig Mac Carron and Ralph Kenna's work on the historicity of epic mythology. These Irish mathematicians believe that network analysis can help resolve long-standing debates concerning whether the characters in the *Iliad, Beowulf,* and *Táin Bó Cúailnge* were completely fictional or based, at least in part, on real historical figures. They argue that since real-world social networks tend to exhibit different properties than fictional ones (i.e., they tend to be assortative, small-world, and scale-free), analyzing the relationships among characters in these epic poems might indicate the type of network to which they are structurally most similar. Their investigations have revealed that the relationships between characters in the *Iliad* are the closest to a real (i.e., historical) social network, while those of *Beowulf* and the *Táin* exhibited patterns similar to fictional networks, such as the Marvel Cinematic Universe, in which the main characters are too well-connected to have been actual historical figures. Interestingly, when Mac Carron and Kenna removed *Beowulf* and the *Táin*'s six main characters from their analysis, the resulting networks were more assortative, which is to say that they more

---

49 The reconstruction of past routes in lowland areas is particularly challenging because of the ineffectiveness of elevation data in determining least-cost paths.

50 Rowin J. van Lanen and Harm Jan Pierik, "Calculating Connectivity Patterns in Delta Landscapes: Modelling Roman and Early-Medieval Route Networks and their Stability in Dynamic Lowlands," *Quaternary International* 501B (2019): 393–412.

closely resembled historical social networks. This led the authors to speculate that these characters may have been an amalgam of several real historical individuals "that became fused as the narrative was passed down orally through the generations."[51]

Challenges of a Network Perspective

Of course, it is important to recognize that network perspectives (like any method) come with their own set of analytical limitations and potential pitfalls. This section identifies three challenges (two methodological and one theoretical) that need to be carefully considered before undertaking network research on the medieval world. The first concerns the kind of data that is amenable to network analysis. As noted above, any set of relational data could potentially be examined from a network perspective, but this approach is generally most valuable for discerning patterns in very large and complex datasets, such as those common to prosopographical, archaeological, and GIS research. Network studies exploring smaller datasets often eschew formal, quantitative methods, instead relying on visualizations to highlight the importance of social connections and relationships in understanding human behavior and decision-making. There are also studies that employ the term "network" in a looser, metaphorical sense (essentially, as a synonym for "social connections") without attempting to build a relational database, display a graph of nodes and edges, or run quantitative tools. While much of this work is valuable in its own right, it is outside the scope of this chapter because it does not employ the

---

51 Pádraig Mac Carron and Ralph Kenna, "Universal Properties of Mythological networks," *EPL: A Letters Journal Exploring the Frontiers of Physics* 99, no. 28002 (2012): 1–6, at 6. A similar kind of analysis has been recently conducted by S.D. Prado and colleagues, who use network algorithms of communicability and importance among characters in Bede's *Ecclesiastical History* to test gender-based peace and diplomacy models. See S.D. Prado, S.R. Dahmen, A.L.C. Bazzan, M. MacCarron, and J. Hillner, "Gendered Networks and Communicability in Medieval Historical Narratives," *Advances in Complex Systems* 23, no. 3 (2020): n.p.

formal methods discussed earlier.[52] The point here is that one needs to have the appropriate kind of dataset in order to benefit fully from a network approach.

A second major challenge to network research is time. As we have seen above, network models provide only a snapshot of relationships among nodes at a given moment. The static, atemporal nature of networks is especially troublesome for historians and archaeologists, whose work necessarily hinges on questions of change, process, and dynamism. Additionally, if there is a lack of chronological precision in the historical or archaeological data used to create the network, the results of any computational measures could be significantly skewed. For example, archaeologists seeking to understand communication between medieval settlements by examining ceramic styles that persisted over the course of decades or even centuries may unintentionally construct a network that never actually existed.

Thankfully, scholars have found various ways to mitigate the problem of time in network analysis. One strategy, applied in several aforementioned studies, is to infer change by comparing multiple networks at different historical moments. As described above, Gramsch-Stehfest created alliance networks for every year of the decade-long coregency of Frederick and Henry, while Preiser-Kapeller sought to understand shifts in Byzantine Thrace by contrasting administrative networks at times of stability (in 1324) and instability (in 1210 and in 1380).

Another promising technique for injecting temporality into network research is agent-based modeling. For medieval Europe, Christian Ewert and Marco Sunder's recent study of Hanseatic trade networks offers an illustrative example. In order to

---

52 A few recent examples of what might be called "informal" network studies include Shannon McSheffrey, "Liberties of London: Social Networks, Sexual Disorder, and Independent Jurisdiction in the Late Medieval English Metropolis," in *Crossing Borders: Boundaries and Margins in Medieval and Early Modern Britain,* ed. Krista J. Kesselring and Sara Butler (Boston and Leiden: Brill, 2018), 216–36, and Serge ter Braake, "Parties and Factions in the Late Middle Ages: The Case of the Hoeken and Kabeljauwen in The Hague (1483-1515)," *Journal of Medieval History* 35 (2009): 97–111.

explain why the kinship-based, heterarchical trading system of Northern Europe differed so sharply from the law-based, institutional system of the ancient and medieval Mediterranean, the authors ran numerous simulations in which they manipulated variables, including the "geographic spread of resources, transportation costs with distance, trade privileges, and information asymmetries" of the long-distance trading system.[53] Their results suggest that one major difference between the two systems was that Northern Europe had a "clear-cut division of geographic specialization [that] slows down network formation and economic development," which may explain why formal institutions developed earlier in the Mediterranean.[54] Another difference lay in trade privileges and market organization, with the Hanseatic merchants enjoying exclusive trade privileges, while the Italian merchants in the Mediterranean competed for them, which in turn encouraged their home communities to support their compatriots with formal institutions.[55]

A third potential danger of network analysis is what I call the "seduction of numbers"; that is, allowing one's preoccupation with the mathematical sophistication of the analysis to crowd out essential aspects of the historical context. As the opening vignette in this chapter illustrates, even relatively minor problematic assumptions about the historical context can lead to erroneous interpretations. For example, one criterion the French mathematicians used to draw links between the nodes in their medieval social network was when two individuals used the same notary within a fifteen-year period. However, as Jarrett pointed out, this is hardly evidence for a true social relationship; it "just means that they came to the same town to get a deal done within 15 years of each other, unless the notary moved in

---

53 Ulf Christian Ewert and Marco Sunder, "Modelling Maritime Trade Systems: Agent-Based Simulation and Medieval History," *Historical Social Research / Historische Sozialforschung* 43, no. 1 (2018): 114–15.

54 Ibid., 135.

55 See also Bernd Wurpts, "Networks into Institutions or Institutions into Networks? Evidence from the Medieval Hansa" (PhD diss., University of Washington, 2018).

that time [...]. This must inevitably lead to a barrage of linked persons who were in reality not linked at all, and therefore results with no social meaning."[56]

Sindbæk has identified an analogous problem in archaeology, where network models too easily become black boxes "whose basis is difficult or impossible to assess, and whose predictions may be equally difficult to validate."[57] We should not forget that advanced network algorithms provide results, but not necessarily answers. Claire Lemercier has offered some useful advice for keeping the historical context in mind, reminding scholars that "our aim is not to 'map social reality' generally, but to understand the patterns of precisely defined ties" as well as distinguishing subjective ties as defined by people in the past with objective ties that are reconstructed by historians.[58] The final section of this paper seeks to add one other item to this very sensible list: developing robust theoretical models to link historical and archaeological questions to network algorithms.

Theory and Network Perspectives

Sociologists have long debated whether social network analysis is best understood as a method, a theory, a paradigm, or a framework. It is not terribly surprising, given its quantitative focus, that network analysis has long had a reputation of being atheoretical. However, this characterization is misleading; although it may not demand fealty to a single theoretical tradition, neither is social network analysis free of underlying assumptions of social ontology. In fact, network approaches going back to Moreno's sociometry are united by the view that human beliefs and behaviors cannot be fully explained by individual essences or properties (e.g., race, gender, class, etc.) but are powerfully informed by the complex web of relationships in

---

56 Jarrett, "Social Networking Gets Medieval, Does It?"

57 Sindbæk, "Broken Links and Black Boxes," 71.

58 Claire Lemercier, "Formal Network Methods in History: Why and How?," in *Social Networks, Political Institutions, and Rural Societies,* ed. Georg Fertig (Turnhout: Brepols, 2010), 281–310.

which they are enmeshed. In other words, network analysis espouses a relational view of social reality in which human agency is shaped as much by location within the network as by one's personality or identity.[59]

With this in mind, it makes sense that relational sociologists such as Mustafa Emirbayer and Harrison White have been strong advocates for a network perspective. At the same time, two of the most influential schools of relational sociology (actor-network theory and Bourdieu's theory of practice) have largely rejected network analysis as a useful analytical tool. Bourdieu believed that social network analysis focused on the wrong type of relationship, so he developed a parallel but distinct "correspondence analysis" that focused on the differential possession of capital (objective relations) rather than interpersonal connections.[60] In a similar way, the "heterogeneous networks" of human and non-human actors that Bruno Latour, Michel Callon, John Law, and others saw as central to the genesis of human agency are qualitatively different from the kinds of networks studied in social network analysis.[61]

Such philosophical debates over the theoretical underpinning of social network analysis have not attracted much attention from those engaged in medieval network research and are arguably less important than developing robust middle-range theories that can help researchers decide which network algorithms are appropriate for answering historical and archaeolog-

---

59 Although her work is beyond the scope of this chapter, Emily Erickson has argued for an underlying tension in social network analysis between the relationalism of Emirbayer and White and the formalism inherited from Georg Simmel. See Emily Erickson, "Formalist and Relationalist Theory in Social Network Analysis," *Sociological Theory* 31, no. 3 (2013): 219–42.

60 Wouter De Nooy, "Fields and Networks: Correspondence Analysis and Social Network Analysis in the Framework of Field Theory," *Poetics* 31, nos. 5–6 (2003): 305–27, at 321.

61 Some have recently argued that despite these differences, social network theory and actor-network theory are potentially compatible. See Lilla Vicsek, Gábor Király, and Hanna Kónya, "Networks in the Social Sciences: Comparing Actor-Network Theory and Social Network Analysis," *Corvinus Journal of Sociology and Social Policy* 7, no. 2 (2016): 77–102.

ical questions. For example, Gramsch-Stehfest utilized cluster analysis to illuminate shifts in political alliances among the German elite in the late Staufer period. However, he was only able to demonstrate why cluster analysis was the appropriate metric for answering this historical question by drawing upon Fritz Heider's structural-balance theory, which argues that certain types of social groups are stable or unstable based on the combination of friendly and hostile relations between individuals within the group.[62] An example of a stable, balanced group would be if two people on friendly terms both are hostile to a third person (i.e., "the enemy of my enemy is my friend" principle), but a situation in which one person is friendly with two people who are hostile to one another creates an inherently unstable group since at some point that person might have to "choose a side," so to speak. Building on this framework, Gramsch-Stehfest developed an algorithm to identify these relationship types, which allowed him to observe how a highly bipolar alliance system at the beginning of Frederick and Henry's coregency fragmented into a smaller set of alliances.

Another application of middle-range theory to medieval network research is found in Peter Jackson's study of the emergence of the term "Kingdom of Scotland" on twelfth- and thirteenth-century charters. Jackson draws upon the "diffusion of innovations" theory developed by Everett Rogers and subsequently applied to network analysis by Thomas Valente.[63] Characterizing the idea of a "Kingdom of Scotland" as a political innovation allowed Jackson to identify specific algorithms (such as network density) that Valente had shown to be useful for identifying "opinion leaders" who were central to the spread of innovations. Using this framework, Jackson was able to demonstrate that most of the opinion leaders already known to historians had low network density scores, which indicated that they served as

---

62 Fritz Heider, *The Psychology of Interpersonal Relations* (New York: John Wiley and Sons, 1958).

63 Everett Rogers, *Diffusion of Innovations* (New York: Free Press of Glencoe, 1962), and Thomas Valente, *Network Models of the Diffusion of Innovations* (Cresskill: Hampton Press, 1995).

bridges between different networks, thereby giving them access to "non-redundant information" that is essential to diffusing innovations. Perhaps more importantly, looking at network density scores also allowed Jackson to identify previously unknown medieval opinion leaders, such as Malcolm, the Earl of Atholl, and to question the influence of others, such as Robert of London, who have long been presumed to be significant figures.[64]

Conclusion

Today, more than a decade after the "Social Networking Gets Medieval" controversy, medieval network research has blossomed into a dynamic and thriving subfield that has explored various aspects of the European and Mediterranean world from the end of antiquity to the beginning of modernity. Although not without its limitations, there should no longer be any doubt that network analysis has the power to shed new light on past social, economic, and political processes. Moreover, its ability to integrate textual, spatial, and material datasets, as well as to provide a shared language and analytical toolkit, holds tremendous promise for facilitating the kinds of interdisciplinary collaboration that will surely be the future of medieval research. At the same time, historians, archaeologists, historical geographers, geoscientists, mathematicians, and network scientists are just beginning to unpack the potential of this method. In the coming decades, innovative and clever applications of network analysis will surely continue to break new ground in our understanding of the medieval past.

---

64 Jackson, "Using Social Network Analysis," 339–40.

Bibliography

Apellániz, Francisco. "Venetian Trading Networks in the Medieval Mediterranean." *Journal of Interdisciplinary History* 44, no. 2 (2013): 157–79. DOI: 10.1162/JINH_a_00535.

Barnes, John A. *Social Networks*. Ann Arbor: Addison-Wesley Publishing Co., 1972.

Bauerfeld, Daniel, and Lukas Clemens, eds. *Gesellschaftliche Umbrüche und religiöse Netzwerke: Analysen von der Antike bis zur Gegenwart*. Bielefeld: Transcript Verlag, 2014. DOI: 10.14361/transcript.9783839425954.

Borchardt, Karl. "Die Templer an der Römischen Kurie im 13. Jahrhundert: Ein Netzwerke?" *Ordines Militares. Colloquia Torunensia Historica* 20 (2015): 25–38. DOI: 10.12775/OM.2015.002.

Bott, Elizabeth. *Family and Social Network: Roles, Norms and External Relationships in Ordinary Urban Families*. London: Tavistock Publications, 1957.

Boulet, Romain, Bertrand Jouve, Fabrice Rossi, and Nathalie Villa. "Batch Kernel SOM and Related Laplacian Methods for Social Network Analysis." *Neurocomputing* 71, nos. 7–9 (2008): 1257–73. DOI: 10.1016/j.neucom.2007.12.026.

Brookes, Stuart, and Hoai Nguyen Huynh. "Transport Networks and Towns in Roman and Early Medieval England: An Application of PageRank to Archaeological Questions." *Journal of Archaeological Science: Reports* 17 (2018): 477–90. DOI: 10.1016/j.jasrep.2017.11.033.

Brughmans, Tom, and Matt Peeples. "Trends in Archaeological Network Research: A Bibliometric Analysis." *Journal of Historical Network Research* 1, no. 1 (2017): 1–24. DOI: 10.1002/9781119188230.saseas0402.

Brumfiel, Geoff. "Social Networking Gets Medieval: Researchers Give a French Province the 'Facebook' Treatment." *Nature News,* May 19, 2008. DOI: 10.1038/news.2008.839.

Cesaretti, Rudolf, José Lobo, Luís M.A. Bettencourt, Scott G. Ortman, and Michael E. Smith. "Population-area Relationship for Medieval European Cities." *PLoS One* 11, no. 10 (2016). DOI: 10.1371/journal.pone.0162678.

Chick, Joe. "Urban Oligarchy and Dissolutioned Voters: The End of Monastic Rule in Reading, 1350-1600." *Cultural and Social History* 16, no. 4 (2019): 387–411. DOI: 10.1080/14780038.2019.1661556.

Cvetković, Angela, and Peter Gemeinhardt, eds. *Episcopal Networks in Late Antiquity: Connection and Communication Across Boundaries.* Berlin and Boston: de Gruyter, 2019. DOI: 10.1515/9783110553390.

De Nooy, Wouter. "Fields and Networks: Correspondence Analysis and Social Network Analysis in the Framework of Field Theory." *Poetics* 31, nos. 5–6 (2003): 305–27. DOI: 10.1016/S0304-422X(03)00035-4.

Ducruet, César, and Theo Notteboom. "The Worldwide Maritime Network of Container Shipping: Spatial Structure and Regional Dynamics." *Global networks* 12, no. 3 (2012): 395–423. DOI: 10.1111/j.1471-0374.2011.00355.x.

Dugdale, Nicholas Wilkerson. "Examining Late Antique Trade through Geospatial and Network Analysis: A Case Study Using Marble Chancel Screen Panels." PhD diss., University of Southampton, 2017.

Erikson, Emily. "Formalist and Relationalist Theory in Social Network Analysis." *Sociological Theory* 31, no. 3 (2013): 219–42. DOI: 10.1177/0735275113501998.

Ewert, Ulf Christian, and Marco Sunder. "Modelling Maritime Trade Systems: Agent-Based Simulation and Medieval History." *Historical Social Research/Historische Sozialforschung* 43, no. 1 (2018): 110–43. DOI: 10.12759/hsr.43.2018.1.110-143.

Fazioli, K. Patrick. "Social Networks, Complex Systems, and the Medieval Frontier: Towards an Interdisciplinary Approach to the Study of Borderlands." Keynote Address at the First Annual Rethinking the Medieval Frontier Conference, Leeds, UK, April 2018.

Fernández-Aceves, Hervin. "Social Network Analysis and Narrative Structures: Measuring Communication and Influence in a Medieval Source for the Kingdom of Sicily." *Intersticios*

Sociales 7, no. 14 (2017): 125–54. https://eprints.whiterose.ac.uk/120755/.

Fernández Riva, Gustavo. "Network Analysis of Medieval Manuscript Transmission: Basic Principles and Methods." *Journal of Historical Network Research* 3 (2019): 30–49.

Gómez, José M., and Miguel Verdú. "Network Theory May Explain the Vulnerability of Medieval Human Settlements to the Black Death Pandemic." *Scientific Reports* 7 (2017): 1–7. DOI: 10.1038/srep43467.

Gramsch-Stehfest, Robert. "Entangled Powers: Network Analytical Approaches to the History of the Holy Roman Empire during the Late Staufer Period." *German History* 36, no. 3 (September 2018): 365–80. DOI: 10.1093/gerhis/ghy049.

Grünbart, Michael. "'Tis love that has warm'd us': Reconstructing Networks in 12th Century Byzantium." *Revue belge de philologie et d'histoire* 83 (2005): 301–13. DOI: 10.3406/rbph.2005.4924.

Hafner-Burton, Emilie M., Miles Kahler, and Alexander H. Montgomery. "Network Analysis for International Relations." *International Organization* 63, no. 3 (2009): 559–92. DOI: 10.1017/S0020818309090195.

Heider, Fritz. *The Psychology of Interpersonal Relations.* New York: John Wiley and Sons, 1958. DOI: 10.1037/10628-000.

Jackson, Cornell. "Using Social Network Analysis to Reveal Unseen Relationships in Medieval Scotland." *Digital Scholarship in the Humanities* 32, no. 2 (2017): 336–43.

Jarrett, Jonathan. "'Social Networking Gets Medieval,' Does It? A Historian's Take on Some Recent Research on Computing in the Humanities." *A Corner of Tenth-Century Europe,* June 5, 2008. https://tenthmedieval.wordpress.com/2008/06/05/social-networking-gets-medieval-does-it-a-historians-take-on-some-recent-research-on-computing-in-the-humanities/.

Jasper, Kathryn Lee, "Peter Damian and the Communication of Local Reform." *The Catholic Historical Review* 104, no. 2 (2018): 197–222. DOI: 10.1353/cat.2018.0024.

Jullien, Eva. "Netzwerkanalyse in der Mediävistik. Probleme und Perspektiven im Umgang mit mittelalterlichen Quellen." *Vierteljahrschrift für Sozial-und Wirtschaftsgeschichte* 100, no. 2 (2013): 135–53. http://hdl.handle.net/10993/9389.

Lemercier, Claire. "Formal Network Methods in History: Why and How?" In *Social Networks, Political Institutions, and Rural Societies,* edited by Georg Fertig, 281–310. Turnhout: Brepols, 2010. DOI: 10.1484/M.RURHE-EB.4.00198.

Mac Carron, Pádraig, and Ralph Kenna. "Universal Properties of Mythological Networks." *EPL (Europhysics Letters)* 99, no. 28002 (2012): 1–6. DOI: 10.1209/0295-5075/99/28002.

McShane, Bronagh Ann. "Visualising the Reception and Circulation of Early Modern Nuns' Letters." *Journal of Historical Network Research* 2 (2018): 1–25.

McSheffrey, Shannon, "Liberties of London: Social Networks, Sexual Disorder, and Independent Jurisdiction in the Late Medieval English Metropolis." In *Crossing Borders: Boundaries and Margins in Medieval and Early Modern Britain,* edited by Krista J. Kesselring and Sara Butler, 216–36. Boston and Leiden: Brill, 2018. DOI: 10.1163/9789004364950_013.

Mersch, Danielle P., Alessandro Crespi, and Laurent Keller. "Tracking Individuals Shows Spatial Fidelity Is a Key Regulator of Ant Social Organization." *Science* 340, no. 6136 (2013): 1090–93. DOI: 10.1126/science.1234316.

Moreno, Jacob Levy. *Who Shall Survive? A New Approach to the Problem of Human Interrelations.* Washington, DC: Nervous and Mental Disease Publishing, 1934. DOI: 10.1037/10648-000.

Mullett, Margaret. *Theophylact of Ochrid: Reading the Letters of a Byzantine Archbishop.* New York: Routledge, 1997.

Nabias, Laurent. "Constellations de Parentés dans la noblesse médiévale d'Île-de-France (1000-1440)." *ARCS — Analyse de réseaux pour les sciences sociales / Network Analysis for Social Sciences* (2018): 1–46.

Ormerod, Paul, and Andrew P. Roach. "The Medieval Inquisition: Scale-Free Networks and the Suppression of Heresy."

Physica A: Statistical Mechanics and Its Applications 339, nos. 3–4 (2004): 645–52. DOI: 10.1016/j.physa.2004.03.020.

Padgett, John F., and Christopher K. Ansell. "Robust Action and the Rise of the Medici, 1400-1434." *American Journal of Sociology* 98, no. 6 (1993): 1259–1319. DOI: 10.1086/230190.

Padgett, John F., and Paul D. McLean. "Organizational Invention and Elite Transformation: The Birth of Partnership Systems in Renaissance Florence." *American Journal of Sociology* 111, no. 5 (2006): 1463–1568. DOI: 10.1086/498470.

Parnell, David Alan. "The Social Networks of Justinian's Generals." *Journal of Late Antiquity* 8, no. 1 (2015): 114–35. DOI: 10.1353/jla.2015.0009.

Pitts, Forrest R. "A Graph Theoretic Approach to Historical Geography." *The Professional Geographer* 17, no. 5 (1965): 15–20. DOI: 10.1111/j.0033-0124.1965.015_m.x.

Prado, S.D., S.R. Dahmen, A.L.C. Bazzan, M. MacCarron, and J. Hillner. "Gendered Networks and Communicability in Medieval Historical Narratives." *Advances in Complex Systems* 23, no. 3 (2020), np.

Preiser-Kapeller, Johannes. "Networks of Border Zones: Multiplex Relations of Power, Religion and Economy in South-Eastern Europe, 1250-1453 AD." Paper presented at CAA2011 — Revive the Past: Proceedings of the 39th Conference on Computer Applications and Quantitative Methods in Archaeology, Beijing, China, April 2011.

Preiser-Kapeller, Johannes, and Falko Daim, eds. *Harbours and Maritime Networks as Complex Adaptive Systems.* Mainz: Verlag des Römisch-Germanischen Zentralmuseums, 2015.

Ragkou, Katerina. "The Economic Centrality of Urban Centers in the Medieval Peloponnese: Late 11th–Mid-14th Centuries." *Land* 7, no. 4 (2018): 153–76.

Raynaud, Dominique. *Optics and the Rise of Perspective: A Study in Network Knowledge Diffusion.* Oxford: The Bardwell Press, 2014.

Rehbein, Malte. "From the Scholarly Edition to Visualization: Re-using Encoded Data for Historical Research." *Interna-*

tional Journal of Humanities and Arts Computing 8, no. 1 (2014): 81–105. DOI: 10.3366/ijhac.2014.0121.

Rogers, Everett. *Diffusion of Innovations.* New York: Free Press of Glencoe, 1962.

Rosé, Isabelle. "Reconstrucción, représentacion gráfica análisis de las redes de poder en la alta edad media. Aproximación a las prácticas sociales de la aristocracia a partir del ejemplo de Odón de Cluny († 942)." *Redes: Revista hispana para el análisis de redes sociales* 21, no. 5 (2011): 139–272. DOI: 10.5565/rev/redes.420.

Rossi, Fabrice, Nathalie Villa-Vialaneix, and Florent Hautefeuille. "Exploration of a Large Database of French Notarial Acts with Social Network Methods." *Digital Medievalist* 9 (2014). DOI: 10.16995/dm.52.

Ruffini, Giovanni. *Social Networks in Byzantine Egypt.* Cambridge: Cambridge University Press, 2008. DOI: 10.1017/CBO9780511552014.

Schor, Adam M. "Becoming Bishop in the Letters of Basil and Synesius: Tracing Patterns of Social Signaling across Two Full Epistolary Collections." *Journal of Late Antiquity* 7, no. 2 (2014): 298–328. DOI: 10.1353/jla.2014.0034.

Scott, John. *Social Network Analysis.* London: Sage, 2017.

Selzer, Stephan, and Ulf Christian Ewert. "Netzwerke im europäischen Handel des Mittelalters. Konzepte-Anwendungen-Fragestellungen." *Vorträge und Forschungen* 72 (2010): 21–47.

Shaw, David Gary. "Social Networks and the Foundations of Oligarchy in Medieval Towns." *Urban History* 32, no. 2 (2005): 200–22. DOI: 10.1017/S096392680500297X.

Sindbæk, Søren. "Broken Links and Black Boxes: Material Affiliations and Contextual Network Synthesis in the Viking World." In *Network Analysis in Archaeology: New Approaches to Regional Interaction,* edited by Carl Knappett, 71–94. Oxford: Oxford University Press, 2013. DOI: 10.1093/acprof:oso/9780199697090.003.0004.

———. "The Small World of the Vikings: Networks in Early Medieval Communication and Exchange." *Norwe-*

gian Archaeological Review 40, no. 1 (2007): 59–74. DOI: 10.1080/00293650701327619.

Skog, Lars, and Hans Hauska. "Spatial Modeling of the Black Death in Sweden." *Transactions in GIS* 17, no. 4 (2013): 589–611. DOI: 10.1111/j.1467-9671.2012.01369.x.

Supekar, Kaustubh, Vinod Menon, Daniel Rubin, Mark Musen, and Michael D. Greicius. "Network Analysis of Intrinsic Functional Brain Connectivity in Alzheimer's Disease." *PLoS Computational Biology* 4, no. 6 (2008) DOI: 10.1371/journal.pcbi.1000100.

ter Braake, Serge. "Parties and Factions in the Late Middle Ages: The Case of the Hoeken and Kabeljauwen in The Hague (1483–1515)." *Journal of Medieval History* 35, no. 1 (2009): 97–111. DOI: 10.1016/j.jmedhist.2008.10.001.

Tilly, Charles. *Trust and Rule.* Cambridge: Cambridge University Press, 2005. DOI: 10.1017/CBO9780511618185.

Valente, Thomas. *Network Models of the Diffusion of Innovations.* Cresskill: Hampton Press, 1995.

Van Lanen, Rowin J., and Harm Jan Pierik. "Calculating Connectivity Patterns in Delta Landscapes: Modelling Roman and Early-Medieval Route Networks and Their Stability in Dynamic Lowlands." *Quaternary International* 501 (2019): 393–412. DOI: 10.1016/j.quaint.2017.03.009.

Vicsek, Lilla Mária, Gábor Király, and Hanna Kónya. "Networks in the Social Sciences: Comparing Actor-Network Theory and Social Network Analysis." *Corvinus Journal of Sociology and Social Policy* 7, no. 2 (2016): 77–102. DOI: 10.14267/CJSSP.2016.02.04.

Volkmann, Armin. "Perspectives for Network Analysis: Roman Roads, Barbarian Paths and Settlement Patterns in the Borderlands at the Limes Germanicus in the Main River Region." *Open Archaeology* 3, no. 1 (2017): 123–38. DOI: 10.1515/opar-2017-0007.

Wetherell, Charles. "Historical Social Network Analysis." *International Review of Social History* 43, Supplement S6 (1998): 125–44. DOI: 10.1017/S0020859000115123.

White, Harrison C. *Identity and Control: A Structural Theory of Social Action.* Princeton: Princeton University Press, 1992.

Wilkinson, Ryan Hayes. "The Last Horizons of Roman Gaul: Communication, Community, and Power at the End of Antiquity." PhD diss., Harvard University, 2015.

Wurps, Bernd. "Networks into Institutions or Institutions into Networks? Evidence from the Medieval Hansa." PhD diss., University of Washington, 2018.

Zweig, Katherina A. *Network Analysis Literacy: A Practical Approach to the Analysis of Networks.* Vienna: Springer, 2016. DOI: 10.1007/978-3-7091-0741-6.

2

Carolingian Schoolbooks and Intellectual Networks: A New Approach

Elizabeth P. Archibald

Early medieval masters who faced the task of assembling introductory materials for their students often described their mission as a sort of raid in the forests and fields of the ancients. The Anglosaxon missionary and grammarian Boniface described the process of compiling a grammatical manual as akin to entering "the ancient tangled forest of the grammarians in order to collect for you the best kinds of various fruits and the diffused perfumes of flowers for you, which are found scattered throughout the glades of the grammarians."[1] In the next generation, Alcuin addressed Charlemagne with a poetic description

---

1   Boniface, *Praefatio ad Sigibertum*. See Vivien Law, "An Early Medieval Grammarian on Grammar: Wynfreth-Boniface and the *Praefatio ad Sigibertum*," in *Grammar and Grammarians in the Early Middle Ages* (London: Longman, 1997), 170.15–20: "tale tricationum molestarum onus [...] ut antiquam perplexae sylvam densitatis grammaticorum ingrederer ad colligendum tibi diversorum optima quaeque genera pomorum et variorum odoramenta florum diffusa, quae passim dispersa per saltum grammaticorum inveniuntur." I owe thanks to a number of individuals for their help navigating the tangled forests of medieval manuscripts and network analysis, especially interlocutors at the Networks and Neighbours conference where this work was first presented in Nijmegen in 2017, members of the Carnegie

of rising early and "running through the fields of the ancients to pluck flowers in order to provide exercises of correct language for the boys."[2] These literary tropes, while somewhat overdramatic, accord with the more mundane relics of early medieval pedagogical activities.

The bouquets — florilegia — that resulted from masters scampering through the landscapes of the ancient grammarians are particularly characteristic of Carolingian literary culture broadly and schoolbooks specifically.[3] Anyone who has had occasion to work with early medieval manuscripts, and schoolbooks in particular, has encountered catalogues identifying codices as "miscellany" and "florilegium." These compilations abound in the liberal arts subjects, especially the trivium. There are several reasons for this phenomenon. Introductory texts tend to be short, lending themselves to shared-living arrangements in medieval codices, where parchment space is of course highly valuable. On the other hand, there is plenty of evidence that the compilers of manuscript miscellanies of the early Middle Ages produced their materials deliberately. Even when working with longer texts, they engaged in activities of excerpting, manipulating, and recombining to create useful compendia.[4] This phenomenon highlights the role of miscella-

---

Mellon University Digital Humanities Faculty Research Group, and the reviewers of this essay.

2 Ernst Dümmler, ed., *Monumenta Germaniae historica, Poetae Latini* 1 (Berlin: Weidmann, 1881), 254 (carm. xlii): "in campos veterum procurrens carpere flores / rectiloquos ludos pangeret ut pueris."

3 The distinctive prevalence of such compilations in Carolingian literary culture was emphasized early on by M.L.W. Laistner, *Thought and Letters in Western Europe, AD 500 to 900* (London: Methuen, 1957), 176: "One important product of monastic industry and of preoccupation with grammatica calls for brief notice. There were obvious advantages, both for use in the schoolroom and for private reading by those whose scholarship was limited, in chrestomathies." On the strategies of grammar instruction in the Carolingian period, see Vivien Law, "The Study of Grammar," in *Carolingian Culture: Emulation and Innovation,* ed. Rosamond McKitterick (Cambridge: Cambridge University Press, 1994), 88–110.

4 The understanding of these processes of knowledge selection underlying early medieval instructional materials continues to develop. Context for

nies as handy collections and, more specifically, points toward an important feature of early medieval schoolbooks: they generally pertain more to the instructor than to the student. In other words, it is often clear that they are collections of material compiled by a particular master, in a particular educational context, for particular instructional exigencies.[5] As such, they hold both promise and problems. In this chapter, I assess a group of early Carolingian grammar miscellanies using methods of digital network analysis, revealing both standardization and originality shaping this corpus of materials.

Early medieval miscellanies are an extremely valuable body of material, offering clues about what their compilers found useful; they are also quite numerous. Unfortunately, a millennium removed from these contexts, their logic is not always evident.

---

understanding the educational goals and practices that informed these materials is found in John J. Contreni, "Learning for God: Education in the Carolingian Age," *The Journal of Medieval Latin* 24 (2014): 89–129. Foundational insights into the dynamics of the relationship between Carolingian manuscripts and educational contexts appear in Bernhard Bischoff, "Libraries and Schools in the Carolingian Revival of Learning," in *Manuscripts and Libraries in the Age of Charlemagne*, trans. Michael Gorman (Cambridge: Cambridge University Press, 1994), 93–114; Rosamond McKitterick, *The Frankish Kingdoms under the Carolingians, 751–987* (London and New York: Longman, 1983), 200–228; as well as in studies of particular manuscript traditions, such as that of Donatus — Louis Holtz, *Donat et la tradition de l'enseignement grammatical: Étude sur l'"Ars Donati" et sa diffusion (IVᵉ–IXᵉ siècle) et édition critique* (Paris: CNRS, 1981) — and studies of particular centers of teaching and learning. See especially John J. Contreni, *The Cathedral School of Laon from 850 to 930: Its Manuscripts and Masters*, Münchener Beiträge zur Mediävistik und Renaissance-Forschung 29 (Munich: Arbeo-Gesellschaft, 1978), and David Ganz, *Corbie in the Carolingian Renaissance*, Beihefte der Francia 20 (Sigmaringen: Jan Thorbecke Verlag, 1990).

5 The categories of schoolbook (or classbook), miscellany, and glossed manuscript overlap but are not coterminous, and there are challenges of definition that attend each. A classic discussion of the distinction between glossed manuscript and schoolbook is Gernot R. Wieland, "The Glossed Manuscript: Classbook or Library Book?," *Anglo-Saxon England* 14 (1985): 153–73. The manuscripts discussed below are all miscellanies, and they are all schoolbooks in that they contain curricular material, though their individual roles in educational contexts were probably varied.

Recent research has begun to recognize and interrogate the significance of early medieval miscellanies, but much work remains to be done.[6] This work has been slow to unfold in part because, while miscellanies are both significant and abundant records of intellectual priorities, they are difficult to manage bibliographically. The miscellaneous character of early schoolbooks was a challenge to medieval catalogers as well as modern, a phenomenon reflected in the earliest library catalogues, such as that of St. Gall. Some texts occupy codices in tidy fashion: "*De doctrina Christiana* in one codex."[7] Then, when the unfortunate medieval cataloger arrives at the section of codices with grammatical content, we find "*Item,* the two *artes* of Donatus, and Honoratus, *De finalibus litteris,* and declensions, and the commentary of Sergius on Donatus, and the book of Isidore, and the book of Caper on orthography, and the *De metrica arte* of Bede. All these things in one codex."[8]

In fact, even this unwieldy description is deceptively tidy. The phrase "all these things in one codex" suggests that the relationship between codex and text is that of container and contents; the miscellaneous codex functions as a sort of receptacle for texts ("all these things"). But modern judgments about texts can be problematic: in the absence of a contemporaneous catalogue like this one, it is not always easy to understand what a compiler

---

6   Anna Dorofeeva has outlined a useful theory of early medieval miscellanies, emphasizing the practical potential of these materials, which fill the role of "local encyclopedias" in many subject areas, as "a response to an increasing need for information." See Anna Dorofeeva, "Miscellanies, Christian Reform and Early Medieval Encyclopaedism: A Reconsideration of the Pre-Bestiary Latin Physiologus Manuscripts," *Historical Research* 90 (2017): 665–82, at 678.

7   St. Gallen, Stiftsbibliothek 728, p. 8: "De doctrina Christiana libri IIII in volumine I." Printed in Paul Lehmann, *Mittelalterliche Bibliothekskataloge Deutschlands und der Schweiz,* vol. 1: *Die Bistümer Konstanz und Chur* (Munich: Beck, 1918), 66–82.

8   St. Gallen, Stiftsbibliothek 728, p. 20: "Item partes Donati minores atque maiores et Onorati de finalibus litteris et declinationes et commentarium Sergii in partes Donati et Ysidori liber et liber Capri de ortographia et Bedae de metrica arte. Haec omnia in volumine I."

or scribe or user of a miscellany saw as a discrete text, especially when they flow together in a codex without rubrication or interruption. And, of course, making a determination about whether a particular document is a witness to a particular work is the fundamental first step in investigating the manuscript tradition of a work. But with miscellanies like these, where each manuscript represents a different approach to excerpting, adapting, interpolating, and recombining materials, it is often surprisingly difficult. There is such variety among the manuscripts that traditional approaches to text editing quickly become problematic.

This is a particularly difficult problem in the case of schoolbooks, where even material that began its curricular life as a well-organized text might end up excerpted and incorporated into different compilations by different masters, with each of the compilations subject to the same kind of manipulations over time. By the Carolingian period, masters and compilers had been raiding the forests of the ancient grammarians for centuries, with constantly changing shopping lists. The typical situation is captured by a description of the *Ars Ambianensis*: "Even where all the versions are extant, none is identical to any other. They all reflect a putative original which each has adapted."[9] In some cases it is possible that the florilegia we are observing are the residue of textual practices that are difficult to trace: some of the innumerable short texts that appear in schoolbooks likely originated as *schedulae*—unbound scraps of parchment that were by-products of book production. Like wax tablets, few *schedulae* survive due to their ephemeral nature, but their use (including as substrate for first drafts of teaching materials) is documented, and some compilations may reflect transit of *schedulae* from one master to another in addition to the direct copying and excerpting of other codices.

As is often observed, a modern editor offering emendations and interventions designed to reconstruct authorial intention

---

9 James E.G. Zetzel, *Critics, Compilers, and Commentators: An Introduction to Roman Philology, 200 BCE–800 CE* (Oxford: Oxford University Press, 2018), 356.

may be reverse-engineering a fantasy text.[10] The miscellanies in question pose a similar problem: in trying to remove the flowers from the florilegium, a modern editor risks imposing anachronistic or inauthentic textual boundaries. The distinction between text and manuscript is evasive: is the thing in our hands a schoolbook in the sense of a canon of material, or a schoolbook in the sense of a physical object?

This problem is mitigated if we focus on the physical object, considering each codex as a self-contained intellectual universe. We can scrutinize a particular manuscript and consider its implications as a material representation of intellectual activity in a particular time and place. A number of schoolbooks have been productively considered in this way — usually those that can be securely attributed to a particular institution, often during the tenure of an important individual.[11] Paleography-based study of manuscript groups tentatively associated with specific institutions, too, is a venerable and indispensable approach that has, over the years, produced much of what we know about institutions of learning in the early Middle Ages. Yet securely dating and localizing manuscripts is an imperfect art: places are intuited from paleographical features, but scribes (and books) traveled, and it is the rare scribe considerate enough to provide precise dates; there is nearly always some uncertainty. Furthermore, scholarship gravitates toward the datable and localizable,

---

10 For a recent reconsideration of theories underpinning text editing and the "tension between classical methodology and medieval texts," see Carmela Vircillo Franklin, "Theodor Mommsen, Louis Duchesne, and the *Liber pontificalis*: Classical Philology and Medieval Latin Texts," in *Marginality, Canonicity, Passion: Classical Presences,* ed. Marco Formisano and Christina Shuttleworth Kraus (Oxford: Oxford University Press, 2018), 99–140, at 103.

11 For example, studies of several of the manuscripts discussed below: Louis Holtz, "Le Paris lat. 7530, Synthèse cassinienne des arts libéraux," *Studi medievali* 16, no. 3 (1975): 97–152, and Bernhard Bischoff, *Sammelhandschrift Diez B. Sant. 66. Grammatici Latini et catalogus librorum. Vollständige Faksimile-Ausgabe im Originalformat der Handschrift aus der Staatsbibliothek Preussischer Kulturbesitz* (Graz: Akademische Druk- und Verlangsanstalt, 1973).

while manuscripts of truly uncertain date and location tend to be overlooked altogether.

The larger problem, though, is this: an early medieval schoolbook, while highly individualized, is decidedly *not* a self-contained intellectual universe, and if we focus on one manuscript, as their idiosyncrasies push us to do, we miss the opportunity to examine the connections among these intellectual objects. We know that masters shared materials, but there is not as much direct evidence of these practices as we would like — and this is the major obstacle to a robust understanding of educational practices across Europe at a moment when these very manuscripts suggest that education had a singularly important role in society.

Thus, there are two fundamental obstacles to using schoolbooks as evidence for early medieval educational practices. Miscellanies, the most characteristic materials of literary and pedagogical culture in the Carolingian period, do not yield easily to traditional textual approaches; this makes it difficult to assess the process of canon formation. Manuscripts of uncertain or unknown provenance restrict our ability to draw broad conclusions about shared educational culture and practices. A potentially fruitful angle of approach to both of the problems posed by these materials involves assessing schoolbooks as elements in a network of learning. This approach allows us to form an impression of the intellectual landscape of the curriculum and the circulation and sharing of curricular content, without needing precise information about particular schoolbooks and their affiliations with masters and institutions.

When it comes to visualizing relationships between manuscripts, medievalists are accustomed to thinking in terms of the stemma, which reconstructs filiation relationships between textual witnesses, branching forth over time. In recent years, scholars have experimented with phylogenetic software (at first, software designed for analysis of evolutionary biology, and more recently, customized software for stemmatology) to assist efforts at reconstructing and visualizing relationships between manuscripts. These efforts have been promising with two important caveats: first, as with any computer-assisted analysis, one should be aware of the assumptions the algorithm applies (e.g., does it admit the possibility of more than two manuscripts having been copied from one exemplar?), and second, one should use it appropriately, as an aid to identifying fruitful areas for further investigation (e.g., highlighting a manuscript of late date whose text is an early witness we might otherwise overlook).[12]

But the quirks of miscellanies, and didactic miscellanies in particular, mean that this corpus lends itself to a different type of analysis, focusing not on texts that change over time but on roughly contemporaneous materials that share content with each other as elements of a network. Network analysis is generally used to analyze the relationships between individuals or communities — correspondents exchanging letters, sites linked by roads, and disease victims connected by disease vectors. But it can help to elucidate any type of data involving a group of entities in relationship with one another — and that is what these miscellanies represent.[13] Miscellanies can be seen as groups of texts in relationship with one another by virtue of existing in the same codex, where they could be encountered together by the same reader. On a larger scale, the manuscripts can be seen as existing in relationship with one another by virtue of containing the same text. Both of these types of relationship can be fruitfully examined with tools of network analysis. Such analysis does not offer a means of access to the masters and students who used these materials, but visualizing the relationships between

---

12 Barbara Bordalejo describes these approaches and problems in "The Genealogy of Texts: Manuscript Traditions and Textual Traditions," *Digital Scholarship in the Humanities* 31, no. 3 (2016): 563–77.

13 The possibilities of network-driven approaches for the humanities in general and for medieval manuscripts in particular are currently being articulated: see the recently published volume by Ruth Ahnert, Sebastian E. Ahnert, Catherine Nicole Coleman, and Scott B. Weingart, *The Network Turn: Changing Perspectives in the Humanities* (Cambridge: Cambridge University Press, 2020), as well as the discussion of analysis of medieval manuscripts and their relationships by Gustavo Fernandez Riva, "Network Analysis of Medieval Manuscript Transmission," *Journal of Historical Network Research* 3, no. 1 (2019): 30–49.

schoolbooks and instructional materials as intellectual elements in a network offers a broad impression of how knowledge was shared and helps to render these problematic sources more tractable. In other words, considering their connections within a wider network gives us a sense of the roads, even if the travelers remain unknown. This approach makes a virtue of the fact that miscellanies are so dynamic: they may vary so much that the distinction between text and manuscript becomes problematic and traditional editing tools cannot represent their complexity, but this variation also allows us to discern the shapes of curricula more clearly and helps to clarify the relationships between the materials.

In what follows, I will suggest some possibilities of two different network analysis approaches to a larger group of early Carolingian schoolbooks. The first analysis seeks to reveal the "communities of texts" within these miscellanies, providing a sense of the contours of the curriculum and a pedagogical canon in formation. The second approach examines affinities between manuscripts and groups of manuscripts based on their shared textual material, suggesting a way to think about intellectual networks that does not directly depend on data about text copying or assumptions about each manuscript's institutional or geographic origin.

Both analyses take as a starting point the group of manuscripts described by Bernhard Bischoff as "grammatical manuscripts from the age of Charlemagne and Louis the Pious."[14] Revealingly, although Bischoff sought to identify not miscella-

---

14 The list appears in Bischoff, "Libraries and Schools in the Carolingian Revival of Learning," 112–13. For additional information about the manuscripts and their contents, I have consulted Paolo de Paolis, "Miscellanee grammaticali altomedievali," in *Grammatica e grammatici latini: Teoria ed esegesi*, ed. Fabio Gasti (Pavia: Ibis, 2003), 29–74. Martin Irvine, *The Making of Textual Culture: "Grammatica" and Literary Theory, 350–1100* (Cambridge: Cambridge University Press, 1994), 395–404, provides a useful though somewhat less granular reckoning of grammatical manuscripts and their contents, and Zetzel, *Critics, Compilers, and Commentators*, offers a monumentally thorough and helpful overview of the efforts to disentangle textual traditions within this body of material.

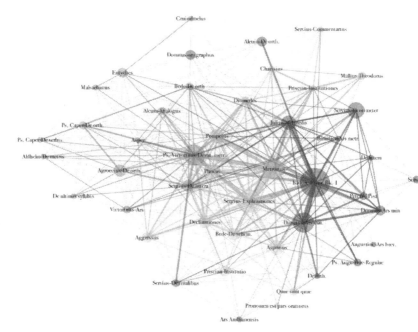

Fig. 1. A graph of relationships between texts, created using the network visualization software Gephi. Graph by the author.

nies in particular but grammatical manuscripts in general, of the twenty-seven surviving manuscripts in Bischoff's list, all but one are miscellanies, containing between a handful and thirty-five or so texts and excerpts (depending, of course, on how one makes a determination about what constitutes a text), primarily but not exclusively dealing with grammar. For the purposes of this project, I have considered only miscellanies where evidence is strong that they existed as a compilation by the ninth century. The goal of the first analysis is to measure and visualize the clusters of texts that appear within the manuscript compilations. In other words, while no two codices among the group contain exactly the same menu of texts, there are groups of texts within that circulate together with greater frequency, and these appear as clusters within a larger network. To some extent, of course, it is possible to identify clusters like these without the assistance of software — such work has been done with some of the manuscripts in this corpus[15] — but even in this relatively manageable group of manuscripts, the dataset consists of more than two thousand relationships between texts, and thus even exhausting manual study of the materials cannot reveal all of the patterns within.

In the first network analysis, I have assigned the texts the role of "nodes," conceptualizing them as elements in relationship with one another by virtue of circulating in the same manuscript. The manuscripts thus serve as the connections between different texts and are assigned the function of "edges" in the network. In effect, we are examining intellectual affinities — the edges represent connections between texts, reflecting the frequency with which Carolingian masters chose to collect specific materials together in a single compilation and Carolingian students and readers encountered them in this way.

Figure 1 is a graph of relationships between texts, created using the network visualization software Gephi. Each node represents a text. Texts appearing more frequently among the group of manuscripts appear as larger nodes. The edges drawn between nodes indicate that the texts represented by these nodes appear together within the same manuscript in at least one manuscript. The weight of each edge (represented visually as its width) is determined by the number of the manuscripts (within this set) in which the two texts appear together. The wider edges thus indicate that the two linked texts circulated more frequently in one another's company. The layout of the graph has been generated using Gephi's ForceAtlas2 algorithm, which causes linked nodes to be drawn toward one another, and non-linked nodes to be pushed apart. (This means that, in general, the more highly connected texts appear more central.) I have used Gephi's modularity function to sort the nodes, allowing the algorithm to identify

---

15 See, for instance, Michael M. Gorman and Elke Krotz, *Grammatical Works Attributed to Peter of Pisa, Charlemagne's Tutor* (Hildesheim: Weidmann, 2014).

clusters of texts that circulate together with disproportionate frequency and on this basis establish communities within the larger network. Each of the clusters identified by Gephi's modularity algorithm has been assigned a different color in this graph. For greater visual clarity I have excluded the texts that appear in a single manuscript in this group. What emerges through this process is a way of visualizing the early Carolingian grammatical curriculum.

Several features are immediately clear. This process trims away much of the "noise" in the schoolbooks since texts that appear in only one manuscript are excluded. Given the personalized nature of the schoolbooks, these are the majority, so the items that remain really do represent the core of the elementary grammar curriculum as it appears in these manuscripts. Unsurprisingly, Donatus (especially the *Ars maior*) appears rather prominent in the network — and closely connected with Isidore's *Etymologies,* since they often circulated together. Although the shift of intellectual energy toward Priscian's *Institutiones* over the course of the ninth century has occupied more attention in the educational history of the Carolingian period, these manuscripts show the importance of Donatus, especially at the introductory level of the curriculum that these compilations represent. Many of the manuscripts seem to be organized around the *Ars minor* and (especially) *Ars maior,* supplementing them with other useful materials. Priscian's monumental *Institutiones* is an insignificant piece of the network, though it appears in numerous manuscripts on its own (especially in the second half of the ninth century). When we see the curriculum in a statistically grounded visualization, certain elements may come as a surprise: we might not immediately cite Isidore as the obvious authority on grammar, but Carolingian masters clearly depended on excerpts from the first book of the *Etymologies* in the elementary phase of the grammar curriculum; similarly, the rather mysterious Sergius (both *De littera* and *Explanationes*) was a clear favorite in grammar pedagogy.[16]

Although the manuscripts, examined in isolation, rarely appear highly planned, several groups of material emerge within the visualization that suggest patterns of organization and delineate comprehensible subject curricula. For instance, it is easy to identify a group of materials on orthography. The fifth-century *Ars de orthographia* of Agroecius is organized as a supplement to the *De orthographia* and *De verbis dubiis,* both attributed to (and neither authentically the work of) the second-century scholar Flavius Caper.[17] Not surprisingly, it circulates frequently with these texts. These texts also circulate disproportionately frequently with Bede's orthographical work. While it is perhaps not surprising for texts on a common subject to appear as a curriculum, this is an interesting result for two reasons: first, it reveals some order within manuscripts that seem rather chaotic on their own, and second, it implies that scribes and compilers who could have chosen one favorite orthography manual from among the available options chose instead to collect several in one place (otherwise these texts would appear more closely linked with other materials). For orthography, then, some of the manuscripts seem to have functioned more as reference manuals than carefully curated pedagogical handbooks. An exception is Alcuin's orthographical manual, which appears more closely connected with other texts: perhaps it superseded the others in the minds of some compilers.

Another link that emerges in this visualization is the frequency of cohabitation between "Metrorius" and Pseudo-Victorinus's *De ratione metrorum,* two texts that have been noted as part of a collection of works often appearing together.[18] The network visualization here shows texts in affinity without indicating the larger causes, and here we have already seen sev-

---

16 On "Sergius" and Servius, see Zetzel, *Critics, Compilers, and Commentators,* 319–24.

17 See ibid., 174–75 and 279–80.

18 Ibid., 334–35, outlines the problem, noting that "This is, as outlined above, extremely confusing" (335).

eral potential reasons for texts to cluster together. In some cases, it appears that texts circulate together due to manuscript traditions: that is, they coalesced as a cluster prior to the copying of an individual manuscript and thus can be seen as more of a discrete compilation than a group of texts; this is the case with "Agroecius"/"Caper" and "Metrorius"/"Victorinus." If texts were placed together at the moment of the manuscript's copying, other explanations abound: they deal with the same material, and compiler(s) found it useful to gather multiple treatments of the same topics in one place; they deal with different materials, and compiler(s) thought they formed a useful curriculum; they share a geographical context (as is the case with, say, *Quae sunt quae* and *Aggressus quidam*[19]); they share origins as new compositions rather than ancient texts. In other words, the network serves to highlight interesting features of the curriculum, for which we can settle on possible historical explanations.

One of the most interesting clusters that emerges in this visualization is the group to which Donatus is assigned, which also includes Isidore of Seville (a variety of excerpts from book I of the *Etymologies* that can be broadly categorized as the *Ars Isidori,* as Evina Steinová discusses in this volume) and an anonymous commentary indicated as "De littera." This material forms a rather comprehensive core of basic instruction about the letters of the alphabet and the parts of speech. The grammar of Peter of Pisa (identified by Einhard as Charlemagne's own grammar teacher) is also assigned to this cluster. With this posited micro-curriculum identified, we can return to the manuscripts for additional information; among those that share this cluster in common are several important manuscripts from ca. 800 with a variety of connections to the court of Charlemagne. Perhaps the fact that these texts are closely linked lends support to the hypothesis that several of these manuscripts reflect the

---

19 On these texts, see Luigi Munzi, *"Multiplex Latinitas": Testi grammaticali latini dell'Alto Medioevo* (Naples: Istituto Universitario Orientale, 2004), 8–15 and 67–72.

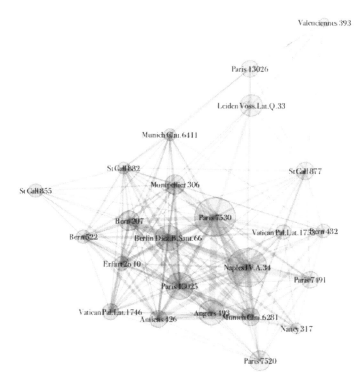

Fig. 1. A graph of relationships between texts, created using the network visualization software Gephi. Graph by the author.

pedagogical interests of the court.[20] Although direct evidence for links between manuscripts in this network is less plentiful than we might like, the larger visualization gives a good sense of curricular clusters. Returning subsequently to the manuscripts with a better grasp of the organization of the curriculum may

---

20 Vivien Law identified the manuscripts Paris, Bibliothèque nationale lat. 13025; Naples, Biblioteca Nazionale IV. A. 34; St. Gallen, Stiftsbibliothek 876; Bern, Burgerbibliothek Cod. 207; and Berlin, Staatsbibliothek, Diez B Sant. 66, as possible reflections of court interests. See Vivien Law, *The Insular Latin Grammarians* (Woodbridge: Boydell Press, 1982), 100–101.

allow for a more thorough assessment of how some groups of material were localized in particular regions and others shared widely — especially having established the larger network as a kind of baseline or control against which to measure the significance of a particular curriculum.

Having identified some of the intellectual relationships between the texts in these miscellanies as curricula or components of an educational canon, a second network analysis approach to the same materials offers another tool that helps to assess the shared intellectual preoccupations of the manuscripts. Like Figure 1, Figure 2 has been created using Gephi and its ForceAtlas2 algorithm. In this visualization, each manuscript is represented as a node, and the texts they share function as the edges connecting them. By considering the manuscripts themselves as nodes in a network that are in relationship with other manuscripts by virtue of their common texts (the same approach applied earlier to visualize the intellectual affinities between a small group of manuscripts), we can enrich our understanding of the intellectual network that includes these materials. While identifying intellectual affinities on the basis of shared material in manuscripts is an exercise that does not automatically necessitate the use of network-analysis tools, once again even in what appears to be a relatively manageable body of material (twenty-seven manuscripts), the connections of this type number well over a thousand, and thus the big picture is difficult to formulate without the assistance of software. Again, the edges do not represent evidence for direct contact between manuscripts as material objects but family affinities via shared materials; that is, the connections are intellectual rather than physical.

What emerges in figure 2, then, is a starting point for additional research on these manuscripts. Do closely linked manuscripts share common geographical origins of which we are aware? For the most part they do not, although there are a few exceptions: Amiens 426 and Paris lat. 13025, for instance, positioned close together, are thought to be Corbie manuscripts. On the other hand, we might expect an opposite phenomenon, where manuscripts of common origin do not share many texts, since that would mean redundancies in institutional collections. If geographical origins do not correlate with textual preoccupations, is there evidence of a broadly shared curriculum across wide regions? Are textual affinities between manuscripts the result of a deliberate program, or of masters independently adopting the same texts? These are central questions to the problem of understanding the way that Carolingian education functioned at local levels. Though this network visualization does not offer easy answers, it offers suggestions for fruitful areas of research.

One observation that can be made on the basis of this group of miscellanies is that compilers of grammatical material were highly independent. Many of the texts (more than eighty of them — or around 60 percent) are not shared with other manuscripts in this group. When we look at shared texts, the numbers drop precipitously. The texts that appear in nine or more manuscripts thus represent a real curricular commitment within this group of manuscripts — excerpts from Isidore's *Etymologies,* the *Explanationes* of Sergius, and Donatus's *Ars maior* being the greatest hits of grammar in the age of Charlemagne and Louis the Pious on the basis of this group. But what compilers did with this common core of material — namely, supplement them with many other, much less popular, texts — seems to have been very much a matter of institutional or individual discretion.

So, while these manuscript miscellanies are complicated in ways that traditional editing tools find difficult to maneuver, their complications are actually of use in understanding them as pieces of a larger intellectual network. In other words, the changing menus of texts in this corpus can function as a sort of larger version of variants within a text, offering useful information about the way that individual masters and scribes worked curricular materials for their own uses. The clusters that emerge in each network analysis have a multiplicity of causes (whether common geographical origins for a group of manuscripts or deliberately selected thematic clusters of texts on a common curriculum), but they suggest broadly the way that these materials — schoolbooks in the sense of both texts and manuscripts — functioned in a wider intellectual network rather than as self-contained intellectual worlds. At the same time, it should be observed that the overall impression of variety and complexity within Carolingian schoolbooks is significant: it is difficult to discern the intellectual networks to which these materials belong precisely because masters felt free to compile ad hoc collections rather than (as is the old stereotype) copying their ancient sources uncritically.[21] Furthermore, the Carolingian reputation for standardization in other spheres has inspired searches for an "official" liberal arts curriculum, but the manuscripts are so varied that these searches have been mostly in vain.[22] Against this backdrop, the curricular and manuscript clusters that emerge in the network analyses here are perhaps especially significant — suggesting that the miscellanies are not evidence of curricular chaos but efforts at making common materials locally useful.

The possibilities of examining these miscellanies and similar categories of evidence in the form of an intellectual network are many: here we see just some of the possible angles of investigation. This technique should be seen as complementary to other, more established approaches, which I have mostly avoided applying in this project in order to assess the utility of the network analyses and visualizations without relying on inferences from other sources. We can localize and date manuscripts and determine their roles in an intellectual network via scrutiny of all sorts of paleographical, codicological, and extra-textual clues, but a network analysis of this sort is complementary to these approaches, suggesting the broad contours of an intellectual landscape. And, like most techniques of digital analysis involv-

---

21 On the issue of originality as it relates specifically to the study of grammar in the Carolingian period, see Louis Holtz, "Les innovations théoriques de la grammaire carolingienne: Peu de chose. Pourquoi?," in *L'héritage des grammariens latins de l'Antiquité aux Lumières,* ed. Irène Rosier (Paris: Société pour l'information grammaticale, 1988), 133–45. The essays in McKitterick, ed., *Carolingian Culture,* provide a multifaceted assessment of Carolingian reception and originality.

22 On the formation of ideas about the liberal arts in Carolingian culture, see John Marenbon, "Carolingian Thought," in *Carolingian Culture,* ed. McKitterick, 171–92.

ing "big data," it allows us to return to the manuscripts with a more precise sense of which threads to pull. Texts that appear unexpectedly as clusters may represent an effort to standardize the curriculum on a particular topic. Manuscripts that seem unexpectedly connected in the network may suggest promising avenues of research (such as St. Gallen Stiftsbibliothek 877, which contains a number of medical texts but which is highly connected with several very important early Carolingian grammatical manuscripts). Furthermore, such analyses could be deployed with other corpora: all sorts of manuscript miscellanies might benefit from this approach (letter collections, legal collections) as well as other types of material (one example is medieval library catalogues, which could be analyzed in this way to assess broad patterns within the intellectual landscape). Although these are preliminary experiments, they suggest the value of adding network visualization to the toolbox of research on medieval manuscripts, schoolbooks, and intellectual worlds.

Bibliography

Manuscripts

Amiens. Bibliothèques d'Amiens Métropole, MS 426. https://gallica.bnf.fr/ark:/12148/btv1b8452180f.

Berlin. Staatsbibliothek, Diez B Sant. 66.

Bern. Burgerbibliothek, Cod. 207. https://www.e-codices.ch/en/list/one/bbb/0207.

Naples. Biblioteca Nazionale IV. A. 34.

Paris. Bibliothèque nationale de France, lat. 13025. https://gallica.bnf.fr/ark:/12148/btv1b8423831v.

St. Gallen. Stiftsbibliothek, Cod. Sang. 728. https://www.e-codices.ch/en/list/one/csg/0728.

St. Gallen. Stiftsbibliothek, Cod. Sang. 876. https://www.e-codices.unifr.ch/fr/list/one/csg/0876.

Primary & Reference

Boniface. *Praefatio ad Sigibertum.* Edited by Vivien Law. "An Early Medieval Grammarian on Grammar: Wynfreth-Boniface and the *Praefatio ad Sigibertum.*" In Vivien Law, *Grammar and Grammarians in the Early Middle Ages,* 169–87. London: Longman, 1997.

Lehmann, Paul. *Mittelalterliche Bibliothekskataloge Deutschlands und der Schweiz,* Vol. 1: *Die Bistümer Konstanz und Chur.* Munich: Beck, 1918.

Monumenta Germaniae historica, Poetae Latini 1. Edited by Ernst Dümmler. Berlin: Weidmann, 1881.

Secondary

Ahnert, Ruth, Sebastian E. Ahnert, Catherine Nicole Coleman, and Scott B. Weingart. *The Network Turn: Changing Perspectives in the Humanities.* Cambridge: Cambridge University Press, 2020. DOI: 10.1017/9781108866804.

Bischoff, Bernhard. "Libraries and Schools in the Carolingian Revival of Learning." In *Manuscripts and Libraries in the Age of Charlemagne,* translated by Michael M. Gorman, 93–114. Cambridge: Cambridge University Press, 1994.

————. *Sammelhandschrift Diez B. Sant. 66. Grammatici Latini et catalogus librorum. Vollständige Faksimile-Ausgabe im Originalformat der Handschrift aus der Staatsbibliothek Preussischer Kultuerbesitz.* Graz: Akademische Druk- und Verlangsanstalt, 1973.

Bordalejo, Barbara. "The Genealogy of Texts: Manuscript Traditions and Textual Traditions." *Digital Scholarship in the Humanities* 31, no. 3 (2016): 563–77. DOI: 10.1093/llc/fqv038

Contreni, John J. "Learning for God: Education in the Carolingian Age." *The Journal of Medieval Latin* 24 (2014): 89–129. DOI: 10.1484/J.JML.5.103276.

————. *The Cathedral School of Laon from 850 to 930: Its Manuscripts and Masters.* Münchener Beiträge zur Mediävistik und Renaissance-Forschung 29. Munich: Arbeo-Gesellschaft, 1978.

de Paolis, Paolo. "Miscellanee grammaticali altomedievali." In *Grammatica e grammatici latini: Teoria ed esegesi,* edited by Fabio Gasti, 29–74. Pavia: Ibis, 2003.

Dorofeeva, Anna. "Miscellanies, Christian Reform and Early Medieval Encyclopaedism: A Reconsideration of the Pre-Bestiary Latin Physiologus Manuscripts." *Historical Research* 90 (2017): 665–82. DOI: 10.1111/1468-2281.12198.

Franklin, Carmela Vircillo. "Theodor Mommsen, Louis Duchesne, and the *Liber pontificalis*: Classical Philology and Medieval Latin Texts." In *Marginality, Canonicity, Passion: Classical Presences,* edited by Marco Formisano and Christina Shuttleworth Kraus, 99–140. Oxford: Oxford University Press, 2018. DOI: 10.1093/oso/9780198818489.003.0005.

Ganz, David. *Corbie in the Carolingian Renaissance.* Beihefte der Francia 20. Sigmaringen: Jan Thorbecke Verlag, 1990.

Gorman, Michael M., and Elke Krotz. *Grammatical Works Attributed to Peter of Pisa, Charlemagne's Tutor.* Hildesheim: Weidmann, 2014.

Holtz, Louis. *Donat et la tradition de l'enseignement grammatical: Étude sur l'"Ars Donati" et sa diffusion (IVe–IXe siècle) et édition critique.* Paris: CNRS, 1981.

————. "Le Paris lat. 7530, Synthèse cassinienne des arts libéraux." *Studi medievali* 16, no. 3 (1975): 97–152.

————. "Les innovations théoriques de la grammaire carolingienne: peu de chose. Pourquoi?" In *L'héritage des grammariens latins de l'Antiquité aux Lumières,* edited by Irène Rosier, 133–45. Paris: Société pour l'information grammaticale, 1988.

Irvine, Martin. *The Making of Textual Culture: "Grammatica" and Literary Theory, 350–1100.* Cambridge: Cambridge University Press, 1994.

Laistner, M.L.W. *Thought and Letters in Western Europe, AD 500 to 900.* London: Methuen, 1957.

Law, Vivien. *The Insular Latin Grammarians.* Woodbridge: Boydell Press, 1982.

————. "The Study of Grammar." In *Carolingian Culture: Emulation and Innovation,* edited by Rosamond McKitterick, 88–110. Cambridge: Cambridge University Press, 1994.

Marenbon, John. "Carolingian Thought." In *Carolingian Culture: Emulation and Innovation,* edited by Rosamond McKitterick, 171–92. Cambridge: Cambridge University Press, 1994.

McKitterick, Rosamond, ed. *Carolingian Culture: Emulation and Innovation.* Cambridge: Cambridge University Press, 1994.

————. *The Frankish Kingdoms under the Carolingians, 751–987.* London and New York: Longman, 1983.

Munzi, Luigi. *"Multiplex Latinitas": Testi grammaticali latini dell'Alto Medioevo.* Naples: Istituto Universitario Orientale, 2004.

Riva, Gustavo Fernandez. "Network Analysis of Medieval Manuscript Transmission." *Journal of Historical Network Research* 3, no. 1 (2019): 30–49.

Wieland, Gernot R. "The Glossed Manuscript: Classbook or Library Book?" *Anglo-Saxon England* 14 (1985): 153–73. DOI: 10.1017/S0263675100001320.

Zetzel, James E.G. *Critics, Compilers, and Commentators: An Introduction to Roman Philology, 200 BCE–800 CE.* Oxford: Oxford University Press, 2018.

3

The Politics of Intellectual Networks in Late Merovingian Francia

Yitzhak Hen

Sometime between 664 and 666 CE, bishop Chrodobert of Tours sent a rhythmic letter to bishop Importun of Paris, complaining about the quality of the grain that was sent by Importun to Tours as the annual payment (*annona*).[1] Importun was furious,

---

1   Chrodobert-Importunus, *Epistulae* 1, ed. and trans. Gerard J.J. Walstra, *Les cinq épîtres rimées dans l'appendice des formules de Sens: La querelle des évêques Frodobert et Importun (an 665/666)* (Boston and Leiden: Brill, 1962), 66–69. On these letters, see Dag Norberg, "Quelques remarques sur les lettres de Frodebert et d'Importun," *Rivista di filologia e di instruzione classica* 92 (1964): 295–303; Dag Norberg, *Manuel pratique de latin médiéval* (Paris: Picard, 1968), 111–23; Michel Banniard, *"Viva voce": Communication écrite et communication orale du IVe au IXe siècle en Occident latin* (Paris: Institut des études augustiniennes, 1992), 292–95; Danuta Shanzer, "The Tale of Frodebert's Tail," in *Colloquial and Literary Latin,* ed. Eleanor Dickey and Anna Chahoud (Cambridge: Cambridge University Press, 2010), 376–405; Yitzhak Hen, "Changing Places: Chrodobert, Boba, and the Wife of Grimoald," *Revue belge de philologie et d'histoire* 90, no. 2 (2012): 225–44; and Alice Tyrrell, *Merovingian Letters and Letter Writers* (Turnhout: Brepols, 2019), 66–81. I would like to thank Michael J. Kelly and Sven Meeder for inviting me to present an earlier version of this paper as a keynote lecture at the workshop *Networks of Knowledge* (Nijmegen, August 31–September 2, 2017). A French version of this paper was published in *L'Austrasie: Pouvoirs,*

and he answered Chrodobert with two acerbic letters — a personal letter to Chrodobert himself and a public letter that was distributed throughout Francia and a copy of which was even sent to the king.[2] The gist of these letters that were addressed "To my lord Chrodobert, [a man] with no God, neither a saint, nor a bishop or a secular cleric, who is ruled by the ancient enemy of mankind"[3] is simple. Because you complained about the grain I had sent to you, I will tell everyone how horrible you are. And the list of calumnies raised by Importun is long and colorful, ranging from heresy to sexual promiscuity, with a caustic comment on the size of Chrodebert's penis, followed by a strong recommendation that he should castrate himself.[4] Chrodobert could not keep quiet, and responded with a vicious circular letter of his own. After quoting king Solomon's proverb — "Do not answer fools according to their folly, or you will be a fool yourself" (Prov. 26:4) — Chrodobert elegantly ignored Importun's accusations and simply asked those who read the letters to ignore the blasphemous allegations made by his infidel enemy, who "lies like an Irishman," "has bad breath," "is worth less than a chicken," and "sings psalms like a babbling devil."[5] A fifth letter, which could have been written by either Importun or Chrodobert (although I think the attribution to Chrodobert is more likely because of its content) was addressed to a religious community of women, asking them not to believe the accusations made in the previous letters.[6]

---

espaces et identités à la charnière de l'Antiquité et du Moyen Âge, ed. Adrien Bayard, Bruno Dumézil, and Sylvie Joye (Paris, forthcoming).

2   Chrodobert-Importunus, *Epistulae* 2–3, ed. Walstra, 68–75.

3   Ibid., 3, ed. Walstra, 70: "Domno meo Frodeberto, sine Deo, nec sancto nec episcopo, nec saeculare clerico, ubi regnat antiquus hominum inimicus."

4   Ibid., 3, ed. Walstra, 72: "Per tua cauta longa — satis est, vel non est? — per omnia iube te castrare, ut non pereas per talis quia fornicatoris Deus iudicabit."

5   Ibid., 4, ed. Walstra, 80, 78, 79: "ut Escotus mentit," "non gaudeas de dentes," "non vales uno coco," and "psallat [...] ut linguaris dilator."

6   Ibid., 5, ed. Walstra, 80–81.

These letters, which are unique and unusual even among the Merovingian letter collections that survive,[7] are an excellent starting point for a discussion on intellectual networks and politics in Merovingian Gaul, for not only do they represent the culmination of a unique cultural phenomenon, whose origins could be traced back to the Frankish royal court and its vibrant elite, but they also give us a rare glimpse of the inventive ways in which the written word was used and abused by leading members of the Merovingian court circle.

The early Merovingian kings and queens, as far as we can tell, were not particularly interested in cultivating cultural activity, unless it was directly associated with exerting their authority over their kingdoms.[8] This situation was about to change, and toward the middle of the sixth century something had happened in Austrasia. It was king Theudebert I who first made an attempt to turn his royal court into an intellectual center by surrounding himself with learned aristocrats, among them Asteriolus and Secundinus, who, according to Gregory of Tours, were both "sapiens et retoricis inbutus litteris,"[9] and Parthenius, the grandson of Emperor Avitus and bishop Ruricius of Limoges, who was educated in Ravenna.[10] Whether this was an attempt to imitate the Ostrogothic court of Theoderic the Great, who had recruited to his service both Boethius and Cassiodorus, is im-

---

7 On Merovingian letter-collections, see Ian N. Wood, "Administration, Law, and Culture in Merovingian Gaul," in *The Uses of Literacy in the Early Middle Ages,* ed. Rosamond McKitterick (Cambridge: Cambridge University Press, 1990), 63–81; Ian N. Wood, "Letters and Letter-Collections from Antiquity to the Early Middle Ages: The Prose Work of Avitus of Vienne," in *The Culture of Christendom: Essays in Medieval History in Commemoration of Denis Bethell,* ed. Marc A. Meyer (London: The Hambledon Press, 1993), 29–43; and Tyrrell, *Merovingian Letters.*

8 See Yitzhak Hen, *Roman Barbarians: The Royal Court and Culture in the Early Medieval West* (Basingstoke: Palgrave Macmillan, 2007), 97–100.

9 Gregory of Tours, *Libri historiarum,* 3.33, ed. Wilhelm Levison and Bruno Krusch, Monumenta Germaniae Historica, Scriptores Rerum Merovingicarum 1.1 (Hanover: Hahn, 1951), 128–29.

10 Ibid., 3.36, ed. Levison and Krusch, 131–32.

possible to gauge.[11] Nevertheless, Theudebert's acts set up a formidable model that was followed suit by future Frankish kings.

Twenty years later, when king Sigibert I recruited the learned Gogo as his advisor and probably as his *maior domus,* Theudebert's and Parthenius's legacy was still prominent in the Austrasian court.[12] Gogo, who was a student of Parthenius himself, was well versed in the culture of Antiquity, as the four letters from him that survive testify.[13] But Gogo was not alone. A group of talented young aristocrats associated in one way or another with the Austrasian court began to crystallize around Gogo, and members of this group joined forces in political, diplomatic, and social struggles, and mobilized forces to protect their own personal interests.[14] The formation of this Austrasian intellectual faction received a further boost with the arrival of the Italian poet Venantius Honorius Clementianus Fortunatus.

Having been cured of an eye infection through the agency of Saint Martin, Fortunatus decided to visit the saint's shrine in Tours.[15] Whether this was a true act of devotion or a mere cover-up story for a secret mission on behalf of the Byzantine exarch of Ravenna is unknown. Nevertheless, Fortunatus's journey

---

11 On the Ostrogothic court of Theoderic the Great, see Hen, *Roman Barbarians,* 27–58.

12 Gregory of Tours, *Libri historiarum,* 5.46, ed. Levison and Krusch, 256.

13 See *Epistolae Austrasicae* 13, 16, 22, and 48, ed. and trans. Elena Malaspina, *Il Liber epistolarum della cancellaria austrasica (sec. V–VI)* (Rome: Herder Editrici, 2001), 116–19, 126–29, 142–45, and 218–21, respectively.

14 See Bruno Dumézil, "Gogo et ses amis: Écriture, échanges et ambitions dans un réseau aristocratique de la fin du VIe siècle," *Revue historique* 309, no. 643 (2007): 553–93.

15 On Venantius Fortunatus and his career, see Peter Godman, *Poets and Emperors: Frankish Politics and Carolingian Poetry* (Oxford: Clarendon Press, 1987), 1–37; Judith W. George, *Venantius Fortunatus: A Poet in Merovingian Gaul* (Oxford: Clarendon Press, 1992); Luce Piétri, "Venance Fortunat et ses commanditaires: Un poète italien dans la société gallo-franque," in *Committenti e produzione artistico-letteraria nell'alto medioevo occidentale,* Settimane di studio del Centro italiano di studi sull'alto medioevo 39 (Spoleto: CISAM, 1992), 729–54; and Michael Roberts, *The Humblest Sparrow: The Poetry of Venantius Fortunatus* (Ann Arbor: University of Michigan Press, 2009).

took him through Francia, and in 566 he arrived at the Austrasian court in Metz just in time for the grand occasion of King
Sigibert's marriage to the Visigothic princess Brunhild. A versed
panegyric and an *epithalamium* in honor of the royal couple on
their wedding night[16] provided Fortunatus with a grand entry
to the Austrasian royal circle and paved his way for success as a
poet in Merovingian Gaul.

This could have hardly been accidental. Wandering poets do
not land out of the blue in royal courts and get admitted just
like that to a royal wedding without any qualms or reservations.
No doubt, Fortunatus's appearance at the wedding of the royal
couple was carefully planned well in advance and orchestrat-
ed by people from the court, if not by Gogo himself. Many of
the Frankish aristocrats whom Fortunatus had met at the royal
wedding in Metz, among them Duke Lupus of Champagne,[17]
the maiores Gogo and Conda,[18] Dynamius and Iovinus of
Provence,[19] as well as various bishops and religious women of
aristocratic origins, became the dedicatees of numerous poems
and epitaphs.[20] This could only mean that by the mid-sixth century the royal court, under the auspices of the Austrasian king,
was indeed becoming a cultural center that attracted talented
intellectuals. But what the nature of this cultural center was, is
very difficult to tell.

The Merovingian *aula regis* is a shadowy institution in the
extreme. Unlike that of the Carolingians, it was never described
in detail by a former member, nor do the documents issued
by the Merovingian chancery provide much information on
its inner workings,[21] let alone its culture and social manifesta-

---

16 Venantius Fortunatus, *Carmina*, 6.1 et 6.1a, ed. and trans. Marc Reydellet, 3
    vols. (Paris: Les Belles Lettres, 1994–2004), vol. 2, 43–52.

17 Ibid., 7.7–8, 2, ed. and trans. Reydellet, 94–100.

18 Ibid., 7.1–2 and 16.2, ed. and trans. Reydellet, 85–88 and 111–14.

19 Ibid., 6.9–10 and 7.11–12, ed. and trans. Reydellet, 80–84 and 102–8.

20 See, for example, ibid., 4.26, 2, ed. and trans. Reydellet, 155–63 et passim.

21 The bibliography on the Carolingian court is enormous and cannot be
    fully listed here. One should only mention here Janet L. Nelson, "Aachen
    as a Place of Power," in *Topographies of Power in the Early Middle Ages*, ed.
    Mayke de Jong, Franz Theuws, and Carine Van Rhijn (Boston and Leiden:

tion. Nevertheless, it seems that during the reign of Sigibert I, a certain group of aristocrats who were associated with the royal court of Austrasia in one way or another, or passed through the royal court, emerged as a unique intellectual group, "les amis de Gogo," as Bruno Dumézil has so nicely called them.[22] The time at court was a formative period for these young members of the Merovingian elite, during which they played a crucial role in the formation of the court's written culture as an audience, producers, and, subsequently, chief disseminators. These young men developed a strong sense of camaraderie (*contubernium*) and friendship (*amicitia*) that were cultivated by the adoption of the insignia and gestures of the late Roman imperial bodyguard, and maintained through the exchange of poetry and letters.[23] At court, these were forms of courtly entertainment and maybe competition; beyond the court, such letters and poetic epistles served as a system for communicating social and political news. As the various letters collected in the so-called *Epistulae Austrasiacae*,[24] and the various poems by Venantius Frotunatus testify, even after they left court these friends exchanged letters

---

Brill, 2001), 217–41; Janet L. Nelson, "Was Charlemagne's Court a Courtly Culture?," in *Court Culture in the Early Middle Ages: The Proceedings of the First Alcuin Conference,* ed. Catherine Cubitt (Turnhout: Brepols, 2003), 39–57; and Matthew Innes, "A Place of Discipline: Carolingian Courts and Aristocratic Youth," in *Court Culture,* ed. Cubitt, 59–76.

22 Dumézil, "Gogo et ses amis."

23 See Pierre Riché, *Education and Culture in the Barbarian West from the Sixth through the Eighth Century,* trans. John J. Contreni (Columbia: University of South Carolina Press, 1976), 236–46; Ian N. Wood, *The Merovingian Kingdoms, 450–751* (London and New York: Longman, 1994), 149–52; Wood, "Administration, Law, and Culture," 67–71; Hope D. Williard, "Letter-writing and Literary Culture in Merovingian Gaul," *European Review of History* 21 (2014): 691–710; and Tyrrell, *Merovingian Letters,* 25–30.

24 On the *Epistulae Austrasicae,* see the edition of Malaspina, 5–46. See also Graham Barrett and George Woodhuysen, "Assembling the Austrasian Letters at Trier and Lorsch," *Early Medieval Europe* 24, no. 1 (2016): 3–57, and compare with Bruno Dumézil, "Private Records of an Official Diplomacy: The Franco Byzantine Letters in the Austrasian Epistular Collection," in *The Merovingian Kingdoms and the Mediterranean World: Revisiting the Sources,* ed. Stefan Esders, Yitzhak Hen, Pia Lucas, and Tamar Rotman (London: Bloomsbury, 2019), 55–62.

to ensure support when needed, and these lines of communication ensured that old friendships were never forgotten.

That such poems and letters were written at all is a clear indication on the one hand of the strength of literary tradition within the court circle of Austrasia, and on the other hand of the innovative and widespread use of the written word in Merovingian Francia. Needless to say, this practice did not emerge *ex nihilo,* and it was deeply rooted in Roman tradition that went back to Cicero, and continued well into Late Antiquity and the early Middle Ages, as attested by the letters of Pliny the Younger, Sidonius Apollinaris, Avitus of Vienne, Ruricius of Limoges, and Ferreolus of Uzès, whose letters unfortunately did not survive.[25] And yet, the Merovingian courtiers of Austrasia gave this tradition a new twist that, eventually, enabled them to mold a political and social support group. Against the background of the political turmoil of the late sixth and early seventh century, they surely needed such support.

Whether the Austrasian court with its intellectual circle was also an educational center for the young members of the Austrasian elite is not at all clear. We know that Gogo was entrusted with the education of the young prince Childebert II.[26] After Gogo's death in 581, the duty was passed on to his successor, Waldelenus,[27] and after Waldelenus's death, Brunhild herself took over and supervised the education of her son.[28] This, in

---

25 See Ian N. Wood, "Continuity or Calamity? The Constraints of Literary Models," in *Fifth-Century Gaul: A Crisis of Identity?,* ed. John Drinkwater and Hugh Elton (Cambridge: Cambridge University Press, 1992), 9–18; Wood, "Letters and Letter-collections"; Jennifer Ebbler, "Tradition, Innovation, and Epistolary Mores," in *A Companion to Late Antiquity,* ed. Philip Rousseau (Chichester: Wiley-Blackwell, 2009), 270–84; Andrew Gillet, "Communication in Late Antiquity: Use and Reuse," in *The Oxford Handbook of Late Antiquity,* ed. Scott F. Johnson (Oxford: Oxford University Press, 2012), 815–46; and Pauline Allen and Brownen Neil, *Crisis Management in Late Antiquity (410–590 CE): A Survey of the Evidence from Episcopal Letters* (Boston and Leiden: Brill, 2013).

26 Gregory of Tours, *Libri historiarum,* 5.46, ed. Levison and Krusch, 256.

27 Ibid., 6.1, ed. Levison and Krusch, 265.

28 Ibid., 8.22, ed. Levison and Krusch, 389.

fact, is the first evidence we have for the education of young princes in Merovingian Gaul, and from Praetextatus's harsh criticism of Fredegund for neglecting the education of her son,[29] we may assume that whatever was going on in Austrasia was quite exceptional. However, the fact that Sigibert and Brunhild took care of the education of their son must not be taken to imply that a school for the education of young aristocrats was founded at the Austrasian court, nor is there any evidence to suggest that other young members of the Austrasian elite joined the young Childebert.

The first vague sign of the formation of some sort of a court school for the education of young aristocrats began to appear only in the next phase of Merovingian rule. Although Pierre Riché lamented the fact that King Chlothar II did not receive proper education at court, albeit the fact that his father, King Chilperic, was by far the most intellectually ambitious monarch of Merovingian Francia,[30] Chlothar was determined to provide a good education for his son, and for that he had to rely on the Austrasian court and its tradition. In 622/623, probably in response to demands from Austrasian magnates, Chlothar II appointed his eleven-year-old son, Dagobert I, as king of Austrasia[31] and placed him under the close supervision of the Austrasian *maior domus* Pippin I and bishop Arnulf of Metz, two of the most prominent members of the Austrasian elite.[32] If we are to believe the seventh-century *Vita Arnulfi,* and there is no

---

29 Ibid., 8.31, ed. Levison and Krusch, 397–98.

30 Riché, *Education and Culture,* 226–27.

31 Fredegar, *Chronicorum liber quartus,* 4.47, ed. and trans. J.M. Wallace-Hadrill (Oxford: Oxford University Press, 1960), 39, and *Liber historiae Francorum,* chap. 4, ed. Bruno Krusch, Monumenta Germaniae Historica, Scriptores Rerum Merovingicarum 2 (Hanover: Hahn, 1888), 311–12. See also Margaret Weidemann, "Zur chronologie der Merowinger in 7. und 8. Jahrhundert," *Francia* 25, no. 1 (1998): 177–230, at 178–82.

32 Fredegar, *Chronicorum liber quartus,* 4.58, ed. and trans. Wallace-Hadrill, 49.

reason why we should not in this case, Arnulf was also entrusted with the young prince's education.[33]

The increasingly sedentary nature of the royal courts after the unification of Francia in 613 facilitated the development of a certain court "school."[34] The existence of such a school is confirmed not only by the writings of its alumni (to which I shall return later), but also by the sole extant listing of dignitaries from the Merovingian kingdom, which is preserved in a compendium of legal material from mid-ninth-century Francia.[35] According to this list, the *praeses* was in charge of the *scola regis* and the *domus palatii,* and the emphasis on his wealth (*multas divitias habet*) and his authority over the *duces civitatum* suggest that this *praeses* was, in fact, the *maior domus* himself.[36] This list of royal officials is traditionally associated with the court of Chlothar II and Dagobert I,[37] but even if one questions its Merovingian authenticity, it is obvious that by the mid-ninth century someone in Francia thought that a school was part and parcel of the Merovingian royal court, and it accords extremely well with the Austrasian scholarly tradition of entrusting the education of

33 *Vita Arnulfi,* chap. 16, ed. Bruno Krusch, Monumenta Germaniae Historica, Scriptores Rerum Merovingicarum 2 (Hanover: Hahn, 1888), 439.

34 Fredegar, *Chronicorum liber quartus,* 4.42–43, ed. and trans. Wallace-Hadrill, 34–36.

35 Vatican City, Biblioteca Apostolica Vaticana, Reg. lat. 1050, fols. 157ᵛ–158ʳ. This treatise was edited in Max Conrat, "Ein Traktat über romanisch-fränkisches Ämterwessen," *Zeitschrift der Savigny-Stiftung für Rechtsgeschichte: Germanistische Abteilung* 29, no. 1 (1908): 239–60, at 248–50. On the Vatican manuscript, see Hubert Mordek, *Biblioteca capitularium regum Francorum manuscripta: Überlieferung und Traditionszusammenhang der fränkischen Herrschererlasse,* нGн Hilfsmittel 15 (Munich: Monumenta Germaniae Historica, 1995), 847–52.

36 Conrat, "Ein Traktat über romanisch-fränkisches Ämterwessen," chap. 2, 248.

37 On this list, see Franz Beyerle, "Das frühmittelalterliche Schulheft vom Ämsterwessen," *Zeitschrift der Savigny-Stiftung für Rechtsgeschichte: Germanistische Abteilung* 69, no. 1 (1953): 6–10, and Yitzhak Hen, "The Merovingian Polity: A Network of Courts and Courtiers," in *Oxford Handbook of the Merovingian World,* ed. Bonnie Effros and Isabel Moreira (Oxford: Oxford University Press, 2020), 217–37.

the young prince in the hands of the *maior domus,* be it Gogo, Waldelenus, or Pippin I.

It seems that aristocrats from all corners of the Merovingian kingdom sent their children to be educated at court with the young princes and under the supervision of the *maior domus.* Such a practice was a direct development of the Austrasian tradition of educating the young prince that we have just seen,[38] but during the first decades of the seventh century it became more prominent and still more widespread. Consequently, a flow of talented young aristocrats frequented the Frankish court and turned it into a lively center of cultural activity.[39] Its fame grew far and wide, so that it even reached the Anglo-Saxon queen Æthelburh, who sent her sons to be educated at Dagobert's court.[40] What was taught at court, and precisely in what context, is not at all clear. Pierre Riché has argued that it was not a school in the scholarly sense of the word, but more of a staff school that trained officers and bureaucrats to ensure a steady supply of loyal officers.[41] This may well be true, but given the fragmentary nature of our evidence it is impossible to reconstruct the court school's syllabus with any certainty.

As far as the elite is concerned, the *aula regis* was the best starting point for a young nobleman, and many of those who gathered at the courts of Chlothar II and Dagobert I became powerful and influential magnates in seventh-century Francia. A certain Desiderius, for example, the son of an aristocratic family from Aquitaine, reached the royal court around 614, where he met the young prince Dagobert and was educated with him. He later became Dagobert's treasurer, and in 630 Dagobert

---

38 See, for example, Gregory of Tours, *Libri historiarum,* 5.46, ed. Levison and Krusch, 256–57; *Vita Arnulfi,* c. 3, 433.

39 See Hen, *Roman Barbarians,* 100–106, and Yitzhak Hen, "Court and Culture in the Barbarian West: A Prelude to the Carolingian Renaissance," in *Le corti nell'alto medioevo,* Settimane di studi del Centro italiano di studi sull'alto medioevo 62 (Spoleto: CISAM, 2015), 627–51.

40 Bede, *Historia ecclesiastica gentis Anglorum,* 2.20, ed. Bertram Colgrave and R.A.B. Mynors (Oxford: Clarendon Press, 1969), 204.

41 Riché, *Education and Culture,* 239–46.

himself nominated him to the bishopric of Cahors.[42] Similarly, Audonius, the son of a Neustrian aristocratic family, was also sent to be educated at the court of Chlothar II, where he spent his youth with Dagobert and other aristocratic youngsters. He was later appointed *referendarius* (i.e., chancellor) by Dagobert, and in 641 he became the bishop of Rouen.[43]

After several years at the service of the Merovingian kings, these successful courtiers retired from royal service and slipped effortlessly into high ecclesiastical offices. Eligius, King Dagobert's counselor, became the bishop of Noyon; Desiderius, as already noted, was appointed to the see of Cahors; Faro, Dagobert's *referendarius,* was appointed to the see of Meaux; Wandregisilus, another one of Dagobert's counselors, found his way to the abbey that later was named after him — Saint-Wandrille; he was succeeded there by Ansbert, Chlothar III's referendarius, who was later nominated to the see of Rouen; Geremer, yet another of Dagobert's counselors, founded the abbey of Saint-Samson-sur-Risle and was its first abbot, while holding at the same time the abbacy of Saint-Germer-de-Fly; and Filibert, another aristocrat that was educated at the court, became the abbot of Rebais, Jumièges, and Noirmoutier.[44] This is by no means an exhaustive list, but it is fairly representative, and it suffices to demonstrate the powerful network nurtured at the royal court — a network

---

42 On Desiderius of Cahors, see *Vita Desiderii episcopi Cadurcensis,* ed. Bruno Krusch, Monumenta Germaniae Historica, Scriptores Rerum Merovingicarum 4 (Hanover: Hahn, 1902), 563–93. See also Wood, *The Merovingian Kingdoms,* 149–52, and Jean Durliat, "Les attributions civiles de l'évêques mérovingiens: L'exemple de Didier, évêque de Cahors (630–655)," *Annales du Midi* 91, no. 143 (1979): 237–54.

43 See *Vita Audoini episcopi Rotomagensis,* ed. Wilhelm Levison, Monumenta Germaniae Historica, Scriptores Rerum Merovingicarum 5 (Hanover: Hahn, 1910), 553–67. See also Paul Fouracre and Richard Gerberding, *Late Merovingian France: History and Hagiography, 640–720* (Manchester: Manchester University Press, 1996), 132–52.

44 On all these functionaries, see Horst Ebling, *Prosopographie der Amtstäger des Merowingerreichs von Chlothar II (613) bis Karl Martell (741),* Beihefte der Francia 2 (Munich: Thorbecke Verlag, 1974), and Pierre Riché and Patrick Périn, eds., *Dictionnaire des Francs: Les temps mérovingiens* (Paris: Éditions Bartillat, 1996).

which Barbara Rosenwein would have defined as an "emotional community."[45]

Throughout their lives, these friends continued to exchange letters. Years after he left the royal court "the memory of the camaraderie and the sweetness of a youth passed under a cloudless sky,"[46] recalled Desiderius of Cahors in a letter addressed to King Dagobert. In another letter, to Audonius of Rouen, Desiderius mentions the good old times at the court of Chlothar II, where they met Eligius, the future bishop of Noyons, and many others:

> May the old affection we had to each other and, indeed, to our Eligius, remain unchanged just as our close brotherhood used to be. In my silent prayers I beg that we shall be worthy to live together in the palace of the supreme heavenly king, just as we had been friends in the court of an earthly prince. And may we also have [with us] the two brothers from our fraternity [Rusticus and Sagitarius], who had already died, the venerable Paul, and the not less laudable Sulpicius.[47]

These were not mere nostalgic sentiments. Desiderius's correspondence with his old friends Eligius of Noyon,[48] Paul of Verdun,[49] and Sulpicius of Bourges,[50] all mentioned in his letter to Audonius, illuminates the ways in which this network of am-

---

45 Barbara H. Rosenwein, *Emotional Communities in the Early Middle Ages* (Ithaca: Cornell University Press, 2006), 135–55.

46 Desiderius of Cahors, *Epistulae*, 1.5, ed. Dag Norberg, Studia Latina Stockholmiensia 6 (Uppsala: Almqvist & Wiksell, 1961), 18: "ipsa tamen recordatio contubernii et dulcido auspicatae indolis pubertatis monet."

47 Ibid., 1.11, ed. Norberg, 30: "Maneat pristina inter nos atque illum tuum, immo nostrum Elegium, inconvulsa caritas, indisiuncta, ut fuit, quondam, fraternitas. Motuis nos iubemus praecibus, ut, quemadmodum in aula terreni principis socii fuimus, ita in illo superni regis caelesti palacio simul vivere mereamur. Et licet de nostro collegio duos iam amiserim germanos, habemus pro his venerabilem Paulum, nec minus praedicabilem meretis Sulpicium."

48 Ibid., 2.6, ed. Norberg, 52.

49 Ibid., 1.12 and 2.11–12, ed. Norberg, 30 and 61.

50 Ibid., 1.13, 2.1, 5, and 10, ed. Norberg, 33, 41–42, 50, and 58.

ity provided moral as well as political support to its members. Moreover, Desiderius's correspondence casts an interesting light on King Chlothar II's court, and on the way of these brilliant young men. They were all talented authors, engaged in literary and artistic work that constituted the very essence of late Merovingian culture. Subsequently, they were the instigators of a creative and prolific literary activity, which some scholars may want to label the "Merovingian Renaissance."

What is remarkable in this process is not so much that the Merovingian kings used their courtiers to control local politics or that royal administrators and churchmen used the written word to cultivate their friendship and sense of identity. Rather it is the fact that all those courtiers, who slowly took control of the highest ecclesiastical ranks in Merovingian Francia, brought with them into the Church the "secular" culture with which they were familiar.[51] They did not stop communicating with each other in writing just because they became ecclesiastical dignitaries. On the contrary, most of the letters written by these courtiers were written after they had left the court for such appointments. Hence, these remarkable courtiers/ecclesiastics/scholars turned the ecclesiastical institutions throughout Gaul into centers of religious cultural activity, marked by their formative experiences at the royal court early in life.

Although the nature of our evidence, and the mobility of the Merovingian elites, especially after 613, make it difficult to discuss Merovingian culture in regional terms, it appears that the emergence of intellectual court circles and *dulcedo* networks of courtiers who used the written word as a means to preserve and cultivate their friendship and support was stronger in Austrasia and lived longer among members of the Austrasian elite, as the evidence from the mid-seventh century clearly points out. And here we get back to our dear old friend Chrodobert, with whom I began my chapter.

There is plenty of evidence to suggest that Chrodobert was an honorable member of the Austrasian elite. The first accusa-

---

51 See Hen, *Roman Barbarians*, 101–11.

tions raised by Importun of Paris in his first letter associate quite explicitly Chrodobert with the Austrasian court of Sigibert and his *maior domus* Grimoald:

> It is disgraceful what you have done in the kingdom of Sigibert concerning the *maior domus* Grimoald, from whom you took his sole sheep, his wife, and consequently he could never have honor again in the kingdom. As soon as [her] company arrived at Tours, you sent her to the holy community of the nunnery that was erected in honor of Saint Peter. There, you did not read [to her] *lectiones divinis,* but exchanged [with her] *sermones libidinis.*[52]

Similar accusations were repeated by Importun in his circular letter:

> Remember Grimoald! What a damage you have done [to him] that neither Jesus Christ, nor God, could ignore. For the good that he had done to you, what did he receive from you? You had his wife, who was innocent […] contrary to canon [law].[53]

Obviously, the purpose of these lines was to defame Chrodobert. Importun did not hesitate to put the blame for Grimoald's fall on Chrodobert and his supposed promiscuous relationship with Grimoald's wife. But even from the biased picture that Importun portrays, it appears that Chrodobert was indeed a prom-

---

52 Chrodobert-Importunus, *Epistulae* 2, chap. 5–8, ed. Walstra, 68–71: "Illud enim non fuit condignum, quod egisti in Segeberto regnum de Grimoaldo maioremdomus, quem ei sustulisti sua unica ove, sua uxor; unde postea in regno numquam habuit honore. Et cum gentes venientes in Toronica regione, misisti ipsa in sancta congregatione in monasterio puellarum, qui est constructus in honore sanctum Petrum. Non ibidem lectiones divinis legistis, sed sermones libidinis inter vos habuistis."

53 Ibid., chap. 11–13, ed. Walstra, 72: "Memores Grimoaldo; qualem fecisti damnum, Iesu Christo et Deo non oblituit. De bona que tibi fecit, quid inde a te recepit. Muliere sua habuisti conscientia nua nec […] norum peracta, sed contra canonica."

inent member of the Austrasian elite. His father, according to Importun, was Grimoald's companion, and it is very likely that Chrodobert himself was deeply involved in Austrasian politics and probably supported Grimoald's moves. The friendship and trust between the two are also reflected in the acts of Grimoald's wife. Soon after it was obvious that the coup had failed, she made her way to Tours, where Chrodobert was a bishop.[54] She knew she could rely on her husband's old ally, and indeed Chrodobert did not disappoint her. He secured for her a place in a nunnery in the vicinity of Tours, where she could spend the rest of her life in relatively comfortable conditions.

As a friend and supporter of Grimoald, Chrodobert was appointed to the see of Paris in 656, when Grimoald was at the peak of his career. Although he was the *maior domus* of Austrasia, there is little place to doubt that he also had some influence on Neustrian politics, and Chrodobert's appointment is a clear sign of that. As long as Grimoald was in control and Childebert the Adopted was sitting on the Austrasian throne, Chrodobert remained the bishop of Paris. But, in 662, when it was clear that the coup had failed, Chrodobert's position in Paris must have been shaken. His involvement in the Grimoald affair, which had enraged the Neustrian nobility, must have made life in Paris very uncomfortable, if not dangerous, for a Grimoald supporter.[55] It was then that Chrodobert decided to look for a way out, and the death of bishop Popolenus of Tours early in 663 opened for Chrodobert a golden opportunity to escape the stifling atmosphere of Paris. Given the fact that Tours was still under Austrasian rule,[56] it was not that difficult to arrange the transfer, and it may well be that Chrodobert received the blessing of Queen Balthild and her *maior domus* Ebroin, both

---

54 See ibid., c. 7, ed. Walstra, 68–71. On the identification of this nunnery, see Hen, "Changing Places," 236, n. 60.

55 On Chrodobert's career and the coup of Grimoald, see Hen, "Changing Places," 234–42.

56 Eugen Ewig, "Das Privileg des Bischofs Berthefrid von Amiens für Corbie von 664 und die Klosterpolitik der Königin Balthid," *Francia* 1 (1973): 62–114, at 108.

of whom were busy at the time securing Childeric II's position in Austrasia. Moreover, the close proximity of bishop Dido of Poitiers, another prominent supporter of Grimoald, might have contributed to securing Chrodobert's new position.[57] It seems that even after the colossal failure of Grimoald's coup, his Austrasian circle of aristocrats was still strong enough to secure the survival of its members.

Chrodobert's worries were not without any basis in reality. His successor as bishop of Paris, the Austrasian Sigobrand, was murdered in 664 by a faction of Neustrian aristocrats, probably at the instigation of Ebroin;[58] and Sigobrand's own successor, Importun, was already replaced by Agilbert in 666.[59] Similarly, Grimoald's daughter, abbess Wulfetrudis of Nivelles, was bullied by the Neustrian nobility. As the author of the *Vita Geretrudis* relates, "it happened [...] out of hatred for her father that kings, queens, and even priests, through envy of the devil, wished to drag her from her place, first by persuasion and later by force, so that they might evilly possess the property of God, which the blessed girl oversaw."[60] No wonder Grimoald's wife sought ref-

---

57 On Dido's role in the coup of Grimoald, see Jean-Michel Picard, "Church and Politics in the Seventh Century: The Irish Exile of King Dagobert II," in *Ireland and Northern France, AD 600–800,* ed. Jean-Michel Picard (Dublin: Four Courts Press, 1991): 27–52, and Yitzhak Hen, "The Structure and Aims of the Visio Baronti," *Journal of Theological Studies* 47, no. 2 (1996): 477–97.

58 *Vita sanctae Balthildis,* chap. 10, ed. Bruno Krusch, Monumenta Germaniae Historica, Scriptores Rerum Merovingicarum 2 (Hanover: Hahn, 1888), 495.

59 Jacques Dubois, "Les évêques de Paris, des origins à l'avènement de Hugues Capet," *Bulletin de la Société de l'Histoire de Paris et de l'Ile-de-France* 96 (1969): 33–97, especially 64–67.

60 *Vita sanctae Geretrudis,* chap. 6, ed. Bruno Krusch, Monumenta Germaniae Historica, Scriptores Rerum Merovingicarum 2 (Hanover: Hahn, 1888), 460: "Contigit autem ex odio paterno, ut reges, reginae, etiam sacerdotes per invidiam diabuli illam de suo loco primum per suasionem, postmodum vellent per vim trahere, et res Dei, quibus benedicta puella praeerat, iniquiter possiderent." On Wulfetrudis, see Richard Gerberding, *The Rise of the Carolingians and the "Liber Historiae Francorum"* (Oxford: Clarendon Press, 1987), 57–59, and Ian N. Wood, "Genealogy Defined by Women: The Case of the Pippinids," in *Gender in the Early Medieval World: East and*

uge in Tours and not in her daughter's nunnery, which, in other circumstances, would have been her obvious choice.[61]

As a member of the Austrasian elite, who belonged to a powerful network of intellectual courtiers, Chrodobert was well versed in the epistolary ways to communicate with his fellow Austrasian courtiers, who now held prominent positions in politics and the Church. Hence, when he encountered a problem with the grain that was sent to him, he communicated his complaint to Importun in a sophisticated rhythmic letter, just as he would have done with his Austrasian expatriates. But he failed to take into account the possibility that Importun, who was not associated with the Austrasian circle of Grimoald, was not familiar with the Austrasian way of doing things. Importun could not believe his eyes when he read Chrodobert's letter, which he mistakenly interpreted as a vicious condescending attack on his position, and accordingly responded with the appropriate Merovingian aggressiveness, which went way out of the *dulcedo* that characterized the correspondence of the Austrasian court circles. This was a simple case of ignorance and misunderstanding that ended up in a bout of name-calling and slanders that resembled a vulgar street fight, albeit in a sophisticated rhythmic guise.

West, 300–900, ed. Leslie Brubaker and Julia M. Smith (Cambridge: Cambridge University Press, 2004), 234–56, especially 240–42.

61 On the connection between Merovingian elite families and the monasteries they had founded, see Régine Le Jan, "Convents, Violence, and Competition for Power in Seventh-Century Francia," in *Topographies of Power,* ed. Mayke de Jong, Franz Theuws, and Carine van Rhijn (Boston and Leiden: Brill, 2001), 243–69; Alain Dierkens, "Saint Amand et la fondation de l'abbaye de Nivelles," *Revue du Nord* 68, no. 269 (1986): 325–34; and Alain Dierkens, "Notes biographiques sur saint Amand, abbé d'Elnone et éphémère évêque de Maastricht († peu après 676)," in *Saints d'Aquitaine: Missionnaires et pèlerins du Haut Moyen Âge,* ed. Edina Bozoky (Rennes: Presses Universitaires de Rennes, 2010), 63–80.

Bibliography

Manuscripts
Vatican City. Biblioteca Apostolica Vaticana, Reg. lat. 1050. https://digi.vatlib.it/view/MSS_Reg.lat.1050.

Primary
Bede. *Historia ecclesiastica gentis Anglorum.* Edited by Bertram Colgrave and R.A.B. Mynors. Oxford: Clarendon Press, 1969.

Chrodobert-Importunus. *Epistulae.* Edited and translated by Gerard J.J. Walstra. *Les cinq épîtres rimées dans l'appendice des formules de Sens: La querelle des évêques Frodobert et Importun (an 665/666).* Boston and Leiden: Brill, 1962.

Desiderius of Cahors. *Epistulae.* Edited by Dag Norberg, Studia Latina Stockholmiensia 6. Uppsala: Almqvist & Wiksell, 1961.

Epistolae Austrasicae. Edited and translated by Elena Malaspina. *Il Liber epistolarum della cancellaria austrasica.* Rome: Herder Editrici, 2001.

Fredegar. *Chronicorum liber quartus.* Edited and translated by J.M. Wallace-Hadrill. Oxford: Oxford University Press, 1960.

Gregory of Tours. *Libri historiarum.* Edited by Wilhelm Levison and Bruno Krusch. Monumenta Germaniae Historica, Scriptores Rerum Merovingicarum I. Hanover: Hahn 1951.

Liber historiae Francorum. Edited by Bruno Krusch. Monumenta Germaniae Historica, Scriptores Rerum Merovingicarum 2. Hanover: Hahn, 1888.

Venantius Fortunatus. *Carmina.* Edited and translated by Marc Reydellet. Collection Budé. 3 Volumes. Paris: Les Belles Lettres, 1994-2004.

Vita Arnulfi. Edited by Bruno Krusch. Monumenta Germaniae Historica, Scriptores Rerum Merovingicarum 2. Hanover: Hahn, 1888.

Vita Audoini episcopi Rotomagensis. Edited by Wilhelm Levison. Monumenta Germaniae Historica, Scriptores Rerum Merovingicarum 5. Hanover: Hahn, 1910.

Vita Desiderii episcopi Cadurcensis. Edited by Bruno Krusch. Monumenta Germaniae Historica, Scriptores Rerum Merovingicarum 4. Hanover: Hahn, 1902.

Vita sanctae Balthildis. Edited by Bruno Krusch. Monumenta Germaniae Historica, Scriptores Rerum Merovingicarum 2. Hanover: Hahn, 1888.

Vita sanctae Geretrudis. Edited by Bruno Krusch. Monumenta Germaniae Historica, Scriptores Rerum Merovingicarum 2. Hanover: Hahn, 1888.

Secondary

Allen, Pauline, and Bronwen Neil. *Crisis Management in Late Antiquity (410–590 CE): A Survey of the Evidence from Episcopal Letters.* Boston and Leiden: Brill, 2013. DOI: 10.1163/9789004254824.

Banniard, Michel. *"Viva voce": Communication écrite et communication orale du IVᵉ au IXᵉ siècle en Occident latin.* Paris: Institut des études augustiniennes, 1992.

Barrett, Graham, and George Woodhuysen. "Assembling the Austresian Letters at Trier and Lorsch." *Early Medieval Europe* 24, no. 1 (2016): 3–57. DOI: 10.1111/emed.12132.

Beyerle, Franz. "Das frühmittelalterliche Schulheft vom Ämsterwessen." *Zeitschrift der Savigny-Stiftung für Rechtgeschichte: Germanistische Abteilung* 69, no. 1 (1953): 6–10. DOI: 10.7767/zrgga.1952.69.1.1.

Conrat, Max. "Ein Traktat über romanisch-fränkisches Ämterwessen." *Zeitschrift der Savigny-Stiftung für Rechtgeschichte: Germanistische Abteilung* 29, no. 1 (1908): 239–60. DOI: 10.7767/zrgga.1908.29.1.239.

Dierkens, Alain. "Notes biographiques sur saint Amand, abbé d'Elnone et éphémère évêque de Maastricht († peu après 676)." In *Saints d'Aquitaine: Missionnaires et pèlerins du Haut Moyen Âge,* edited by Edina Bozoky, 63–80. Rennes: Presses Universitaires de Rennes, 2010. DOI: 10.4000/books. pur.131820.

———. "Saint Amand et la fondation de l'abbaye de Nivelles." *Revue du Nord* 68, no. 269 (1986): 325–34. DOI: 10.3406/rnord.1986.4215.

Dubois, Jacques. "Les évêques de Paris, des origins à l'avènement de Hugues Capet." *Bulletin de la Société de l'Histoire de Paris et de l'Ile-de-France* 96 (1969): 33–97.

Durliat, Jean. "Les attributions civiles de l'évêques mérovingiens: L'exemple de Didier, évêque de Cahors (630–655)." *Annales du Midi* 91, no. 143 (1979): 237–54. DOI: 10.3406/anami.1979.1762

Dumézil, Bruno. "Gogo et ses amis: Écriture, échanges et ambitions dans un réseau aristocratique de la fin du VIe siècle." *Revue historique* 309, no. 643 (2007): 553–93. DOI: 10.3917/rhis.073.0553.

———. "Private Records of an Official Diplomacy: The Franco-Byzantine Letters in the Austrasian Epistular Collection." In *The Merovingian Kingdoms and the Mediterranean World: Revisiting the Sources,* edited by Stefan Esders, Yitzhak Hen, Pia Lucas, and Tamar Rotman, 55–62. London: Bloomsbury, 2019.

Ebbler, Jennifer. "Tradition, Innovation, and Epistolary Mores." In *A Companion to Late Antiquity,* edited by Philip Rousseau, 270–84. Chichester: Wiley-Blackwell, 2009. DOI: 10.1002/9781444306101.ch19

Ebling, Horst. *Prosopographie der Amtsträger des Merowingerreichs von Chlothar II (613) bis Karl Martell (741).* Beihefte der Francia 2. Munich: Thorbecke Verlag, 1974.

Ewig, Eugen. "Das Privileg des Bischofs Berthefrid von Amiens für Corbie von 664 und die Klosterpolitik der Königin Balthid." *Francia* 1 (1973): 62–114.

Fouracre, Paul, and Richard Gerberding. *Late Merovingian France: History and Hagiography, 640–720.* Manchester: Manchester University Press, 1996.

George, Judith. *Venantius Fortunatus: A Poet in Merovingian Gaul.* Oxford: Clarendon Press, 1992.

Gerberding, Richard. *The Rise of the Carolingians and the "Liber Historiae Francorum."* Oxford: Clarendon Press, 1987.

Gillet, Andrew. "Communication in Late Antiquity: Use and Reuse." In *The Oxford Handbook of Late Antiquity,* edited by Scott F. Johnson, 815–46. Oxford: Oxford University Press, 2012. DOI: 10.1093/oxfordhb/9780195336931.013.0025.

Godman, Peter. *Poets and Emperors: Frankish Politics and Carolingian Poetry.* Oxford: Clarendon Press, 1987.

Hen, Yitzhak. "Changing Places: Chrodobert, Boba, and the Wife of Grimoald." *Revue belge de philologie et d'histoire* 90, no. 2 (2012): 225–44. DOI: 10.3406/rbph.2012.8320.

———. "Court and Culture in the Barbarian West: A Prelude to the Carolingian Renaissance." In *Le corti nell'alto medioevo.* Settimane di studi del Centro italiano di studi sull'alto medioevo 62, 627–51. Spoleto: CISAM, 2015.

———. *L'Austrasie: pouvoirs, espaces et identités à la charnière de l'Antiquité et du Moyen Âge,* edited by Adrien Bayard, Bruno Dumézil, and Sylvie Joye. Paris, forthcoming.

———. *Roman Barbarians: The Royal Court and Culture in the Early Medieval West.* Basingstoke: Palgrave Macmillan, 2007.

———. "The Merovingian Polity: A Network of Courts and Courtiers." In *Oxford Handbook of the Merovingian World,* edited by Bonnie Effros and Isabel Moreira, 217–237. Oxford: Oxford University Press, 2020. DOI: 10.1093/oxfordhb/9780190234188.013.17.

———. "The Structure and Aims of the Visio Baronti." *Journal of Theological Studies* 47, no. 2 (1996): 477–97. DOI: 10.1093/jts/47.2.477

Innes, Matthew. "A Place of Discipline: Carolingian Courts and Aristocratic Youth." In *Court Culture in the Early Middle Ages: The Proceedings of the First Alcuin Conference,* edited by Catherine Cubitt, 59–76. Turnhout: Brepols, 2003. DOI: 10.1484/M.SEM-EB.3.3819.

Le Jan, Régine. "Convents, Violence, and Competition for Power in Seventh-Century Francia." In *Topographies of Power,* edited by Mayke de Jong, Franz Theuws, and Carine van Rhijn, 243–69. Boston and Leiden: Brill, 2001.

Mordek, Hubert. *Biblioteca capitularium regum Francorum manuscripta: Überlieferung und Traditionszusammenhang der fränkischen Herrschererlasse.* HGH Hilfsmittel 15. Munich: Monumenta Germaniae Historica, 1995.

Nelson, Janet. "Aachen as a Place of Power." In *Topographies of Power in the Early Middle Ages,* edited by Mayke de Jong, Franz Theuws and Carine Van Rhijn, 217–41. Boston and Leiden: Brill, 2001.

―――. "Was Charlemagne's Court a Courtly Culture?" In *Court Culture in the Early Middle Ages: The Proceedings of the First Alcuin Conference,* edited by Catherine Cubitt, 39–57. Turnhout: Brepols, 2003. DOI: 10.1484/M.SEM-EB.3.3818.

Norberg, Dag. *Manuel pratique de latin médiéval.* Paris: Picard, 1968.

―――. "Quelques remarques sur les lettres de Frodebert et d'Importun." *Rivista di filologia e di instruzione classica* 92 (1964): 295–303.

Picard, Jean-Michel. "Church and Politics in the Seventh Century: The Irish Exile of King Dagobert II." In *Ireland and Northern France, AD 600–800,* edited by Jean-Michel Picard, 27-52. Dublin: Four Courts Press, 1991.

Piétri, Luce. "Venance Fortunat et ses commanditaires: Un poète italien dans la société gallo-franque." In *Committenti e produzione artistico-letteraria nell'alto medioevo occiden-tale,* 729–54. Settimane di studio del Centro italiano di studi sull'alto medioevo 39, Spoleto: CISAM, 1992.

Riché, Pierre. *Education and Culture in the Barbarian West from the Sixth through the Eighth Century.* Translated by John J. Contreni. Columbia: University of South Carolina Press, 1976.

Riché, Pierre, and Patrick Périn, eds. *Dictionnaire des Francs: Les temps mérovingiens.* Paris: Éditions Bartillat, 1996.

Roberts, Michael. *The Humblest Sparrow: The Poetry of Venantius Fortunatus.* Ann Arbor: University of Michigan Press, 2009. DOI: 10.3998/mpub.353844

Rosenwein, Barbara. *Emotional Communities in the Early Middle Ages.* Ithaca: Cornell University Press, 2006.

Shanzer, Danuta. "The Tale of Frodebert's Tail." In *Colloquial and Literary Latin,* edited by Eleanor Dickey and Anna Chahoud, 376–405. Cambridge: Cambridge University Press, 2010. DOI: 10.1017/CBO9780511763267.024.

Tyrrell, Alice. *Merovingian Letters and Letter Writers.* Turnhout: Brepols, 2019. DOI: 10.1484/M.PJML-EB.5.116644.

Weidemann, Margaret. "Zur chronologie der Merowinger in 7. und 8. Jahrhundert." *Francia* 25, no. 1 (1998): 177–230.

Williard, Hope. "Letter-writing and Literary Culture in Merovingian Gaul." *European Review of History* 21 (2014): 691–710. DOI: 10.1080/13507486.2014.949223.

Wood, Ian N. "Administration, Law, and Culture in Merovingian Gaul." In *The Uses of Literacy in the Early Middle Ages,* edited by Rosamond McKitterick, 63–81. Cambridge: Cambridge University Press, 1990. DOI: 10.1017/CBO9780511584008.005

———. "Continuity or Calamity? The Constraints of Literary Models." In *Fifth-Century Gaul: A Crisis of Identity?,* edited by John Drinkwater and Hugh Elton, 9–18. Cambridge: Cambridge University Press, 1992.

———. "Genealogy Defined by Women: The Case of the Pippinids." In *Gender in the Early Medieval World: East and West, 300–900,* edited by Leslie Brubaker and Julia M. Smith, 234–56. Cambridge: Cambridge University Press, 2004.

———. "Letters and Letter-Collections from Antiquity to the Early Middle Ages: The Prose Work of Avitus of Vienne." In *The Culture of Christendom: Essays in Medieval History in Commemoration of Denis Bethell,* edited by Marc A. Meyer, 29–43. London: The Hambledon Press, 1993.

———. *The Merovingian Kingdoms, 450–751.* London and New York: Longman, 1994.

4

Networks of Learning and Political Legitimacy in Ninth-Century Asturias: Toward Mozarabic Authorship of the *Chronicle of Alfonso III*

Ksenia Bonch Reeves

Introduction[1]

The manifestation of a Visigothic political consciousness and adherence to the Isidorian tradition of historical writing is a commonality shared by two Iberian chronicle traditions, the mid-eighth-century Mozarabic[2] and the late-ninth-century

---

1   I wish to express my sincere gratitude to Ann Christys for insightful remarks on the earlier version of this paper. I am, however, fully responsible for any and all shortcomings thereof.

2   It is useful to define the term "Mozarabic," one that is more widely accepted in Spanish and French scholarship than in British and North American sources. The latter often refer to Christians living under Islam as Andalusi Christians. In fact, neither Christians nor Arabs of al-Andalus used the term "Mozarab." Christians referred to themselves as *Gothi, Latini, christicolae, catholici,* while Arabs used terms such as *dhimmī* (protected communities subject to tax), *naṣāra* (Nazarenes), or *'ajam* (speakers of languages other than Arabic). The term, derived from *musta'rib,* "arabicized," appears for the first time in eleventh-century León. It can also be found in local

Asturian.[3] Yet the ideological and stylistic chasm that separates them is nothing short of striking.[4] The earliest witnesses of the Islamic conquest of the Iberian Peninsula, the Mozarabic *Chronicle of 741* and the *Chronicle of 754,* are replete with Old Testament apocalyptic imagery that projects an ethos of political pessimism and resignation to Islam.[5] By contrast, the late-ninth-century Asturian *Chronicle of Alfonso III* and the *Chronica Albeldensia* boldly claim political independence and continuity with the Visigothic kingdom. These differences have long been invoked to justify the view that the Mozarabs, or Andalusi Christians, had little to contribute to the development of Spain as a nation, while the Asturians articulated the ideological foundations of the *reconquista,* the recovery of the Iberian Peninsula from the Arabs, as an existential purpose of the Asturian Kingdom and subsequently León and Castile.[6]

---

charters (*fueros*) posterior to the reconquest of Toledo by Alfonso VI in 1085. Although disagreement exists as to which particular Christian groups can be properly termed Mozarabs, the use of the adjectival form "Mozarabic" with regard to various forms of Andalusi Christian cultural production, from writing and liturgy to manuscript illumination and architecture, is a more established and less problematized term. It is in this sense that I refer to "Mozarabic" authorship. For critical studies, see note 27 below.

3   For more on this, see Ksenia Bonch Reeves, *Visions of Unity after the Visigoths: Early Iberian Latin Chronicles and the Mediterranean World* (Turnhout: Brepols, 2016), 4–16.

4   Citations of the Asturian *Chronicle of Alfonso III* and the *Chronica Albeldensia* follow Juan Gil Fernández, José Luis Moralejo, and Juan Ignacio Ruiz de la Peña, eds., *Crónicas asturianas. Crónica de Alfonso III (Rotense y 'A Sebastián'). Crónica Albeldense (y 'Profética').* Universidad de Oviedo. Publicaciones del Departamento de Historia y Arte. Área de Historia Medieval 11 (Oviedo: Universidad de Oviedo, 1985). Citations of other texts, unless otherwise noted, follow Juan Gil, ed., *Corpus Scriptorum Muzarabicorum,* 2 vols. (Madrid: CSIC, Instituto Antonio de Nebrija, 1973).

5   That imagery is analyzed by Bonch Reeves, *Visions of Unity,* 71–112. See also Robert G. Hoyland, *Seeing Islam as Others Saw It: A Survey and Evaluation of Christian, Jewish, and Zoroastrian Writings on Early Islam* (Princeton: Darwin Press, 1997).

6   Roger Collins, *The Arab Conquest of Spain: 710–797* (Oxford and New York: Blackwell, 1989), 50. These Asturian texts have been linked with the nascent reconquest ideology since 1932. See Manuel Gómez-Moreno, "Las primeras crónicas de la Reconquista: El ciclo de Alfonso III," *Boletín de la*

While the textual sources and models of legitimation of both of these traditions have been undergoing a vigorous reassessment, the assumption of a disconnect between the two continues to inform their reading.[7] Nothing appears to exemplify — and problematize — this notion better than the episode of the battle of Covadonga in the *Chronicle of Alfonso III*, which depicts the first, likely mythologized, Christian military triumph over the Arabs and Islam in 718 or 722. Having taken refuge in the Peaks of Europe, local chieftain Pelayo, whom the chronicle identifies as a descendant of Visigothic nobility and the arms-bearer of the last Visigothic kings Witiza and Rodrigo, responds to another Visigothic descendant, Toledan bishop Oppas, whom the chronicle names Witiza's son. Acting as a proxy for an Arab governor, Oppas, who now represents the *dhimmī* Christian community living under Islam, urges Pelayo to accept Muslim tutelage by emphasizing that Visigothic sovereignty had been irrevocably lost:

Bishop Oppas, having stepped up upon a mound in front of the cave [of Covadonga], addresses Pelagius by saying: "Pelagius, Pelagius, where are you?" The said Pelagius responds by saying: "Here I am." To whom [says] the bishop: "I assume it is not lost on you, my nephew and [spiritual] son, how previously all of Spain was governed by a single law under the rule

---

Real Academia de la Historia 100 (1932): 562–628, at 563. See also Ramón Menéndez Pidal, "La historiografía medieval sobre Alfonso II el Casto," in *Estudios sobre la monarquía asturiana: Colección de trabajos realizados con motivo del XI centenario de Alfonso II el Casto, celebrado en 1942,* 2nd edn. (Oviedo: Artur-Graf, 1971), 10–41.

7 See, for example, Cyrille Aillet, *Les mozarabes: Christianisme, islamisation et arabisation en péninsule Ibérique (IXe–XIIe siècle)* (Madrid: Casa de Velázquez, 2010); José Carlos Martín, "Los *Chronica Byzantia-Arabica.* Contribución a la discusión sobre su autoría y datación, y traducción anotada," *e-Spania* 10 (2010), https://journals.openedition.org/e-spania/329; Roger Collins, *Caliphs and Kings: Spain, 796–1031* (Malden: Wiley-Blackwell, 2012); and Julio Escalona, "Family Memories: Inventing Alfonso I of Asturias," in *Building Legitimacy: Political Discourses and Forms of Legitimation in Medieval Societies,* ed. Isabel Alfonso, Hugh Kennedy, and Julio Escalona (Boston and Leiden: Brill, 2004), 223–62.

of the Visigoths, and shined beyond other lands in doctrine and knowledge; and how, when the entire Gothic army came together, it was unable to resist the onslaught of the Ishmaelites. How much better will you be able to defend yourself on top of this mountain?"[8]

To this solicitation, Pelayo responds: "We put our hope in Christ that, by means of this little mountain […], the well-being of Spain and the army of the Gothic people will be restored […]. I despise this multitude [of Muslim troops] and do not fear them in the least."[9] A battle ensues, with Pelayo winning what the chronicler proclaims to be a providential victory for Asturias.

The Covadonga scene not only represents a dialogue between two competing forms of Christian political legitimation — the Andalusi model, which, in the absence of political power, relied solely on continuity with the Visigothic church, and the northwestern Iberian model, characterized by the assertion of Asturian political independence and legitimation of the Asturian royal dynasty from the victory at Covadonga onward. This scene also stands out in the Asturian chronicle corpus as unusually detailed in its literary elaboration as it includes the only known example of a dramatic dialogue between historical characters in the early Iberian chronicles.

---

8   *Chronicle of Alfonso III, Rotensis* version, ls. 3–9, ed. Fernández, Moralejo, and Ruiz de la Peña, 126: "Oppa episcopus in tumulum ascendens ante Couam Dominicam, Pelagium sic adloquitur dicens: 'Pelagi, Pelagi, ubi es?' Qui ex fenestra respondens ait: 'Adsum.' Cui episcopus: 'Puto te non latere, confrater et fili, qualiter omnis Spania dudum in uno ordine sub regimine Gotorum esset ordinata et pre ceteris terris doctrina atque scientia rutilaret. Et quum […] omnis exercitus Gotorum esset congregatus, Ismaelitarum non ualuit sustinere impetum; quanto magis tu in isto montis cacumine defendere te poteris."

9   Ibid., 120, 122, 124, and 126: "Spes nostra Christus est quod per istum modicum monticulum […] sit Spanie salus et Gotorum gentis exercitus reparatus […] hanc multitudinem despicio et minime pertimesco."

Because of its stylistic rarity, the origin of the Covadonga scene has been commonly attributed to the oral tradition.[10] Yet this is not a casually written dialogue or an accidental impression of oral culture on the historical narrative, for it closely follows the rhetorical precepts of *adlocutio* as outlined, for instance, by Priscian: "the rhetorical development unfolds in three time frames; and begins in the present, returns to the past, and transitions to the future; and let it have the style appropriate to the characters."[11] In fact, the elaboration of the entire battle episode likely reveals a kind of rhetorical preparation by the chronicler that has not been found anywhere in the ninth-century Iberian north but has been attested among contemporary Christian communities of al-Andalus. Not only does this possibility raise intriguing questions concerning the authorship of this portion of the text, but it also points to a high degree of textual networking between politically independent and *dhimmī* Iberian Christian learning communities. A stylistic analysis of the Covadonga episode that follows aims at illustrating the interconnected nature of Iberian Latin centers of power and learning. Paradoxically, while rejecting the Andalusi political model of *dhimmī*tude in favor of political independence, the Asturian *Chronicle of Alfonso III* likely avails itself of the Andalusi Christian tradition of Latinate learning for its articulation.

---

10 James D'Emilio, "The Legend of Bishop Odoario and the Early Medieval Church in Galicia," in *Church, State, Vellum, and Stone: Essays on Medieval Spain in Honor of John Williams,* ed. Therese Martin and Julie A. Harris (Boston and Leiden: Brill, 2005), 46–81, at 64.

11 *Codex Parisinus* n. 75530, 8th c., Priscian, *Praeexcercitamina,* in *Rhetores Latini Minores: Ex codicibus maximam partem primum adhibitis,* ed. Carl Halm (Leipzig: B.G. Teubner, 1863), XVII, 558: "operatio procedit in tria tempora, et incipit a praesentibus, recurrit ad praeterita et transit ad futura; habeat autem stilum suppositis aptum personis." A recent English translation can be found in George A. Kennedy, ed. and trans., *Progymnasmata: Greek Textbooks of Prose Composition and Rhetoric* (Boston and Leiden: Brill, 2003), 73–88. See also Hermogenes, *Praeexcercitamina,* in *Prisciani Caesariensis Opuscula,* vol. 1, ed. Marina Passalacqua (Rome: Edizione di Storia e Letteratura, 1987).

Approaching the *Chronicle of Alfonso III*: Competing Versions

The painstaking elaboration of the battle of Covadonga episode and Pelayo's character led to a long-standing belief that the year 718 marked the beginning of the Asturian Kingdom. In fact, it was not until the reign of Alfonso II (791–842) that the title of *rex* would be used in official charters of an established monarchy.[12] The *Chronicle of Alfonso III* and its contemporary, the *Chronicle of Albelda,* are the principal narrative legitimation tools of the Asturian political project, which ended with the transfer of the royal capital from Oviedo to León in 910. The former text, fashioned as a continuation of Isidore's *Chronicle,* contains the succession of kings from Recceswinth (r. 653–672) to Ordoño I (r. 850–866), father of Alfonso III (r. 866–910). The chronicle is believed to have been finalized between 911 and 914, shortly after the king's death, and is known in two redactions. The so-called *Rotensis* (*Rot.*) version of the *Chronicle of Alfonso III,* named after the cathedral of Roda in the region of Ribagorza where it was discovered, is believed to predate another version known as *Ad Sebastianum* (*Ad Seb.*), named after the monk whose name appears in the dedication.[13] The *Rot.* served as a source for several posterior histories — the twelfth-century *Historia Legionensis* and the Leonese-Castilian *Chronica Naierensis,* the *Chronicon mundi* by Lucas of Tuy (1236), and the *Historia de Rebus Hispanie* by Rodrigo Jiménez de Rada (1243–46).[14] Whereas none of the extant manuscripts of *Ad Seb.* predate the sixteenth century, it

---

12 Collins, *Caliphs and Kings,* 50 and 59–60.

13 Claudio Sánchez-Albornoz dates the *Rotensis* version to between 883 and 886 and the *Ad Sebastianum* to 886. See Claudio Sánchez-Albornoz, "Otra vez sobre la crónica de Alfonso III," *Cuadernos de Historia de España* 13 (1950): 90–100.

14 Gil Fernández, introduction to *Crónicas asturianas,* 79; Sánchez-Albornoz, "Las crónicas de Albelda y de Alfonso III," in *Investigaciones sobre historiografía hispana medieval (siglos VIII al XII)* (Buenos Aires: Instituto de Historia de España, 1967), 17–108, at 42.

has been long believed that the existing redactions reliably point to the existence of a lost Asturian original.[15]

Because both versions of the *Chronicle of Alfonso III* are thought to depend on one common source, a lost chronicle putatively composed around the year 800, during the reign of Alfonso II, it is likely that neither of the extant versions may in fact represent the original composition.[16] Still, for purposes of this analysis, it is useful to determine the version that would have been the closest relative to the hypothetical original text.

An argument in support of the earlier redaction of the *Rotensis* can be made based on the progressive linking of Asturian leaders to the Visigothic royal bloodline, a strategy that both chronicles employ to corroborate royal legitimacy. The Asturian legitimation strategy sought to level the political effects of a power vacuum that arose after the demise of the Visigothic kingdom and elevate the Asturian royal dynasty vis-à-vis other newly emerging centers of power, both Christian and Muslim, in the Iberian north.[17] An important programmatic document of the Asturian dynasty, the *Testamentum* of donation to the basilica of San Salvador in Oviedo, made by Alfonso II on November 16, 812, is the earliest proclamation of Pelayo, the protagonist of the battle of Covadonga, as the providential redeemer of the errors of the last Visigothic kings and the founder of the new

15 See Zacarías García Villada, *Crónica de Alfonso III* (Madrid: Sucesores de Rivadeneyra, 1918), 13–33.

16 Zacarías García Villada articulated the hypothesis of the common source of these chronicles in "Notas sobre la Crónica de Alfonso III," *Revista de Filología Española* 8 (1921): 252–80, at 264–66, and was sustained by Claudio Sánchez-Albornoz, "¿Una crónica asturiana perdida?," *Revista de Filología Hispánica* 7, no. 2 (1945): 105–46.

17 See Escalona, "Family Memories," 223–62; Manuel Carriedo Tejedo, "Nacimiento, matrimonio y muerte de Alfonso III el Magno," *Asturiensia Medievalia* 7 (1993–1994): 129–45; Lucy K. Pick, "Gender in the Early Spanish Chronicles: From John of Biclar to Pelayo of Oviedo," *La Corónica* 32, no. 3 (2004): 227–49; and Georges Martin, "Linaje y legitimidad en la historiografía regia hispana de los siglos IX al XIII," *e-Spania* 11 (2011), https://journals.openedition.org/e-spania/20335.

Asturian dynasty.[18] The *Testamentum*, however, does not contain any indication of blood ties between Pelayo and Visigothic royalty. In fact, it is believed that Asturians showed no concern with their Visigothic identity prior to the 880s.[19]

Such a concern appears to be patently manifest in the *Chronica Albeldensia*, the earlier of the two Asturian chronicle compositions, whose narrative ends in 883. By stating that Pelayo was expelled from Toledo by Witiza (r. 694–710), it seeks to leave no doubt about Pelayo's Visigothic origins and link the Arab success in conquering Spain with Pelayo's absence from the heart of the kingdom.[20] The *Rot.* version of the *Chronicle of Alfonso III*, a composition chronologically posterior to the *Albeldensia*, further strengthens the Asturian legitimation claim by identifying Pelayo as a spatarius of two of the last Visigothic kings, Witiza and Rodrigo (r. 710–711).[21] Finally, the *Ad Seb.* version of the *Chronicle of Alfonso III* adds that Pelayo was of royal lineage and chosen to rule by representatives of the royal Visigothic bloodline, as had been Rodrigo, the last of the Visigothic kings.[22]

With regard to Alfonso I of Asturias (693–757, r. 739–757), son of local duke Pedro, both chronicles affirm the Cantabrian origin of the king. The *Albeldensia* merely seeks to underscore Alfonso's ties by marriage to the dynasty founder Pelayo

---

18 Antonio C. Floriano Cumbreño, *Diplomática española del período astur (718–910)*, 2 vols. (Oviedo: Instituto de Estudios Asturianos, 1949–1951), 120: "In era dcc xl viiii simul cum rege roderico regni amisit gloria merito etenim arabico sustinuit gladium, ex quia peste tua dextera Christe famulum tuum eruisti pelagium, qui in principis sublime tus potential uictorialiter dimicant." Although there is no doubt about the authenticity of the *Testamentum*, the surviving copy was likely made during the reign of Alfonso III. See Elena Rodríguez Díaz, "Notas codicológicas sobre el llamado Testamento del Rey Casto," *Asturiensia Medievalia* 8 (1995–1996): 71–78.

19 Escalona, "Family Memories," 232–33; Jocelyn Hillgarth, *Visigoths in History and Legend* (Toronto: Pontifical Institute of Medieval Studies, 2009), 67–68.

20 *Chronica Albeldensia* 14, ed. Fernández, Moralejo, and Ruiz de la Peña, 171–73.

21 *Chronicle of Alfonso III, Rot.* 8, ed. Fernández, Moralejo, and Ruiz de la Peña, 122.

22 *Chronicle of Alfonso III, Ad Seb.* 8, ed. Fernández, Moralejo, and Ruiz de la Peña, 123.

by stating that Alfonso I was Pelayo's son-in-law by marriage to his daughter Hermenesinda, and later became the maternal grandfather of Alfonso II (759–842, r. 791–842).[23] The *Rot.* states that Alfonso was elected king by the people of Asturias ("ab uniuerso populo Adefonsus elegitur in regno"), drawing a close parallel with the elective nature of the Visigothic monarchy. *Ad Seb.* omits this fact, instead claiming that Alfonso was an army chief during the reigns of Visigothic kings Egica (r. 687–702) and Witiza.[24] However, *Ad Seb.* strengthens Alfonso's claim to legitimacy by adding that Pedro was of Visigothic royal lineage, since he counted kings Liuvigild (r. 568–586) and Reccared (r. 586–601) among his ancestors ("ex semine Leuuegildi et Reccaredi regum progenitus").[25]

The Asturian chronicle narrative thus appears to progressively bolster claims of legitimacy by linking Asturian kings to the Visigothic monarchy by ties of consanguinity, marriage, or service, with the *Ad Seb.* making the boldest claims. One might therefore assume that the *Rot.* could represent an earlier redaction of the *Chronicle of Alfonso III.* In light of the above, if the argument of Andalusi authorship were to be made, it should more properly apply to the earlier, *Rot.* version of the chronicle on the premise that it may follow the hypothetical common source of both *Rot.* and *Ad Seb.* more closely.[26]

Migration and Tradition: Mozarabs in the North

Andalusi Christians were a geographically, linguistically, and culturally heterogeneous group that traced its origins to the aftermath of the invasion of Spain in 711. Their attitude toward

---

23 *Albeldensia* 15, ed. Fernández, Moralejo, and Ruiz de la Peña, 173: "Petri Cantabrie ducis filius fuit. Et dum Asturias uenit, Bermisindam Pelagi filiam Pelagio precipiente accepit."

24 *Rot.* 11, ed. Fernández, Moralejo, and Ruiz de la Peña, 130; *Ad Seb.* 13, ed. Fernández, Moralejo, and Ruiz de la Peña, 131 and 133: ("tempore Egicani et Uittizani princeps militie fuit.")

25 *Ad Seb.* 13, ed. Fernández, Moralejo, and Ruiz de la Peña, 131.

26 Sánchez Albornoz, "¿Una crónica asturiana perdida?," 98.

Arabization and Islamization varied from active resistance to assimilation, and their textual heritage includes writings in both Latin and Arabic.[27] What united this group, according to eighth- and ninth-century historical and hagiographical production, was their acknowledgment of the transfer of political power to the Arabs and their staunch adherence to the Visigothic church, the only remaining institutional pillar of that community. The Andalusi ecclesiastical networks found themselves under constant political pressure, absent formal recognition of their legitimacy both from Muslims in the south and from the nascent Christian kingdoms of the north. Still, as late as 1243, Mozarabic, or Visigothic, liturgy was still practiced in several of Toledo's parishes.[28]

Andalusi Christian clerics have long been regarded as having provided "a key link between Muslim south and Christian

---

27 On this, see Cyrille Aillet, Mayte Penelas, and Philippe Roisse, eds., ¿Existe una identidad mozárabe? Historia, lengua y cultura de los cristianos de al-Andalus (siglos IX–XII) (Madrid: Casa de Velázquez, 2008).

28 Rodrigo Jiménez de Rada, Historia de rebus Hispanie, in Roderici Ximenii de Rada Historia de rebus Hispaniae siue Historia gothica, ed. Juan Fernández Valverde, Corpus Christianorum, Continuatio Mediaeualis 72C (Turnhout: Brepols, 1987), 118. Rodrigo characterizes the Mozarabs of Toledo as "those who, having been subjected to the barbaric rule, preferred to live in [the Arab-dominated portion of] Spain under tribute and obtained permission to continue using their laws and ecclesiastical norms, conserve their bishops and priests, and the ecclesiastical rite as set forth by Isidore and his brother Leander, which still survives in six of Toledo's parishes today" ("qui in Hispaniis seruituti barbarice mancipati elegerunt degere sub tributo, permissi sunt uti lege et ecclesiasticis institutis et habere pontifices et euangelicos sacerdotes, apud quos uiguit officium Isidori et Leandri et uiguet hodie in VI parrochiis Toletanis.") The most comprehensive recent study of Andalusi Christians is Cyrille Aillet, Les mozarabes. For the relationship between the Andalusi Christian south and Asturias, also indispensable is Aillet, "La formación del mozarabismo y la remodelación de la Península Ibérica (s. VIII–IX), in De Mahoma a Carlomagno. Los primeros tiempos (siglos VII–IX). Actas de la XXXIX Semana de Estudios Medievales de Estella. 17 al 20 de julio de 2012, ed. Philippe Sénac et al. (Pamplona: Gobierno de Navarra, 2013), 285–310. For Andalusi Christian political thought, see Luís García Moreno, "Spanish Gothic Consciousness among the Mozarabs in Al-Andalus (VIII–Xth Centuries)," in The Visigoths: Studies in Culture and Society, ed. Alberto Ferreiro (Boston and Leiden: Brill, 1999), 303–24.

north."[29] The northward migration of Andalusi clerics is thought to have begun during the reign of Alfonso I of Asturias, under the rapidly increasing pressure of assimilation to Islam. Asturian ecclesiastical charters, though believed to be interpolations by twelfth-century forgers, are the first documents to both bear witness to the northward migration and give notice of Pelayo's victory.[30] But already in 760, long before the most elaborate form of this narrative appeared in the *Chronicle of Alfonso III,* Pelayo's exploits are alluded to by Odoarius, a North African or Andalusi cleric who reestablished the episcopal see of Lugo as part of the repopulation effort undertaken by Alfonso I. Odoarius states that he headed northward alongside his *familia* (monastic community), upon hearing of Pelayo's victories and Alfonso I's ascent to the throne.[31] Odoarius, depicted as a quasi-Mosaic figure, mentions having been in a long exile before undertaking his journey. However, it cannot be established with certainty whether the exile took place in al-Andalus or North Africa.[32]

Following a migratory wave encouraged by Alfonso I, another peak occurred during the reign of Ordoño I (850–866),

---

29 John Tolan, *Saracens: Islam in the Medieval European Imagination* (New York: Columbia University Press, 2002), 98 and n. 123.

30 Floriano Cumbreño, *Diplomática,* vol. 1, 4–8, 40–65.

31 Ibid., 62–63: "In territorio Africae surrexerunt quidam gentes Hismaelitarum et tulerunt ipsam terram a Christianis, et uiolauerunt Sanctuarium Dei et Christicolas Dei miserunt in captiuitatem et a iugo servitutis, et Ecclesias Dei dextruxerunt, et fecerunt nos exules a patria nostra, et fecimus moram per loca deserta multis temporibus. Postquam Dominus per seruum suum Pelagium in hac regione [Asturias/Galicia] respicere iussit, et christianos in hac patria dilatauit; siue etiam, et diuae memoriae Princeps Dominus Adephonsus in sedem ipsius sublimauit qui ex ipsa erat de stirpe Regis Recaredi et Ermegildi. Dum talia audiuimus perducti fuimus in Sedem Lucensem cum nostris multis familiis, et cum otros populis tam nobiles quam inobiles; et inuenimus ipsam Sedem desertam et inhabitabilem factam." See also Aillet, *Les mozarabes,* 248–50, and D'Emilio, "The Legend," 46–81.

32 Odoarius, above, uses the same words, "loca deserta," to both describe his place of exile and refer to the recently reconquered Lugo province ("et inuenimus ipsam Sedem desertam et inhabitabilem factam"). We therefore interpret "deserta" as "devoid of Christian presence," suggesting that Odoarius had spent considerable time living in Muslim-dominated lands, either in al-Andalus or in North Africa.

when Astorga, León, Amaya, and Tuy were repopulated by those *ex Spania aduenientibus,* or Christians who had resided in the Muslim-occupied Iberian Peninsula.[33] The geography of northwestern migrations thus evolved from Galicia and Oviedo in the eighth century to Bierzo and Astorga by the mid-ninth, and eventually to León.[34]

One must consider that migration was likely an ongoing and protracted phenomenon outside of the waves of displacements encouraged by particular kings. Whereas the *Chronicle of 754* states that Christian emigration northwards began in the early days of the Arab conquest, after the surrender of Toledo, recent archeological findings suggest that the former capital of the Visigothic kingdom was not abandoned until the very end of the ninth century, when large groups of resident Christians are thought to have fled to Asturias and León. This puts the time of this migration very close to the date of the Asturian chronicles' composition.[35]

---

33 *Chronicle of Alfonso III, Rot.* 25, ed. Fernández, Moralejo, and Ruiz de la Peña, 114. See Aillet, *Les mozarabes,* 269.

34 See Jean-Pierre Molénat, "Le passage des mozarabs d'al-Andalus vers l'Espagne Chrétienne," in *Passages: Déplacements des hommes, circulation des textes et identités dans l'Occident médiéval. Actes du colloque de Bordeaux (2–3 février 2007),* ed. Joëlle Ducos and Patrick Henriet (Toulouse: CNRS-Université de Toulouse-Le Mirail-[FRAMESPA], 2013): 69–70. Apart from testimonies, there is an attested presence of Arabicized names in the Iberian northwest; however, these do not necessarily prove the fact of migrations but rather reflect the Arabization of local populations, as is the case of the lords of Pamplona Banū Qasī, or the presence of Muslim slaves or servants captured in combat. See Aillet, *Les mozarabes,* 268–76. See also Carlos Manuel Reglero de la Fuente, "Onomástica arabizante y migraciones en el Reino de León (siglos IX–X)," in *Anthroponymie et migrations dans la Chrétienté médiévale,* ed. Monique Bourin and Pascual Martínez Sopena (Madrid: Casa de Velázquez, 2010), 89–104, at 101.

35 "Ad montana temti iterum effugientes fame et diuersa morte periclitant"; "[The Toledans] tried to flee to the mountains where they risked hunger and various forms of death," *Chronicle of 754,* 44–45, 32–33 (includes the flight of Sinderedus, bishop of Toledo, to Rome). See Ricardo Izquierdo Benito, "Toledo entre visigodos y omeyas," in *De Mahoma a Carlomagno. Los primeros tiempos (siglos VII–IX). Actas de la XXXIX Semana de Estudios Medievales de Estella. 17 al 20 de julio de 2012,* ed. Philippe Sénac et al.

The Mozarabic tradition may have been familiar with the legend of Covadonga already in 754, when the *Chronicle of 754*, now widely believed to be of Andalusi origin, mentions certain Christians who found refuge in the mountains of the north as Hishām 'Abd al-Malik made a failed expedition to the Pyrenees *in era DCCLXXX* (742):

> After launching further attacks here and there in those re-mote places [in the Pyrenees] with his strong army and los-ing many of his soldiers, ['Abd al-Malik] was convinced of the power of God, from whom the small band of Christians holding the pinnacles was awaiting mercy.[36]

Aside from this brief note, there is no mention of the Asturian kingdom in the mid-eighth-century Mozarabic chronicles or in the contemporary corpus of the Mozarabic martyrdom move-ment, the two principal sources of Andalusi political thought.

The "Mozarabism" of the Asturian Chronicles

The contemporary of the *Chronicle of Alfonso III,* the *Chronica Albeldensia,* contains a wealth of material that is believed to be of Andalusi Christian origin. This text bears witness that the

---

(Pamplona: Gobierno de Navarra, 2013), 99–130, at 128; Luis Serrano Pie-decasas Fernández, "El primer siglo de la meseta bajo el dominio islámico," in *Mundos medievales. Espacios, sociedades y poder: Homenaje al Prof. Jose Ángel García de Cortázar y Ruiz de Aguirre,* ed. Beatriz Arízaga Bolumburu et al. (Santander: Universidad de Cantabria, 2012), 901–14, at 904 and 912; Sonia Gutiérrez Lloret, "De Teodomiro a Tudmir. Los primeros tiempos desde la arqueología (ss. VII–IX)," in *De Mahoma a Carlomagno,* ed. Sénac et al., 229–84, at 244–46.

36 *Chronicle of 754,* 66, 44: "Abdelmelic [...] nititur Pirinaica inabitantium iuga et expeditionem per loca dirigens angusta nihil prosperum gessit conuictus de Dei potentia, a quem Xp<isti>ani tandem preparui pinnacula retinentes prestolabant misericordiam." Translation follows Tolan, *Sara-cens,* 82. On the scholarly polemic regarding this passage, and on additional Arabic sources that appear to corroborate the legend, see David Arbesú, "De Pelayo a Belay: la batalla de Covadonga según los historiadores árabes," *Bulletin of Spanish Studies* 88, no. 3 (2011): 321–40, at 326–27.

Andalusi Christian worldview, characterized by the adaptation of the Old Testament apocalyptic discourse to Iberian reality, was known in Asturias. One example includes the succession tables of Roman emperors, Arab caliphs, and Umayyad emirs of Córdoba, in addition to Visigothic and Asturian kings. This is done in a manner reminiscent of the two mid-eighth-century Mozarabic chronicles. Both texts create quadruple chronologies mirroring the four kingdoms in Daniel's Old Testament prophecy, which these texts interpret to be the Byzantine Empire, Persia (implicit in Byzantine events), the Visigothic kingdom, and Arabia.[37] The *Albeldensia* follows the Roman provincial division of Spain, and its list of episcopal sees includes al-Andalus — a probable echo of the detailed interest the *Chronicle of 754* takes in Visigothic church councils and ecclesiastical affairs.[38] Importantly, the *Albeldensia* upholds the Mozarabic chronicles' basic assumption in that it acknowledges the loss of Visigothic political power to the Arabs as a consequence of disobeying God's orders. It briefly mentions the fall of Toledo and its aftermath, an episode more thoroughly elaborated in the *Chronicle of 754*.[39] The *Albeldensia* also follows the *Chronicle of 754* rather closely by narrating the Arab conquest of Spain.[40]

Of particular interest in the *Albeldensia* is the miscellany of history and apocalyptic prophecy known as the *Prophetic Chronicle*, if only because it demonstrates that the Mozarabic worldview was not only known in Asturias but also that an attempt was made to adapt it to the political needs of the Asturian

---

37 Dan 7. On this, see Bonch Reeves, *Visions of Unity*, chap. 2, 71–111.

38 *The Chronicle of 754* mentions the following Visigothic councils in some detail: II Seville (619), IV Toledo (633), V Toledo (636), XI Toledo (675), XV Toledo (688). The *Albeldensia*'s list confirms the organization of sees as given in the Acts of the Councils of Córdoba in 839 (Toledo, Seville, Mérida, Braga, Tarracona, and Tangiers), with the addition of Narbonne, and mentions all of the thirteen bishoprics mentioned by Samson in his *Apologeticus*, except Martos. See Edward Colbert, *The Martyrs of Córdoba (850–859): A Study of the Sources* (Washington, DC: The Catholic University of America Press, 1962), 92–93.

39 *Chronicle of 754*, 54, 70–72.

40 *Albeldensia* 17, ed. Fernández, Moralejo, and Ruiz de la Peña, 182–83.

kingdom. This fragment follows Isidore's *History of the Goths* in linking the Visigoths with the people of Gog,[41] but the figure of the last Byzantine emperor in the prophecy is replaced with that of Alfonso III of Asturias, with the reckoning that Muslim rule in Spain would end by 884:

> The Saracens themselves, having observed certain portents and signs of the stars, predict their own approaching ruin and the restoration of the kingdom of the Goths by our prince. And also, according to revelations and observations made by many of the Christians, this prince of ours, the glorious Lord Alfonso [III], is said to reign in all of Spain in the near future.[42]

This fragment represents a marked departure from the preceding portion of the text that acknowledges the *translatio imperii* to the Arabs. Given that the political thought of Andalusi Christians rested on the acknowledgment of the loss of political power to Islam, as evidenced by the *Chronicle of 741* and the *Chronicle of 754,* what this fragment demonstrates is that some in Asturias may have deemed the Andalusi Christian apocalyptic narrative to be adaptable to the political goals of the Asturian kingdom. However, the *Chronicle of Alfonso III* develops instead a more suitable model of royal legitimacy — one based not on prophecy but rather on a combination of two mutually reinforcing claims: (1) a genealogical link to Visigothic royalty via the figure of Pelayo, and (2) continuity with the *Lex Visigothorum* created by presenting Asturian kings as the true keepers of the norms governing Visigothic royal power.[43]

---

41 Ibid., 19, 186–87.

42 Ibid., 19, 188: "Ipsi Sarrazeni quosdam prodigiis uel austrorum signis interitum suum adpropinquare predicunt et Gotorum regnum restaurari per hunc nostrum principem dicunt; etiam et multorum Christianorum reuelationibus atque ostensionibus hic princebs noster gloriosus domnus Adefonsus proximiore tempore in omni Spania predicetur regnaturus."

43 See Bonch Reeves, *Visions of Unity,* 153–94.

Finally, not unlike the Mozarabic chronicles, the *Albeldensia* styles itself as a continuation of the Isidorian historiographical tradition. The *Chronicle of 741* begins with the death of King Reccared in 601 and ends with the beginning of the reign of Umayyad caliph Hishām (r. 724–743). It has been deemed a possible continuation of the *Chronicle* by John of Biclar, since this text ends with the reign of Reccared (r. 586–601); there is some speculation about its relationship to Isidore's *Historia Gothorum,* which it follows in earlier chapters.[44] The *Chronicle of 754* covers the years between 611 and 754, from the beginnings of the reign of Heraclius in Byzantium and of Sisebut in Hispania, which makes it a likely continuation of Isidore's *Historia Gothorum.* The *Albeldensia* inscribes the history of the Goths into Roman and universal history in a manner that makes it a continuation of Isidore's *Chronicle.* By contrast, the *Chronicle of Alfonso III* is dedicated to local history, which it inscribes into Visigothic history: it begins with the death of Recceswinth (672) and the election of Wamba (r. 672–680), contains a succession of Visigothic kings including Rodrigo, proceeds to link Pelayo with the Visigothic royal court, and continues with a succession of Asturian kings, terminating either with the death of Ordoño II in 866 (*Ad Seb.*) or the beginning of the reign of Alfonso III (*Rot.*).

Owing to these considerations, it is typically the *Albeldensia* that is associated with Andalusi Christian culture and authorship.[45] Conversely, the more limited geographical scope of the *Chronicle of Alfonso III* has so far precluded a systematic consideration of its connection to Andalusi Christian culture. Yet the elaboration of the battle of Covadonga scene in the *Rotensis* may reveal the chronicler's exposure to organized learning practices

---

44 Collins, *The Arab Conquest of Spain,* 53, and Carlos Martín, "Los Chronica Byzantia-Arabica."

45 See Manuel Díaz y Díaz, "Isidoro en la Edad Media hispana," in *Isidoriana: Estudios sobre San Isidoro en el XIV centenario de su nacimiento,* ed. Manuel Díaz y Díaz (León: Centro de Estudios "San Isidoro," 1961), 345–87, at 371. The *Alb.* conserves the memory of the "disciplina atque scientia de Toleto" (7, ed. Fernández, Moralejo, and Ruiz de la Peña, 155).

that would have survived among Andalusi Christians but have not been attested in the ninth-century Iberian northwest.

The Rhetorical Elaboration of the Covadonga Scene in the *Rotensis*

We might find a remarkable consistency between the tropes in the Covadonga scene and those prescribed in minor rhetorical treatises, such as, for example, the *Progymnasmata,* a compendium composed between the second half of the second century and sometime during the fourth century CE and attributed to Hermogenes or Libanus.[46] Known in the Latin West via a revised translation by Priscian (ca. 500) and under the title of *Praeexcercitamina,* this collection of preparatory exercises prescribes the characterization of royal and military leaders through the use of commonplaces structured around praise and blame. It also contains easy rhetorical "recipes" for *amplificatio,* allowing for the easy creation of battle scenes in descriptions of war. Given that we lack any evidence of the circulation of rhetorical treatises on the Iberian Peninsula, and particularly in the north, such an argument might initially seem tenuous and far-fetched. However, because organized learning practices have been attested among Andalusi Christians, particularly in mid-ninth-century Córdoba, and are reflected in the Mozarabic historiographical and hagiographical production, this assumption merits further analysis.[47]

In the *Praeexcercitamina,* as well as in other examples of the *progymnasmata* genre, personal descriptions are subdivided into internal characteristics (those independent of the individual) and external ones (those referring to the individual's circumstances or those created by the individuals). The former include ethnicity (*gens*), citizenship (*ciuitas*), family (*genus*), portents

---

46 See note 6, above.

47 In Charles Faulhaber, *Latin Rhetorical Theory in Thirteenth and Fourteenth Century Castile* (Berkeley: University of California Press, 1972), and Charles Faulhaber, "Retóricas clásicas y medievales en bibliotecas castellanas," *Ábaco* 4 (1973): 151–300.

announcing the individual's birth, education, physical appearance ("quod pulcher, quod magnus, quod citus, quod fortis"), character traits ("de animo [...] quod iustus, quod moderatus, quod sapiens, quod strenuus"), and occupation ("quod officium professus est philosophum uel rhetoricum uel militare"). The "external" set of characteristics comprises friendships, wealth, and fortune. Individuals were to be praised and blamed according to their actions, which were considered of greatest importance, and a tone of impartiality was to be maintained in personal descriptions. For example, a military leader ought to be evaluated on his prowess in combat and on the manner of his death, e.g., whether he died while defending his homeland, by being struck by an enemy, or by an external, miraculous force.[48]

The portraits of Oppas and Pelayo, the two descendants of Visigoths who hold competing views on the future of post-Visigothic Iberia — one subjected to Arab rule by way of a peace treaty, the other politically independent — incorporate several of these commonplaces. The chronicler names Oppas bishop of Toledo and son of king Witiza, adding that he had been complicit in the fall of the Visigothic capital. Pelayo is said to have been the arms-bearer of the last Visigothic kings, Witiza and Rodrigo; upon his escape to Asturias, he is elected "prince." Pelayo's military deeds are discussed at length in the *Rot.*, which is much more detailed than the *Ad Seb.* in describing the logistics of Pelayo's escape to Asturias, his election as Asturian leader, and the manner in which he found refuge in the remote mountain.[49]

This manner of personal characterization was a salient feature of the mid-eighth-century Mozarabic chronicles, where it applied to both Christians and Muslims. The first Mozarabic presentation of the prophet Muḥammad in Spain, which we

---

48 Priscian, *Praexcercitamina,* ed. Halm, 556: "In omnibus autem est exquisitissimum de gestis dicere, ut militarem vitam degens quid in ea gessit. [...] Ad haec qualitate mortis, ut pro patria pugnans, vel si quid mirabile in ipsa morte evenit, vel etiam ab eo qui illum interfecit."

49 See *Rot.* 8 in the appendix to this chapter.

find in the so-called *Chronicle of 741,* follows this pattern in that it mentions the prophet's noble origin and military prudence:

Having amassed a most copious multitude [of troops], Saracens invaded the [Byzantine] provinces of Syria, Arabia and Mesopotamia, under the governorship of a man named Muḥammad, of their tribe, of most noble origin, a rather prudent man and a foreseer of some future events.[50]

In both Mozarabic chronicles, attributes such as *belliger, iustus, prouidus, prudens, strenuus* are applied to Christians and Muslims. In the *Chronicle of 754,* which portrays the first Iberian Muslim governors and the last Visigothic kings, both Governor Odiffa and King Reccared II (d. 621) are said to have not accomplished anything worthy of praise or blame given the brevity of their respective reigns.[51] Employed in personal descriptions, this imperative of impartiality may be somewhat responsible for the modern perception of these chronicles as indifferent to the rise of Islam.

In addition to personal characterizations, historical narration encouraged limited use of descriptions. Priscian affirms that description promotes greater cohesion and the impression of immediacy in the narrative.[52] Mentioned among objects worthy of description are scenes of naval or overland combat,

---

50 *Chronicle of 741,* 12–14, 8–9: "Adgregata Sarracenorum copiosissima multitudo Syriae, Arabiae et Mesopotamiae prouincias inuaserunt, supra ipsos principatum tenente Mahmet nomine, de tribu illius gentis nobilissima natus, prudens admodum uir et aliquantorum futurorum prouisor gestorum."

51 *Chronicle of 741,* 64, 40 and 12, 20: "Odiffa, uir leuitate plenus [...] pre paucitate regni nihil dignum aduersumque ingeminat"; "Reccharedo [...] dum tre per menses solummodo regnat, huius uite breuitas nichil dignum prenotat."

52 Priscian, *Praexcercitamina,* ed. Halm, 558–59: "Descriptio est oratio colligens et praesentans oculis quod demonstrat." Cf. Cicero suggests that historiographical exposition calls for the description of regions ("rerum ratio ordinem temporum desiderat, regionum descriptionem"). See Cicero, *De Oratore,* ed. and trans. Antonio Tovar and Aurelio R. Bujaldyn, 2nd edn. (Madrid: CSIC, 1992), XV, 62–64.

climates, seasons, phases of peace and war, and objects of interest, such as riverbanks or shores, plains, mountains, and cities. Correspondingly, we find a relatively detailed description of the natural setting that served as Pelayo's refuge in *Rot.* 8 (but not in *Ad Seb.*):

> He arrived to the shore of the river Piloña. He found it very swollen, but he was able to swim across on horseback and climb up the mountain. [...] he ascended a tall mountain called Auseva and hid himself in the side of the mountain in a cave he knew to be the most safe; a large cave from which a river came out by the name of Güeña.[53]

Similarly, the *Rot.* (and in this case, also *Ad Seb.*) are generously detailed in the description of military action in a manner that creates an effect of immediacy and projects the chronicler as a personal witness of the battle. In *Praeexcercitamina* and similar rhetorical manuals, descriptions of military actions followed an established pattern by first exposing the causes of the war and proceeding to relate the course of military action and its outcomes both for the victors and the vanquished. These commonplaces served to increase the persuasive force of the narrative:

> May we attempt to describe events beginning with the preceding events and what comes out and results of them; so that, if we describe a war, first we must say what happened before the war, characteristics such as preparations, fears that were; then treaties, blood, deaths, the joy of the victors and the tears of servitude of the vanquished.[54]

---

53 *Rot.* 8, ed. Fernández, Moralejo, and Ruiz de la Peña, 202: "Ad ripam flubii Pianonie peruenit. Que fortis litus plenum inuenit, sed natandi adminiculum super equum quod sedebat ad aliam ripam se trantulit et montem ascendit.[...] ad montem magnum, cui nomen est Aseuua, ascendit et in latere montis antrum quod sciebat tutissimum se contulit; ex qua spelunca magna flubius egreditur nomine Enna."

54 Priscian, *Praexcercitamina,* ed. Halm, 63: "Conemur igitur res quidem describere ab antefactis et quae in ipsis eueniunt uel aguntur, ut, si belli di-

Similarly, the description of the Covadonga battle includes events that precede military action: the Arab conquest of Toledo, Pelayo's flight to Asturias, Tāriq's orders directing the troops to Asturias to capture Pelayo and secure his alliance, and Pelayo's refuge in the mountain. The description of the battle itself begins with the failed effort of Oppas to establish a peace treaty similar to those that had been procured by the Arabs elsewhere on the Iberian Peninsula.[55] One might ask whether the vivid description of the battle we find in the two extant versions of the chronicle — "they take on arms, rise catapults, ready slingshots; spears bristle, swords are being brandished, and arrows are being flown incessantly"[56] — was necessarily elaborated by an ocular witness of the battle or by an avid student of the *amplificatio*. The latter possibility seems sufficient, and it reminds us of the similarly vivid and detailed battle descriptions in the *Chronicle of 754* (e.g., the battle of Poitiers, 732).[57]

---

camus descriptionem, primum quidem ante bellum dicere debemus dilectus habitos, sumptus paratos, timores qui fuerunt; hinc congressus caedes mortes uictorias laudes uictorum, illorum uero qui uicti sunt lacrimas seruitutem."

55 We know of at least four such treaties between 711 and 724. See Alfred M. Howell, "Some Notes on Early Treaties between Muslims and the Visigothic Rulers of al-Andalus," in *Andalucía medieval: Actas del I Congreso de historia de Andalucía, diciembre de 1976,* vol. 1: *Andalucía medieval,* ed. Emilio Cabrera Muñoz (Córdoba: Monte de Piedad y Caja de Ahorros de Córdoba, 1978), 3–14, and Collins, *The Arab Conquest of Spain,* 87. On Theodemir, see also Luís A. García Moreno, "Teudemiro de Orihuela y la invasión islámica," in *Mindos medievales: espacios, sociedades y poder: Homenaje al Profesor José Ángel García de Cortázar y Ruiz de Aguirre,* ed. Beatriz Arízaga Bolumburu et al. (Santander: Universidad de Cantabria, PubliCan, 2012), 529–44.

56 *Rot.* and *Ad Seb.*10, ed. Fernández, Moralejo, and Ruiz de la Peña, 128–29: "arma adsumunt, eriguntur fundiuali, abtantur funde, migantur enses, crispantur aste hac incessanter emittuntur sagitte."

57 "Dum acriter dimicant, gentes septentrionales in hictu oculi, ut paries inmobiles permanentes sicut et zona rigoris glacialiter manent adstricti, Arabes gladio enecant. Sed ubi gens Austrie mole membrorum preualida et ferrea manu perardua pectorabiliter ferientes regem inuentum exanimant, statim nocte prelio dirimente despicabiliter gladios eleuant atque in alio die uidentes castra Arabum innumerabilia ad pugnam sese reseruant." *Chronicle of 754,* 65, 42; see also *Chronicle of 754,* 64, 45–46. Due to the vivid and

The Covadonga battle scene ends in a miracle when, according to the chronicler, the mountain that gave refuge to the Christians trembles, unleashing a stream of water on the retreating Muslim troops:

> But [the Arabs] would not escape God's revenge. As soon as they proceeded over the top of the mountain, which is situated on the bank of the river called Deva, near the town of Cosgaya, the judgment of God would have it that as the mountain shook from its foundations, it threw 63,000 men into the river; and there the mountain crushed all of them, whereby the said river, in claiming its path, displayed many of their battle standards.[58]

The chronicler is careful at this point in billing his account as historical rather than fictitious, in accordance with the Isidorian distinction between history as *narratio res gestae*[59] and fiction as *fabulae* [...] *quia non sunt res factae.*[60] Such rhetorical distinction between history as an expository account created for pur-

---

detailed nature of battle descriptions in this chronicle, its editor assumes that the author was an ocular witness of, or participant in, the battles he described. See José Eduardo López Pereira, *Estudio crítico sobre la Crónica mozárabe de 754* (Zaragoza: Anubar, 1980), 107. This appears not to be necessary, as the effect of immediacy appears to have been achieved with rhetorical elaboration alone.

58 *Rot.* 10, ed. Fernández, Moralejo, and Ruiz de la Peña, 128: "Set nec ipsi Domini euaserunt uindictam. Quumque per uerticem montis pergerent, qui est super ripam fluminis cui nomen est Deua, iuxta uillam qui dicitur Causegaudia, sic iudicio Domini hactum est, ut mons ipse a fundamentis se rebolbens LXa tria milia uirorum in flumine proiecit et ibi eos omnes mons ipse opressit, ubi nunc ipse flumen, dum limite suo requirit, ex eis multa signa euidentia ostendit."

59 Isidore, *Etymologiae,* in *Etimologías: Edicion bilingüe,* ed. and trans. José Oroz Reta and Manuel A. Marcos-Casquero, 3rd edn., 2 vols. (Madrid: Biblioteca de Autores Cristianos, 2000), vol. 1, 41, 358.

60 Isidore, *Etymologiae,* 1.40, ed. Oroz Reta and Marcos-Casquero, 356, and Hermogenes/Priscian, *Progymnasmata,* 177–78. Coincidentally, in further identifying the fabula with Aesop and by distinguishing between *fabulae Aesopicae* and *Lybisticae,* Isidore appears to be following Hermogenes/Priscian almost verbatim.

poses of persuasion and literary fiction as a more frivolous genre survives in al-Andalus until the mid-ninth century is evidenced in the work of Eulogius of Córdoba, archivist of the movement of Cordovan martyrs. In the *Documentum martyriale* (851), the author vows to limit himself "to referring faithfully to what happened [...]. For in fact truth stands firm and undiminished in whichever manner it is revealed, while the falsehood of the most ornate fiction is gradually discovered."[61]

Finally, in concluding the battle scene, the *Rot.* links history to scripture, much in the manner preached by Isidore and practiced by the Andalusi Christian community: "Do not believe this [miracle] to be vain or fictitious: but remember that He who opened the waves of the Red Sea to the passage of the sons of Israel, He himself buried these Arabs, who have persecuted the church of the Lord, under the immense weight of the mountain."[62]

Sources of Learning in Ninth-Century Iberia

The elaboration of the Covadonga scene may reveal a chronicler versed in classical rhetoric of a kind that would most likely be taught in organized schools. We have scant evidence of such learning practices in the northwestern Iberian region. Cordo-

---

61 Eulogius, *Documentum martyriale,* in *Corpus Scriptorum Muzarabicorum,* ed. Gil, vol. 1, 334: "Et sat nobis est fideliter referre quod fuit [...]. Illibata namque veritas, quoquo modo proferatur, firmiori gressu constitit, et ornatissimi fictum mendacium paululum perseverat."

62 *Rot.* and *Ad Seb.* 10, ed. Fernández, Moralejo, and Ruiz de la Peña, 128–29: "Non istut inannem aut fabulosum putetis, sed recordamini quia, qui Rubri Maris fluenta ad transitum filiorum Israhel aperuit, ipse hos Arabes persequentes eclesiam Domini immenso mole oppressit." On history and prophecy in al-Andalus, see Luís A. García Moreno, "Monjes y profecías cristianas próximo-orientales en el al-Andalus," *Hispania Sacra* 51, no. 103 (1999): 91–100. For the bishop of Seville, the meaning of history was inseparable from its mystical and moral meaning, and the three were to be taught in tandem: "Tripliciter autem scribitur, dum non solum historialiter, uel mystice, sed etiam moraliter, quid in unumque gerere debeat edocetur." Isidore of Seville. "De fide catholica contra judaeos," in *Hispalensis episcopi opera omnia,* ed. Faustino Arévalo, Patrologia Latina 83, 2.20.2, 528–29.

van monks are known to have occasionally traveled to monastic communities of Asturias and Navarre in the middle of the ninth century, but little is known about the precise nature of monastic networking.[63] The *Albeldensia* describes Alfonso II of Asturias as distinguished in learning (*scientiae clarus*), yet no specific evidence exists of where and how the learning took place nor to whom the education would have been available.[64] According to Roger Collins, "Few of the monasteries we know about […] appear to have been centers of learning," and most of the surviving documents appear to be of legal and economic nature.[65] While we know that Isidore's works continued to circulate, evidence of manuscript donations to monasteries tends to be dated mostly to the tenth century, posterior to the chronicle's composition, while any such instances may themselves be a consequence of Andalusi Christian migrations to the monasteries in Galicia and León.[66]

Apart from monastic migrations, the principal ways books from al-Andalus would be brought to Asturias were diplomatic gifts and the transfer of relics.[67] Thus, the body of Eulogius, the spiritual leader of the martyrdom movement who was ex-

---

63 Ann Christys, "Educating the Christian Elite in Umayyad Córdoba," in *Die Interaktion von Herrschern und Eliten in imperialen Ordnungen des Mittelalters,* ed. Wolfram Drews, Das Mittelalter. Perspektiven mediävistischer Forschung. Beihefte 8 (Berlin and Boston: Walter de Gruyter, 2018), 118.

64 *Alb.* 15.12, ed. Fernández, Moralejo, and Ruiz de la Peña, 178.

65 Collins, *Caliphs and Kings,* 107. Collins believes that Alfonso III would have had Orosius's *History* and Isidore's *Chronicle* and *Historia Gothorum* at his disposal, and manuscripts of *Etymologiae* would have likely also been in circulation in the northwest (ibid., 109).

66 See Claudio Sánchez Albornoz, "Notas sobre los libros leídos en el reino de León hace mil años," *Cuadernos de Historia de España* 1–2 (1944): 222–38; Díaz y Díaz, "Isidoro en la Edad Media hispana"; and Díaz y Díaz, "La historiografía hispana." Aillet states that Galician and Leonese monastic charters contain between 5% and 15% of Arabic or Arabicized names in the tenth and eleventh centuries (*Les mozarabes,* 264–69). Further evidence of textual circulation, in the form of textual allusions and citations of sacred and legal texts, has recently been established in the corpus of Asturian charters. See Graham Barrett, "The Written and the World in Early Medieval Iberia" (PhD diss., University of Oxford, 2015).

67 Collins, *Caliphs and Kings,* 96.

ecuted in Córdoba in 859, was transferred to Oviedo in 884 "as part of diplomatic negotiations between Alfonso III and emir Muḥammad I (r. 852–886)."[68] Collins believes that the extensive list of theological, historical, poetic, legal, liturgical, and exegetic texts found at the Asturian court in late ninth century may represent the catalogue of Eulogius's personal library.[69] The transfer of Eulogius's remains and his manuscripts would have been brokered by Dulcidius, a Mozarab priest from Toledo, who according to the *Albeldensia* had been tasked by Alfonso III to negotiate a peace treaty with Muḥammad in 883.[70] Dulcidius the *presbiter* is mentioned in *Ad Seb.* as perhaps a possible collaborator in the composition and/or transmission of the text.[71] Some interpret the suitability of Dulcidius for the task as proof of the existence of a Christian Arabicized population, or Mozarabic "diaspora" in Asturias with active links to al-Andalus.[72] Others go as far as to believe that Dulcidius was the creator of the *Rot.*, which he would have compiled from sources he had brought from Córdoba. That version would have then been reworked by Sebastian, bishop of Ourense, and attributed the official authorship of Alfonso III.[73]

Dulicidius's travel to Córdoba on royal charge is testimony of northwestern Iberian links to the foremost center of Latin learning. In the preceding decades, Córdoba had replaced Toledo as the organizational center of Andalusi Christianity[74] — not

---

68 Ibid., 108.

69 Escorial Lib. Ms. R. II. 18. Collins, *Caliphs and Kings,* 54.

70 *Alb.* 15.13, ed. Fernández, Moralejo, and Ruiz de la Peña, 181.

71 *Ad Seb.* 1, ed. Fernández, Moralejo, and Ruiz de la Peña, 115: "Adefonsus rex Sabastiano nostro salutem. Notum tibi sit de istoria Gotorum, pro qua nobis per Dulcidium presbiterem notuisti."

72 Aillet, *Les mozarabes,* 275. See also Tolan, *Saracens,* 98, and Colbert, *The Martyrs,* 95.

73 Yves Bonnaz, *Chroniques asturiennes (fin IXᵉ siècle)* (Paris: CNRS, 1987), xlvlI-xv; Tolan, *Saracens,* 99 and n. 129.

74 Cyrille Aillet, "Islamisation e évolution du peuplement chrétien en al-Andalus," in *Islamisation et arabisation de l'occident musulman médiéval (VIIᵉ-XIIᵉ siècle),* ed. Dominique Valérian, Bibliothèque Historique des Pays d'Islam 2 (Paris: Publications de la Sorbonne, 2011), 151–92, at 154.

least owing to the proximity of the emiral court, which ensured Muslim protection of the church.[75] By the second third of the ninth century, Córdoba was experiencing a revival of Latin culture as an antidote to the increasing pace of Arabization. One may glean Cordovan learning practices by perusing the literary heritage left by the so-called Cordovan martyrdom movement. Between 850 and 859, a number of Christians sought to publicly challenge Islam, while Muslims from mixed families reverted to Christianity. Both types of offenders risked and often deliberately provoked execution, which was carried out in accordance with Islamic law.[76] The chief literary exponents of the movement are its chief archivist and apologist cleric Eulogius of Córdoba (d. 859), his lay friend Paulus Alvarus, or Alvar of Córdoba (d. 861), and their mentor abbot Samson (d. 890). Collectively, the authors outline the doctrinal and political divisions within the Cordovan Christian community with regard to martyrdom. Occasionally, they support their cause by leveling arguments regarding the utility and manner of learning, providing us with invaluable information regarding Andalusi Christian education and schooling.

In the first part of the *Indiculus luminosus* (ca. 854), which represents a doctrinal apology of martyrdom, Alvar of Córdoba famously complains about the decline of Latin culture among Cordovan laity.[77] Although he first identifies with the learned, citing his own background in liberal arts and ecclesiastical studies, he later draws a contrast between his own *rusticitas* (lack of sophistication) and the rhetorical eloquence of the *peritissimi,* the most learned members of the Latinate community. In doing

---

75 Aillet, "La formación del mozarabismo," 310.

76 For comprehensive sources on Cordovan martyrs, see Kenneth Baxter Wolf, *Christian Martyrs in Muslim Spain* (Cambridge: Cambridge University Press, 1988); Jessica Coope, *The Martyrs of Córdoba: Community and Family Conflict in an Age of Mass Conversions* (Lincoln: University of Nebraska Press, 1995); and Ann Christys, *Christians in al-Andalus, 711–1000* (London: Routledge, 2010).

77 Paulus Alvarus, *Indiculus luminosus,* in *Corpus Scriptorum Muzarabicorum,* ed. Gil, vol. 1, 270–314, 35, 314–15.

so, he prides himself on eschewing the language of philosophers and grammarians ("philosophi et Donatiste, grammatici") and instead practicing the simplicity of a true follower of Christ, which he shares with other supporters of martyrdom ("nos uero evangelici servi, Christi discipuli, rusticanorum sequipedi").[78] In Alvar's polemic, purely scholastic or formal learning is unfavorably contrasted with the simplicity of a true Christian who likens himself to apostolic figures.[79]

While Samson's polemical tone against Cordovan ecclesiastical hierarchy is consistent with that of Alvar, his argument is not. In a departure from Alvar's ostentatious simplicity, Samson proudly displays his own eloquence. Samson was abbot at the Cordovan basilica of St. Zoilus, where Eulogius served as priest, and would later become abbot at the monastery of Pinna Mellaria. His *Apologeticus* (864) attacks the excesses of two *exceptores reipublicae,* or Christian intermediaries between the Muslim government and the Cordovan *dhimmī* community. Part II of the treatise, which contains an invective against Samson's enemy Hostegesis, points to the Cordovan tradition of organized learning and briefly sketches the curriculum practiced in Cordovan schools.

In this exchange, it is Hostegesis, Samson's adversary and persecutor, who claims to profess Christian simplicity while accusing Samson of idolatry. Samson retorts:

[Samson on Hostegesis's language:] If anyone looks there for Latin, it will be difficult for him to find it. If he looks for orthography, he will find there is none. If he examines his sense, he will at once recognize the words of a madman. Who will fail to hold him deserving of ridicule? Who, not to say a grammarian, or a rhetorician, or a dialectician, or a philosopher, or an orthographer, but anyone so to say, trained only in common letters, who will not say that he is to be laughed

---

78 Ibid., 20, 291–93. See Colbert, *Martyrs of Córdoba,* 285.
79 Colbert sees this as a sign that the *peritissimi* themselves were divided regarding their attitude to the martyrdom movement (ibid., 268, 285, 357).

at by boys, seeing him trusting in his own folly and having a mind inflated four times over with scum, still ignorant of the sequence of syllables, and not knowing the tenses of the verbs, and daring to dictate in the name of the bishops such offensive words with the puffing mouth of an old woman? For he is known to be more a barbarian than a speaker of Latin eloquence.[80]

Whereas Hostegesis undermines Samson's religious beliefs by stating that they are expressed in an idolatrous fashion, Samson retaliates by attacking Hostegesis's Latin ("Why do you presume to teach when you do not know the errors of prose and poetry?"). He proceeds to list Hostegesis's many grammatical mistakes (e.g., his use of *contempti* vs. *contenti*; *idolatrix* vs. *idolater* with reference to Samson); he mocks Hostegesis's lack of knowledge of Cicero, Cyprian, Jerome, and Augustine; and boasts of his own knowledge of Virgil, whose verses he quotes verbatim.

Samson's passionate defense of learning betrays an educator's background and points to both the Christian orientation of rhetorical education in Córdoba and the pagan bases of Cordovan Latin learning. In Córdoba's learning establishments, mostly housed in monasteries and basilicas, pagan letters would continue to be taught alongside sacred texts, and such schools would educate both clergy and laity.[81] That the Christian culture

---

80 Samson, *Apologeticus* 2.13.2, in *Corpus Scriptorum Muzarabicorum*, ed. Gil, vol. 2, 506–658, 591; trans. Colbert, 373: "Ubi si Latinitatem quis querat, difficile poterit inuenire, si ortografie disciplinam, nullam sentiet esse, si sensum discutiat, insani capitis uerba mox poterit censere. Quis non dicam grammaticus, non retoricus uel dialecticus, non filosofus uel ortografus, sed, ut ita dicam, communium tantummodo litterarum utcumque imbutus non illum risui dignum poterit definire, non a pueris subsannandum peribere, quem confidentem in stultitia sua et mentem cutvrno fuco inflatam conspicans habere, adhuc ordinem sillabarum ignarum nec tempora uerborum doctum, tam rancidola orsa inflatis bucis sub nomine episcoporum aniliter audit dictare, quum constet eum magis barbarum quam oratorem Latine facundie esse?"

81 The works of Eulogius contain references to at least four basilicas and nine monasteries in Córdoba and the immediate vicinity, at least some of which would have served as centers of Latin learning. See Wolf, *Christian Martyrs*,

of Córdoba was steeped in late-antique and Latin culture was due to two factors: (1) the originally archaic nature of Iberian Christianity, which traced its roots to Rome and North Africa,[82] and (2) the subsequent fossilization of the Latin culture in Arab-dominated al-Andalus.[83] The mid-/late-ninth-century testimo-

---

13. See also Pedro Herrera Roldán, "Las escuelas cristianas de la Córdoba del siglo IX," in *Actas del I Congreso de la Cultura Mozárabe (Historia, Arte, Literatura y Música)*, org. Schola Gregoriana Cordubensis (Córdoba: Publicaciones Obra Social y Cultural Cajasur, 1996), 195–200. Similar practices have been observed among the Christians of Maghreb. See Dominique Valérian, "La permanence du christianisme au Maghreb: L'apport problématique des sources latines," in *Islamisation et arabisation de l'occident musulman médiéval (VIIe–XIIe siècle)*, ed. Dominique Valérian, Bibliothèque Historique des Pays d'Islam 2 (Paris: Publications de la Sorbonne, 2011), 131–49.

82 The geographical closeness of Hispania to Africa contributed to its reputation as a relatively safe haven for clerics who fled the invasions of Alans, Vandals, and Suevi in 409. See Jacques Fontaine, *Isidore de Séville et la culture classique dans l'Espagne wisigothique*, 2 vols., 2nd edn. (Paris: Études augustiniennes, 1983), 1:7–9. The relatively heavier Romanization of the Visigoths compared to other barbarian tribes resulted in the reliance of Visigothic literary culture on classical models. Some documentary evidence is discussed in Roger Collins, "Literacy and Laity in Early Medieval Spain," in *Uses of Literacy in Early Mediaeval Europe*, ed. Rosamond McKitterick (Cambridge: Cambridge University Press, 1992), 109–33. See also Nicholas Everett, "Lay Documents and Archives in Early Medieval Spain and Italy, c. 400–700," in *Documentary Culture and the Laity in the Early Middle Ages*, ed. Warren C. Brown, Marios Costambeys, Matthew Innes, and Adam J. Kosto (Cambridge: Cambridge University Press, 2012), 63–94.

83 The school system may have been similar to the one that had existed in Roman North Africa in the second half of the fourth century, as described in Augustine's *Confessions*. Jorge Luis Cassani, "Aportes al estudio del proceso de la romanización de España. Las instituciones educativas," *Cuadernos de Historia de España* 18 (1952): 50–70; María Angeles Alonso Alonso, "Profesionales de la educación en la Hispania romana," *Gerión: Revista de Historian Antigua* 33 (2015): 285–310; and Robert Kaster, *Guardians of Language: The Grammarian and Society in Late Antiquity* (Berkeley: University of California Press, 1988). On the education of Saint Augustine, see Martin Irvine, *The Making of Textual Culture: "Grammatica" and Literary Theory, 350–1000*, Cambridge Studies in Medieval Literature 19 (Cambridge: Cambridge University Press, 2006), 169–71. Peninsular epigraphic evidence confirms the existence of rhetorici, along with *ludimagistri* (elementary tutors), and *grammatici* (tutors in Greek and Latin who imparted knowledge

nies reflect an intensification of Latin study in al-Andalus as a means of resistance to Arabization and Islamization. According to Aillet, "the works of Eulogius, Alvar, and Samson effectively possess all characteristics of an attempt of a Latin revival, aimed at revitalizing cultural norms that were in danger of sinking into oblivion."[84]

History books were well known in mid-ninth-century Córdoba, as stated by Alvar in his praise of Eulogius: "Where were books of poetry and prose, where were history books that escaped his study?"[85] Alvar's testimony that Eulogius dedicated himself to collecting, restoring, and reading manuscripts from all over Spain, depicts a scholar desperately clinging to a vanishing past: "He corrected mistakes, consolidated fragments, restored rare works, discovered the old, revived the forgotten, and was constantly busy consuming works where he could find the deeds of men of times past."[86] That Andalusi Christians cherished the shared memory of Visigothic cultural splendor transpires in the words of bishop Oppas addressed to Pelayo at Co-

---

through the reading of texts). According to the Iberian Roman rhetorician Quintilian (35–100 CE), rhetorical education began with the reading of histories, the task considered all the more difficult since exposition of true facts required a high level of erudition and persuasive power: "grammaticis autem poeticas dedimus: apud rhetore minitium sit historica, tanto robustior quanto uerior." Marcus Fabius Quintilian, *The Institutio Oratoria of Quintilian,* ed. and trans. H.E. Butler, 4 vols., Loeb Classical Library (Cambridge: Harvard University Press; London: William Heinemann, 1961), vol. 4, 75. Education in rhetoric included readings of Titus Livius and Sallust, small historical compositions, exercises in the praise and blame of historical characters, confirmation and refutation of historical narrations, and memorization of histories (ibid., 2.1, 2.4, 2.8, 12.4).

84 Aillet, *Les mozarabes,* 139.

85 Alvar, *Vita Eulogii,* in *Corpus Scriptorum Muzarabicorum,* ed. Gil, vol. 1, 330–43, 335: "Ubi libri erant metrici, ubi prosatici, ubi historici qui ejus investigationem effugerent?"

86 Ibid., 335. See also Gonzalo Menéndez Pidal, *Mozarabes y asturianos en la cultura de la Edad Media en relación especial con la historia conocimientos geográficos* (Madrid: Imprenta y Editorial Maestre, 1954), 25. See also Colbert, *Martyrs of Córdoba,* 181–82: "Vitiata corrigens, fracta consolidans, inusitata restaurans, antiqua repriorans, neglecta renouans, et quaeque poterat ex antiquis uiris gesta petere, satagebat operibus adimplere."

vadonga: "puto te non latere [...] qualiter omnis Spania dudum pre ceteris terris doctrina atque scientia rutilaret".[87] In much the same vein, the Mozarabic *Chronicle of 754* invokes the wisdom, eloquence, and literary acumen of Visigothic clergy, including Isidore of Seville, Braulio of Saragossa, and Ildefonsus of Toledo.[88] Given the rich character of the Andalusi Latin textual tradition, were the Asturian court to avail itself of a kind of learning useful for historical composition, the Andalusi Latin revival could have conceivably germinated in the Iberian northwest, albeit for a very different cause — that of supporting the political independence of the emerging Asturian kingdom and the legitimation of its royal dynasty, whose political birth is linked to Pelayo's consequential victory at Covadonga.

Conclusion

The manifestly local scope of the *Chronicle of Alfonso III* has typically precluded discussion of its Andalusi Christian authorship, while the rare presence of a dramatic dialogue between Oppas and Pelayo has provoked speculations that its origin is to be sought in the oral tradition. This paper argues that the composition of the scene is consistent with the rhetorical precepts of Hermogenes/Priscian and exhibits a level of education in rhetoric that, in light of extant evidence, was likely unavailable anywhere in the Christian north in the late ninth century. Conversely, the rhetorical model employed in the *Chronicle of Alfonso III* can be found in eighth- and ninth-century Mozarabic chronicles and hagiographical compositions. It is suggestive of a kind of education in rhetoric, inherited from Late Antiquity, that was likely still practiced at Andalusi parochial schools in the mid-ninth century and perhaps preserved ever-more fervently against the backdrop of the intensifying Arabization of al-Andalus. In particular, the author of the *Chronicle of Alfonso III* appears to be familiar with the models of *amplificatio* and

---

87 See the introduction section to this chapter.
88 *Chronicle of 754* 17, 34 and 36, 54.

adlocutio outlined in the *Praeexcercitamina* by Hermogenes/ Priscian, and, like the Mozarabic chroniclers of the preceding century, is equally skilled at creating an impression of having been an ocular witness of historical events.

The ability to fulfill the Late-Antique precepts for writing history, incorporate scriptural quotations into the historical narrative, employ the *amplificatio* in order to create a vivid description of a battle, carefully sequence events involving the causes, preparations, and the outcome of military action, and add a touch of the *adlocutio* to the encounter between Pelayo and Oppas betray a writer who is all too familiar with rhetorical conventions of written composition. This gives us reason to think that the eloquent formulation of the Asturian political project found in the battle of Covadonga episode could have been a brainchild of someone who may have fled *dhimmi*tude and found his voice in service of the Asturian monarchy, or at the very least had been educated in and/or maintained close ties with the Andalusi Christian tradition.

Appendix
The Battle of Covadonga, *Chronicle of Alfonso III, Rotensis*
Version[89]

8. [III Idus Nouembris era DCCLII] Araues tamen regionem
simul et regno opresso plures gladio interfecerunt, relicos uero
pacis federe blandiendo siui subiugauerunt. Urbs quoque To-
letana, cunctarum gentium uictris, Ismaeliticis triumfis uicta
subcubuit et eis subiugata deseruit. Per omnes prouincias Spanie prefectos posuerunt et pluribus annis Bauilonico regi tribu-
ta persoluerunt <quousque sibi regem eligerunt>, et Cordoba
urbem patriciam regnum sibi firmaberunt. Per idem ferre tem-
pus in hac regione Asturiensium prefectus erat in ciuitate Ieio-
ne nomine Munnuza conpar Tarec. Ipso quoque prefecturam
agente, Pelagius quidam, spatarius Uitizani et Ruderici regum,
dicione Ismaelitarum oppressus cum propria sorore Asturias est
ingressus. Qui supra nominatus Munnuza prefatum Pelagium
ob occassionem sororis eius legationis causa Cordoua misit; sed
antequam rediret, per quodam ingenium sororem illius sibi in
coniungio sociauit. Quo ille dum reuertit, nulatenus consen-
tit, set quod iam cogitauerat de salbationem eclesie cum omni
animositate agere festinauit. Tunc nefandus Tarec ad prefatum
Munnuza milites direxit, qui Pelagium conprehenderent et Cordoua usque ferrum uinctum perducerent. Qui dum Asturias
peruenissent uolentes eum fraudulenter conprendere, in uico
cui nomen erat Brece per quendam amicum Pelagium manifestum est consilio Caldeorum. Sed quia Sarraceni plures erant,
uidens se non posse eis resistere de inter illis paulatim exiens
cursum arripuit et ad ripam flubii Pianonie peruenit. Que foris
litus plenum inuenit, sed natandi adminiculum super equum
quod sedebat ad aliam ripam se trantulit et montem ascendit.
Quem Sarraceni persequere cessaberunt. Ille quidem montana petens, quantoscumque ad concilium properantes inuenit,
secum adiuncxit adque ad montem magnum, cui nomen est
Aseuua, ascendit et in latere montis antrum quod sciebat tu-

---

89 *Rot.,* 122–28.

tissimum se contulit; ex qua spelunca magna flubius egreditur nomine Enna. Qui per omnes Astores mandatum dirigens, in unum colecti sunt et sibi Pelagium principem elegerunt. Quo audito, milites qui eum conprehendere uenerant Cordoua reuersi regi suo omnia retulerunt, Pelagium, de quo Munnuza suggestionem fecerat, manifestum esse reuellem. Quo ut rex audiuit, uessanie ira commotus hoste innumerauilem ex omni Spania exire precepit et Alcamanem sibi socium super exercitum posuit; Oppanem quendam, Toletane sedis episcopum, filium Uitizani regis ob cuius fraudem Goti perierunt, eum cum Alkamanem in exercitum Asturias adire precepit. Qui Alkama sic a consorte suo consilio aceperat ut, si episcopo Pelagius consentire noluisset, fortitudine prelii captus Corduua usque fuisset adductus. Uenientesque cum omni exercitu CLXXXVII ferre milia armatorum Asturias sunt ingressi.

9. Pelagius uero in montem erat Asseuua cum sociis suis. Exercitus uero ad eum perrexit et ante ostium cobe innumera fixerunt temptoria. Predictus uero Oppa episcopus in tumulo ascendens ante coba dominica Pelagium sic adloquitur dicens: "Pelagi, Pelai, ubi es?" Qui ex fenestra respondens ait: "Adsum." Cui episcopus: "Puto te non latere, confrater et fili, qualiter omnis Spania dudum in uno ordine sub regimine Gotorum esset ordinata et pre ceteris terris doctrina atque scientia rutilaret. Et quum, ut supra dixi, omnis exercitus Gotorum esset congregatus, Ismaelitarum non ualuit sustinere impetum; quamto magis tu in isto montis cacumine defendere te poteris, quod mici difficile uidetur! Immo audi consilium meum et ab hac uolumtate animum reuoca, ut multis uonis utaris et consortia Caldeorum fruaris." Ad hec Pelagius respondit: "Non legisti in scripturis diuinis quia eclesia Domini ad granum sinapis deuenitur et inde rursus per Domini misericordia in magis eregitur?" Episcopus respondit: "uere scriptum sic est." Pelagius dixit: "Spes nostra Xp<isto>s est quod per istum modicum monticulum quem conspicis sit Spanie salus et Gotorum gentis exercitus reparatus. Confido enim quod promissio Domini impleatur in nobis quod dictum est per Dauid: "Uisitauo in uirga iniquitates eorum et in flagellis

peccata eorum; misericordia autem meam non abertam ab cis. Et nunc ex oc fidens in misericordia Ihesi Xp<ist>i [...] qui ab istis paucis potens est liuerare nos. Et conuersus episcopus ad exercitum dixit: "Properate et pugnate." Uos enim audistis qualiter mici respondit. Ut uolumtatem eius preuideo, nisi per gladii uindicta non habebitis cum eo pacis federe.

10. Iam nunc uero prefatus Alkama iubet comitti prelium. Arma adsumunt, eriguntur fundiuali, abtantur funde, migantur enses, crispantur aste hac incessanter emittuntur sagitte. "Sed in hoc non defuisse Domini magnalia": nam quum lapides egresse essent a fundiualis et ad domum sancte uirginis Marie peruenissent, qui intus est in coba, super mittentes reuertebant et Caldeos fortiter trucidabant. Et quia Dominus non dinumerat astas, set cui uult porrigit palmas, egressique de coba ad pugnam, Caldei conuersi sunt in fugam et in duabis diuisi sunt turmas. Ibique statim Oppa episcopus est conprehensus et Alkama interfectus. In eodem namque loco CXXIIII milia ex Caldeis sunt interfecti, sexaginta uero et tria milia qui remanserunt in uertize montis Auseuua ascenderunt atque per locum Amossa ad Liuanam descenderunt. Set nec ipsi Domini euaserunt uindictam. Quumque per uerticem montis pergerent, qui est super ripam fluminis cui nomen est Deua, iuxta uillam qui dicitur Causegaudia, sic iudicio Domini hactum est, ut mons ipse a fundamentis se rebolbens LXa tria milia uirorum in flumine proiecit et ibi eos omnes mons ipse opressit, ubi nunc ipse flumen, dum limite suo requirit, ex eis multa signa euidentia ostendit. Non istut inannem aut fabulosum putetis, sed recordamini quia, qui Rubri Maris fluenta ad transitum filiorum Israhel aperuit, ipse hos Arabes persequentes eclesiam Domini immenso montis mole oppressit.

Bibliography

Primary

Crónicas asturianas. *Crónica de Alfonso III (Rotense y 'A Sebastián'). Crónica Albeldense (y 'Profética').* Edited by Juan Gil Fernández, José Luis Moralejo, and Juan Ignacio Ruiz de la Peña. Universidad de Oviedo. Publicaciones del Departamento de Historia y Arte. Área de Historia Medieval, 11. Oviedo: Universidad de Oviedo, 1985.

Cicero, Marcus Tullius. *De Oratore.* Edited and translated by Antonio Tovar and Aurelio R. Bujaldyn. 2nd edition. Madrid: CSIC, 1992.

Floriano Cumbreño, Antonio C. *Diplomática española del período astur (718–910).* 2 volumes. Oviedo: Instituto de Estudios Asturianos, 1949–1951.

Gil, Juan, ed. *Corpus Scriptorum Muzarabicorum.* 2 Volumes. Madrid: CSIC, Instituto Antonio de Nebrija, 1973.

Hermogenes. *Praeexcercitamina.* In *Prisciani Caesariensis Opuscula,* edited by Marina Passalacqua, Vol. 1: 33–49. Rome: Edizione di Storia e Letteratura, 1987.

Isidore of Seville. "De fide catholica contra judaeos." In *Sancti Isidori, Hispalensis episcopi opera omnia,* edited by Faustino Arévalo, 450–538. Patrologia Latina 83.

———. *Etymologiae.* In *Etimologías: Edicion bilingüe,* 2 Volumes, edited and translated by José Oroz Reta and Manuel A. Marcos-Casquero. Madrid: Biblioteca de Autores Cristianos, 2000.

Jiménez de Rada, Rodrigo. *Historia de rebus Hispanie.* Edited by Juan Fernández Valverde. Corpus Christianorum, Continuatio Mediaeualis 72C. Turnhout: Brepols, 1987.

Paulus Alvarus. *Indiculus luminosus.* In *Corpus Scriptorum Muzarabicorum,* edited by Juan Gil, Vol. 1: 270–315. Madrid: CSIC, Instituto Antonio de Nebrija, 1973.

Priscian. *Praeexcercitamina.* In *Rhetores Latini Minores: Ex codicibus maximam partem primum adhibitis,* edited by Carl Halm, 551–60. Leipzig: Teubner, 1863.

Quintilian, Marcus Fabius. *The Institutio Oratoria of Quintilian.* Edited and translated by H.E. Butler. Loeb Classical Library. Cambridge: Harvard University Press, 1961.

Reche Martínez, María Dolores, ed. and trans. *Teón, Hermógenes. Aftonio. Ejercicios de Retórica.* Biblioteca Clásica Gredos 158. Madrid: Gredos, 1991.

Secondary

Aillet, Cyrille. "Islamisation e évolution du peuplement chrétien en al-Andalus." In *Islamisation et arabisation de l'occident musulman médiéval (VIIe–XIIe siècle),* edited by Dominique Valérian, 151–92. Bibliothèque Historique des Pays d'Islam 2. Paris: Publications de la Sorbonne, 2011. DOI: 10.4000/books.psorbonne.2512.

———. "La formación del mozarabismo y la remodelación de la Península Ibérica (s. VIII–IX)." In *De Mahoma a Carlomagno. Los primeros tiempos (siglos VII–IX). Actas de la XXXIX Semana de Estudios Medievales de Estella. 17 al 20 de julio de 2012,* edited by Philippe Sénac et al., 285–310. Pamplona: Gobierno de Navarra, 2013.

———. *Les mozarabes: Christianisme, islamisation et arabisation en péninsule Ibérique (IXe–XIIe siècle).* Madrid: Casa de Velázquez, 2010.

Aillet, Cyrille, Mayte Penelas, and Philippe Roisse, eds. *¿Existe una identidad mozárabe? Historia, lengua y cultura de los cristianos de al-Andalus (siglos IX–XII).* Madrid: Casa de Velázquez, 2008.

Alonso Alonso, María Angeles. "Profesionales de la educación en la Hispania romana." *Gerión: Revista de Historian Antigua* 33 (2015): 285–310. DOI: 10.5209/rev_GERI.2015.v33.50983.

Arbesú, David. "De Pelayo a Belay: La batalla de Covadonga según los historiadores árabes." *Bulletin of Spanish Studies* 88, no. 3 (2011): 321–40. DOI: 10.1080/14753820.2011.574357.

Barrett, Graham. "The Written and the World in Early Medieval Iberia." PhD diss., University of Oxford, 2015.

Bonch Reeves, Ksenia. *Visions of Unity after the Visigoths: Early Iberian Latin Chronicles and the Mediterranean World.* Turnhout: Brepols, 2016. DOI: 10.1484/M.CURSOR-EB.5.111940.

Bonnaz, Yves. *Chroniques asturiennes (fin IXe siècle).* Paris: CNRS, 1987.

Carriedo Tejedo, Manuel. "Nacimiento, matrimonio y muerte de Alfonso III el Magno." *Asturiensia Medievalia* 7 (1993–1994): 129–45.

Cassani, Jorge Luis. "Aportes al estudio del proceso de la romanización de España. Las instituciones educativas." *Cuadernos de Historia de España* 18 (1952): 50–70.

Christys, Ann. *Christians in al-Andalus, 711–1000.* London: Routledge, 2010.

———. "Educating the Christian Elite in Umayyad Córdoba." In *Die Interaktion von Herrschern und Eliten in imperialen Ordnungen des Mittelalters,* edited by Wolfram Drews, 114–24. Das Mittelalter. Perspektiven mediävistischer Forschung. Beihefte 8. Berlin and Boston: Walter De Gruyter, 2018. DOI: 10.1515/9783110574128-006.

Colbert, Edward P. *The Martyrs of Córdoba (850–859): A Study of the Sources.* Washington, DC: The Catholic University of America Press, 1962.

Collins, Roger. *Caliphs and Kings: Spain, 796–1031.* Malden: Wiley-Blackwell, 2012. DOI: 10.1002/9781118273968.

———. "Literacy and Laity in Early Medieval Spain." In *Uses of Literacy in Early Mediaeval Europe,* edited by Rosamond McKitterick, 109–33. Cambridge: Cambridge University Press, 1992).

———. *The Arab Conquest of Spain: 710–797.* Oxford and New York: Blackwell, 1989.

Coope, Jessica. *The Martyrs of Córdoba: Community and Family Conflict in an Age of Mass Conversions.* Lincoln: University of Nebraska Press, 1995.

D'Emilio, James. "The Legend of Bishop Odoario and the Early Medieval Church in Galicia." In *Church, State, Vellum, and Stone: Essays on Medieval Spain in Honor of John Williams,* edited by Therese Martin and Julie A Harris, 46–81. Boston and Leiden: Brill, 2005.

Díaz y Díaz, Manuel. "Isidoro en la Edad Media hispana." In *Isidoriana: Estudios sobre San Isidoro en el XIV centenario de su nacimiento,* edited by Manuel Díaz y Díaz, 345–87. León: Centro de Estudios "San Isidoro," 1961.

———. "La historiografía hispana desde la invasión árabe hasta el año 1000." In *De Isidoro al siglo XI: ocho estudios sobre la vida literaria peninsular,* 203–34. Barcelona: Ediciones El Albir, 1976.

Escalona, Julio. "Family Memories: Inventing Alfonso I of Asturias." In *Building Legitimacy: Political Discourses and Forms of Legitimation in Medieval Societies,* edited by Isabel Alfonso, Hugh Kennedy and Julio Escalona, 223–62. Boston and Leiden: Brill, 2004.

Everett, Nicholas. "Lay Documents and Archives in Early Medieval Spain and Italy, c. 400–700." In *Documentary Culture and the Laity in the Early Middle Ages,* edited by Warren C. Brown, Marios Costambeys, Matthew Innes, and Adam J. Kosto, 63–94. Cambridge: Cambridge University Press, 2012. DOI: 10.1017/CBO9781139177993.004.

Faulhaber, Charles. *Latin Rhetorical Theory in Thirteenth and Fourteenth Century Castile.* Berkeley: University of California Press, 1972.

———. "Retóricas clásicas y medievales en bibliotecas castellanas." *Ábaco* 4 (1973): 151–300.

Fontaine, Jacques. *Isidore de Séville et la culture classique dans l'Espagne wisigothique.* 2 Volumes. 2nd Edition. Paris: Études augustiniennes, 1983.

García Moreno, Luís A. "Monjes y profecías cristianas próximo-orientales en el al-Andalus." *Hispania Sacra* 51, no. 103 (1999): 91–100. DOI: 10.3989/hs.1999.v51.i103.600.

———. "Spanish Gothic Consciousness among the Mozarabs in Al-Andalus," in *The Visigoths: Studies in Culture and Society,* edited by Alberto Ferreiro, 303–24. Boston and Leiden: Brill, 1999.

———. "Teudemiro de Orihuela y la invasión islámica." In *Mundos medievales: Espacios, sociedades y poder: Homenaje al Profesor José Ángel García de Cortázar y Ruiz de Aguirre,* edited by Beatriz Arízaga Bolumburu, Dolores Mariño Verias, Carmen Díez Herrera, Esther Peña Bocos, Jesús Ángel Solórzano Telechea, Susana Guijarro González, and Javier Añíbarro Rodríguez, 529–44. Santander: Universidad de Cantabria, PubliCan, 2012.

García Villada, Zacarías. *Crónica de Alfonso III.* Madrid: Sucesores de Rivadeneyra, 1918.

———. "Notas sobre la Crónica de Alfonso III." *Revista de Filología Española* 8 (1921): 252–70.

Gómez-Moreno, Manuel. "Las primeras crónicas de la Reconquista: el ciclo de Alfonso III." *Boletín de la Real Academia de la Historia* 100 (1932): 562–628.

Gutiérrez Lloret, Sonia. "De Teodomiro a Tudmīr. Los primeros tiempos desde la arqueología (ss. VII–IX)." In *De Mahoma a Carlomagno. Los primeros tiempos (siglos VII–IX). Actas de la XXXIX Semana de Estudios Medievales de Estella. 17 al 20 de julio de 2012,* edited by Philippe Sénac et al., 229–84. Pamplona: Gobierno de Navarra, 2013.

Herrera Roldán, Pedro. "Las escuelas cristianas de la Córdoba del siglo IX." In *Actas del I Congreso de la Cultura Mozárabe (Historia, Arte, Literatura y Música),* organized by Schola Gregoriana Cordubensis, 195–200. Córdoba: Publicaciones Obra Social y Cultural Cajasur, 1996.

Hillgarth, Jocelyn N. *Visigoths in History and Legend.* Toronto: Pontifical Institute of Medieval Studies, 2009.

Howell, Alfred M. "Some Notes on Early Treaties between Muslims and the Visigothic Rulers of al-Andalus." In *Andalucía medieval: Actas del I Congreso de historia de Andalucía, diciembre de 1976,* Vol. 1: *Andalucía medieval,* edited by Emilio Cabrera Muñoz, 3–14. Córdoba: Monte de Piedad y Caja de Ahorros de Córdoba, 1978.

Hoyland, Robert G. *Seeing Islam as Others Saw It: A Survey and Evaluation of Christian, Jewish, and Zoroastrian Writings on Early Islam.* Princeton: Darwin Press, 1997.

Irvine, Martin. *The Making of Textual Culture: "Grammatica" and Literary Theory, 350–1000*. Cambridge Studies in Medieval Literature 19. Cambridge: Cambridge University Press, 2006.

Izquierdo Benito, Ricardo. "Toledo entre visigodos y omeyas." In *De Mahoma a Carlomagno. Los primeros tiempos (siglos VII–IX). Actas de la XXXIX Semana de Estudios Medievales de Estella. 17 al 20 de julio de 2012*, edited by Philippe Sénac et al., 99–130. Pamplona: Gobierno de Navarra, 2013.

Kaster, Robert A. *Guardians of Language: The Grammarian and Society in Late Antiquity*. Berkeley: University of California Press, 1988. DOI: 10.1525/9780520342767.

Kennedy, George A., ed. and trans. *"Progymnasmata": Greek Textbooks of Prose Composition and Rhetoric*. Boston and Leiden: Brill, 2003.

López Pereira, José Eduardo. *Estudio crítico sobre la Crónica mozárabe de 754*. Zaragoza: Anubar, 1980.

Martin, Georges. "Linaje y legitimidad en la historiografía regia hispana de los siglos IX al XIII." *e-Spania* 11 (2011). https://journals.openedition.org/e-spania/20335. DOI: 10.4000/e-spania.20335.

Martín, José Carlos. "Los *Chronica Byzantia-Arabica*. Contribución a la discusión sobre su autoría y datación, y traducción anotada." *e-Spania* 10 (2010). https://journals.openedition.org/e-spania/329 DOI: 10.4000/e-spania.329.

Menéndez Pidal, Gonzalo. *Mozarabes y asturianos en la cultura de la Edad Media en relación especial con la historia conocimientos geográficos*. Madrid: Imprenta y Editorial Maestre, 1954.

Menéndez Pidal, Ramón. "La historiografía medieval sobre Alfonso II el Casto." In *Estudios sobre la monarquía asturiana: Colección de trabajos realizados con motivo del XI centenario de Alfonso II el Casto, celebrado en 1942*, 10–41. Oviedo: Artur-Graf, 1971.

Molénat, Jean-Pierre. "Le passage des mozarabs d'al-Andalus vers l'Espagne Chrétienne." In *Passages: Déplacements des hommes, circulation des textes et identités dans l'Occident médiéval. Actes du colloque de Bordeaux (2–3 février 2007),* edited by Joëlle Ducos and Patrick Henriet, 67–76. Toulouse: CNRS-Université de Toulouse-Le Mirail-[FRAMESPA], 2013. DOI: 10.4000/books.pumi.38158.

Pick, Lucy K. "Gender in the Early Spanish Chronicles: From John of Biclar to Pelayo of Oviedo." *La Corónica* 32, no. 3 (2004): 227–49. DOI: 10.1353/cor.2004.0026.

Piedecasas Fernández, Luis Serrano. "El primer siglo de la meseta bajo el dominio islámico." In *Mundos medievales. Espacios, sociedades y poder: Homenaje al Prof. Jose Ángel García de Cortázar y Ruiz de Aguirre,* edited by Beatriz Arízaga Bolumburu, Dolores Mariño Verias, Carmen Díez Herrera, Esther Peña Bocos, Jesús Ángel Solórzano Telechea, Susana Guijarro González, and Javier Añíbarro Rodríguez, 901–14. Santander: Universidad de Cantabria, 2012.

Reglero de la Fuente, Carlos Manuel. "Onomástica arabizante y migraciones en el Reino de León (siglos IX–X)." In *Anthroponymie et migrations dans la Chrétienté médiévale,* edited by Monique Bourin and Pascual Martínez Sopena, 89–104. Madrid: Casa de Velázquez, 2010.

Rodríguez Díaz, Elena. "Notas codicológicas sobre el llamado *Testamento del Rey Casto.*" *Asturiensia Medievalia* 8 (1995–1996): 71–78.

Sánchez-Albornoz, Claudio. "Las crónicas de Albelda y de Alfonso III." In *Investigaciones sobre historiografía hispana medieval (siglos VIII al XII),* 17–108. Buenos Aires: Instituto de Historia de España, 1967.

———. "Notas sobre los libros leídos en el reino de León hace mil años." *Cuadernos de Historia de España* 1–2 (1944): 222–38.

———. "Otra vez sobre la crónica de Alfonso III." *Cuadernos de Historia de España* 13 (1950): 90–100.

———. "¿Una crónica asturiana perdida?" *Revista de Filología Hispánica* 7, no. 2 (1945): 105–46.

Tolan, John. *Saracens: Islam in the Medieval European Imagination.* New York: Columbia University Press, 2002.

Torrente Fernández, Isabel. "Relaciones de parentesco en Asturias durante la Edad Media (siglos VIII a IX)." *Asturiensia Medievalia* 6 (1991): 39–57.

Valérian, Dominique. "La permanence du christianisme au Maghreb: L'apport problématique des sources latines." In *Islamisation et arabisation de l'occident musulman médiéval (VIIᵉ–XIIᵉ siècle)*, edited by Dominique Valérian, 131–49. Bibliothèque Historique des Pays d'Islam 2. Paris: Publications de la Sorbonne, 2011. DOI: 10.4000/books.psorbonne.2511.

Wolf, Kenneth Baxter. *Christian Martyrs in Muslim Spain*. Cambridge: Cambridge University Press, 1988.

5

Novalesa's Networks between Gaul and Italy: Restoring Institutional Memories and Libraries in the Twilight of the Early Middle Ages

Edward M. Schoolman

Introduction

Nestled in a mountain valley on the southern side of the Alps, the Monastery of St. Peter at Novalesa played many roles throughout its history. It was an early outpost of aristocratic patronage, founded by a nobleman named Abbo of Provence in 726 as an expression of piety and to consolidate control over the Mount Cenis pass, an important route between Frankish Gaul and northern Italy.[1] Its early history tied it to the communities north of the Alps far more than it did to those in the rest of Italy, until the first decade of the tenth century when the monks were forced to flee under the threat and eventual arrival of a Muslim raid. Following almost a century of exile, a new generation of

---

1   On Abbo, see Patrick J. Geary, *Aristocracy in Provence: The Rhône Basin at the Dawn of the Carolingian Age,* Middle Ages Series (Philadelphia: University of Pennsylvania Press, 1985).

monks returned to reclaim the site of the monastery and their history; while the reconstituted Novalesa thrived, it did so in a radically different time. And although it reclaimed aspects of its past, it would never regain its stature.

In considering its place between Frankish and Italian influence, regional and local patronage, and the evolution of monastic movements, the history of Novalesa presents a number of compelling questions. Given the history at the site and its two periods of occupation, how can we trace the informal personal, intellectual, and institutional networks to which Novalesa belonged? How did these networks change for the monastic community during the two discrete phases at the site? And finally, how did the century-long processes of rebuilding Novalesa's library and the reclaiming of its history reframe its position?

While these types of questions are difficult to answer for most monastic institutions, they are especially complex for Novalesa, given that its abandonment at the beginning of the tenth century resulted in the loss of nearly all of its manuscripts and charters, some of which were later recovered, others forged, and some lost entirely. Following the reestablishment of the monastic community in the eleventh century, the texts and manuscripts composed served as witnesses of the effort to recapture its past and affirm its present status, and offer a glimpse of the links shared between its patrons and abbots, and most importantly its connections to other institutions through shared texts. These sources illustrate Novalesa's historical and imagined reliance on Frankish patronage and ties to other monasteries beyond the Alps, from Cluny to Reichenau, as well as how the reinstituted community utilized its memory and links to rebuild its library and reconstruct its past.

These diverse facets reveal a monastery that began its existence in the eighth century as an outpost of Carolingian monasticism and patronage and that retained personal ties to Gaul, notably Provence. After its exile from the Novalesa site in 906, the community retained some knowledge of its history despite the loss of institutional memory and the papers and charters that protected it. In the eleventh century, the exiled community returned to the site of Novalesa, and began to collect texts to build a new library while relying on its connections to other monasteries. In addition to navigating its new position within local Italian networks, members of this latter community would produce new texts that recreated its lost history.

Given the nature of the surviving sources from Novalesa, this study aims to be exploratory rather than exhaustive, seeking the contours of Novalesa's place within a radically altered intellectual landscape primarily through two manuscripts composed following its reestablishment: the *Chronicle of Novalesa* and a miscellany now at the Newberry Library in Chicago. The following sections describe the various ways to imagine monastic networks, the history of Novalesa and certain manuscripts produced following its reestablishment, the history of the abbots and their personal and geographic links, and projections of the monastery's status in memory and its role in the eleventh century.

Recovering Novalesa's Monastic Links

As the primary engines of manuscript production in the early Middle Ages, monasteries held a privileged position in the transfer of knowledge, maintained through the activities of the *scriptoria* in particular and monastic schools. Because monasteries had other responsibilities, such as the care and spiritual health of the monks and their supporters, and served as the objects of elite patronage, these various facets often became intertwined. Given these traits, there is no consensus as to what makes a *monastic network,* which could be informal and driven by personal as well as institutional connections, on the one hand, or part of more formal arrangements through shared patronage or extended monastic communities, on the other. In considering their role in education and the production of texts for that purpose, monasteries were often central nodes in larger educational networks, especially under the Carolingians.[2] Beyond their educational structures, individual monasteries also formed the locus of "horizontal learning" in informal pathways.[3] Examples of important imperially sponsored monastic houses, such as Farfa, underscore the continuities and mutual benefits of monastic patronage networks.[4] Both within and beyond the confines of monastic walls, monastic spiritual and emotional networks bound together monks and nuns into families.[5] Finally, with the rise of Cluny, monastic networks could also be formal agreements of support. Even early in the tenth century, Cluny had become part of a *Klosterverband* and later would become the motherhouse to a network of smaller monasteries and reformer to even more.[6]

In this study, I am most concerned with the ephemera of networks in which only individual links remain visible: the

2   See Chap. 5, "Education Exchange: The Monastic Network," in Madge M. Hildebrandt, *The External School in Carolingian Society* (Boston and Leiden: Brill, 1992), 108–29.

3   Nicolangelo D'Acunto, "Forms of Transmission of Knowledge at Saint Gall (Ninth to Eleventh Century)," in *Horizontal Learning in the High Middle Ages: Peer-to-Peer Knowledge Transfer in Religious Communities,* ed. Micol Long, Tjamke Snijders, and Steven Vanderputten, Knowledge Communities (Amsterdam: Amsterdam University Press, 2019), 207–15.

4   Marios Costambeys, *Power and Patronage in Early Medieval Italy: Local Society, Italian Politics and the Abbey of Farfa, c.700–900* (Cambridge: Cambridge University Press, 2008).

5   Although "spiritual families" as such are largely a product of the later Middle Ages, notably those connected to Catherine of Siena, the connection between spiritual parents and their children, and more notably between brothers, reaches back to the origins of Christian monasticism in Late Antiquity. See Claudia Rapp, *Brother-Making in Late Antiquity and Byzantium* (Oxford: Oxford University Press, 2016).

6   On the Cluniac reforms, see Giles Constable, "Cluniac Reform in the Eleventh Century," in *Vom Umbruch zur Erneuerung? Das 11. und beginnende 12. Jahrhundert,* ed. Nicola Karthaus, Jörg Jarnut, and Mattias Wemhoff (Munich: Fink Wilhelm GmbH, 2006), 231–46, repr. *The Abbey of Cluny: A Collection of Essays to Mark the Eleven-Hundredth Anniversary of Its Foundation,* ed. Giles Constable (Münster: LIT, 2010), 81–112. See also Steven Vanderputten, *Monastic Reform as Process: Realities and Representations in Medieval Flanders, 900–1100* (Ithaca: Cornell University Press, 2013).

transmission of texts and manuscripts, the relationships between patrons and monasteries, and the careers of abbots and monks. Together they help to illuminate the position of the historical "Novalesas": the Carolingian monastery in northern Italy through 906, this early monastery as it was imagined during the period of exile and resettlement, and the renewed Italian monastery of the eleventh century.

Although many manuscripts survive from the reconstituted monastery of Novalesa, this chapter will focus on two with clear provenance and a record of critical study. The foundational scholarship on the majority of Novalesa's medieval manuscripts and history was undertaken by Carlo Cipolla, who in the last decades of the nineteenth century consulted a significant portion of the manuscripts and texts associated with the monastery. His scholarship incorporated his research and updated editions of texts specific to Novalesa in the two-volume *Monumenta novaliciensia vetustiora,* among others.[7]

The *Chronicle of Novalesa*

The *Chronicle* survives as a single medieval rotolus written around 1050 and covers the period from the monastery's mythical establishment through 1014. The manuscript today is imperfect, as the first sections were damaged and, along with others, only preserved in an eighteenth-century transcription. Known as the *Chronicon Novaliciense,* the work consists of a five-part "history" of the monastery from its initial mythical establishment to its re-foundation by the abbot Gezo, and an "appendix" of brief notices and anecdotes designed to be later inserted into the main text.

---

7   These include Carlo Cipolla, *Monumenta novaliciensia vetustiora: Raccolta degli atti e delle chronache riguaardanti l'abbazia della Novalesa,* 2 vols., FSI 32 (Rome: Isituto Storico Italiano, 1898–1901); Carlo Cipolla, *Ricerche sull'antica biblioteca del monastero della Novalesa* (Turin: Carlo Clausen, 1894); an Carlo Cipolla, "Notizia di alcuni codini dell'antica biblioteca novalicense," *Memorie della reale accademia della scienze di Torino* 2, no. 44 (1894): 193–213.

The *Chronicle of Novalesa* was composed in inelegant Latin, with clear historical embellishments, problematic chronology, and incoherent organization. The chapter titles listed at the beginning of each book inconsistently describe the chapter's content. The text has often been seen as a creation of its age, using the cultural resources available to monks lacking refined literary skills yet attempting to bring together the surviving history of their institution. Due to its apparent disorganization, it may also have been a work-in-progress or a "scratch pad" for a more formal record. The value of the text has centered on its accounts of Novalesa's connections to the most important figures of the Carolingian age, including Charlemagne and his successors, and its reliance on the history of the ninth-century poem about the life of Walter of Aquitaine, the *Waltharius*.

The text received its first published edition by Celestinus Combetti in 1843; another edition was made for the Monumenta Germaniae Historica (MGH) by Lodovico Bethmann, published in the seventh volume of the Scriptores series in 1846.[8] A fully annotated edition of the text appears in the second volume of Carlo Cipolla's *Monumenta novaliciensia,* with a detailed introduction on the history of the manuscript's publication up to that point. More recently, the *Chronicle* received an Italian translation with an edition by Gian Carlo Alessio in 1982 and a complete English translation in 2017 in the dissertation of Elizabeth Artemis Clark.[9] Several scholars, most notably Patrick Geary and Uwe Ludwig, have scrutinized stories about the monastery's various destructions, reconstructions, and the patronage of roy-

---

8 *Chronicon Novaliciense,* in MGH, Scriptores Rerum Langobardorum, ed. Ludwig Bethmann (Hanover: Hahn, 1846), 73–133, and *Chronicon Novaliciense,* ed. Celestino Combetti (Turin: ex Regio Typographeo, 1843). Hereafter CN.

9 *Cronaca di Novalesa,* ed. Gian Carlo Alessio (Turin: G. Einuadi, 1982), and Elizabeth Artemis Clark, "The Chronicle of Novalese: Translation, Text, and Literary Analysis" (PhD diss., UNC–Chapel Hill, 2017). I have chosen here to follow the conventional book and chapter divisions used by Cipolla and Bethmann.

al and aristocratic families, many of which are fictional but serve to construct a plausible past for the monks.[10]

The *Novalesa Miscellany*

The manuscript of a miscellany from Novalesa, now housed at the Newberry Library in Chicago, was formed from two distinct eleventh-century manuscripts bound together later in the Middle Ages.[11] The better-known second half includes the first two books of Paul the Deacon's *Historia Langobardorum* with a spurious description of the oblation of Charlemagne's illegitimate son Hugo to the monastery of Novalesa (which appears in the *Chronicle*).[12] The first half, composed of 107 folios, contains a true miscellany created for a monastic audience. The main portion contains sixty-eight folios of the *Expositio missae* of Amalarius of Metz, as well as sermons, saints' lives, penitential texts, epigrams, and a "glossary" of Greek terms. Other notable works included were a letter on the Hungarians attributed to Remigius of Auxerre, a short poem on the double creation of life by Eugenius of Toledo, *Quid sit ceroma,* a tract once thought to have been authored by Lupus of Ferrières but now attributed to his student Heiric of Auxerre, and finally on the last folio a list of small donations made by the local laymen who supported the monastery. Despite their disparate origins, these texts collectively imply that the network from which Novalesa rebuilt

---

10 Chapter 4, "Unrolling Institutional Memories," in Patrick J. Geary, *Phantoms of Remembrance: Memory and Oblivion at the End of the First Millennium* (Princeton: Princeton University Press, 1994), 115–33, and Uwe Ludwig, "Die Gedenklisten des Klosters Novalese — Möglichkeiten einer Kritik des Chronicon Novaliciense," in *Memoria in der Gesellschaft des Mittelalters,* ed. Dieter Geuenich and Otto Gerhard Oexle (Göttingen: Vandenhoeck & Ruprecht, 1994), 32–55.

11 On the history of this manuscript, see Edward M. Schoolman, "Of Lost Libraries and Monastic Memories: Creating the Eleventh-Century Novalesa Miscellany," *Haskins Society Journal* 28 (2017): 39–61. A short study of the contents also appears in Cipolla, *Monumenta novaliciensia,* vol. 1, 428–29.

12 Cipolla, "Notizia di alcuni," 211.

its library (or portions of it) had nodes ranging from Cluny to Reichenau to Santa Maria in Ripoll, Catalonia.

Abbots in Monastic Networks

In trying to understand Novalesa's place before and after its tenth-century exile, the abbots who served its community demonstrate patterns of connections that increasingly looked northward, reflecting their communities' orientations. Three others with more conventional careers illustrate this northward-facing gaze, including its most famous abbot, Eldrad, who later became the monastery's saint and spiritual patron. The careers of Eldrad and his predecessor, Frodoin, representing Novalesa's first phase, and Gezo and Aldradus representing the second, appear to reveal the long-lasting pull of increasing intensity toward communities in the Frankish heartland, though this is a conclusion not without complications. The most significant uncertainty rests with the historically unreliable *Chronicle of Novalesa,* which serves as our primary source for the abbacies of Frodoin, Eldrad, and Gezo. In the cases of these three abbots as recorded in the *Chronicle,* what appears are the projection of an idealized past and aspirations of the reconstituted monastery. From these, we find reflections of the actual institutional networks of the abbots through their personal connections to locations and people.

Frodoin

Our knowledge about the career and network of Frodoin is based both on the *Chronicle of Novalesa* and on charters, some original and others preserved in later copies. The charters include the issuance of two immunities to the monastery in 773 and 779 by Charlemagne and are useful because they document the most important events in Frodoin's career as abbot.[13] Along with the *Chronicle,* these sources formed the basis for a forged charter

---

13 MGH, Diplomatica Karolinorum 1, ed. Michael Tangl (Hanover: Hahn, 1906), no. 74, 106–8 and no. 125, 174–75.

reaffirming early grants under Pippin and the monastery's first patron, Abbo, as well as the spurious oblation of Charlemagne's son Hugo in 774. Given these details, the forgery was likely a product of the monastic reconstitution in the eleventh century, as the details also appear in the *Chronicle* as well as in a description of the forged renewal requested by Frodoin.[14]

While the immunities reflect the standing of both Frodoin and Novalesa at its height, including multiple visits by Charlemagne as he traveled between Gaul and Italy, the *Chronicle* suggests that Frodoin himself had a strong and visible connection to Frankish elite society. In book 3, he is described as one of the sons of Magfred, presumably a noble Frank who, like his predecessor as abbot, Asinarius, "was of the Frankish race, and was of the greatest renown among the nobility of the Franks. His father gave to him many estates of land and entrusted him to the monastic community for his education."[15] The *Chronicle* places this event during the reign of Pippin.

Following the deaths of Asinarius and his immediate successor, Witgar, the *Chronicle* describes the unanimous support for and election of Frodoin, along with his charismatic gifts. Perhaps most importantly (at least for the eleventh-century author), the abbot had overseen the continued growth and development of its resources. This proved useful in an anecdote when Charlemagne's army settled in Novalesa on its way to Italy (presumably in 773), and the monks' provisions were consumed at royal meals. This occurred because "the monastery in those days was extremely wealthy and most rich in resources and had been well-stocked by the most holy father," that is, Frodoin.[16] This generosity was rewarded, as later Charlemagne granted "a huge estate called Gabiana, where there were a thousand manses with

---

14 MGH, Diplomatica Karolinorum 1, ed. Tangl, no. 225, 301–4, and Cipolla, *Monumenta novaliciensia,* vol. 1, 57.

15 CN, 3.2: "fuerat siquidem et ipse Francicus genere, hac nominatissimus inter proceribus Francorum. Dedit ergo pater multa terrarum predia eidem filio suo, quem tradidit monastico ordini erudiendum."

16 CN, 3.8, trans. Clark.

their dependencies" to the monastery, which he provided specifically "to Novalesa because of his reverence for the abbot."[17]

This Gabiana appears in the forged charter of 774, as does the oblation of Hugo, which is mentioned on the return of Charlemagne following his defeat of the Lombard king Desiderius. With the oblation came more property and gifts, along with relics belonging to Cosmas and Damian (connecting the monastery, at least hagiographically, to Rome) and those of Walaric (who appears as Walericus in the text and known more widely as Valery), the founder of the abbey of Leuconay. More reliable evidence from the mid-eleventh-century *Vita Walarici abbatis Leuconaensis* posits a different final location for Walaric's relic: that Charlemagne gave them to Corbie, but that in the tenth century they were translated to Saint-Bertin, and to Saint-Valery-sur-Somme.[18] This translation would have been widely known, and the account of the *Chronicle* perhaps attempts to position Novalesa among these royally supported monasteries in Gaul. Indeed, the majority of the career of Frodoin as described in the *Chronicle* relates to the pull of, and relationship with, the Carolingians and Gaul. In light of the situation of the monastery in the eleventh century, the imagined eighth century must have seemed a past worthy of their ambition.

Eldrad

The history of Eldrad contains as much fiction as does that of Frodoin, complicated by the fact that he was venerated as a saint whose *vita* emanated from the monastic community of Novalesa before, during, and after the exile of 906 in various forms.[19]

---

17 CN, 3.14, trans. Clark.
18 The *Vita Walarici* can be found in Monumenta Germaniae Historica, Scriptores Rerum Merovingicarum 4, ed. Bruno Krusch (Hanover: Hahn, 1902), 157–75. On the later peregrinations of Walaric's relics, see Kate M. Craig, "Bringing Out the Saints: Journeys of Relics in Tenth to Twelfth Century Northern France and Flanders" (PhD diss., University of California–Los Angeles, 2015).
19 Bibliotheca Hagiographica Latina, 2443–46. The chapel dedicated to Eldrad, with thirteenth-century frescos and twelfth-century inscriptions, remains the center of his cult.

Like with Frodoin, the main biographical element highlighted in all of the *vitae,* such as the impartially preserved *vita rythmica* and the historical account preserved in one of Novalesa's *Martyrologium Adonis,* were his origins in Gaul and his elevation by an unnamed Carolingian monarch.[20]

The historical account in the large *martyrologium* in Berlin (Hamilton 4), written as an addition to the main text, presents the geographic context of Eldrad:

> In the monastery of Novalesa: The deposition of the blessed abbot Eldrad. This distinguished man was a native of the Gallic Provence [...]. He finally came to Novalesa, where he led a celibate life and he was made the worthiest father of nearly 500 monks by the grace of his king.[21]

According to the *Chronicle,* Eldrad's tenure as abbot began with the death of his predecessor, Hugo (considered by the author to be the illegitimate son of Charlemagne). While the *Chronicle* describes the final years of Hugo's career as having been spent building monastic communities "under the dominion of Novalesa" in Francia, as well as a gift of a monastery dedicated to Medard in Soisson, the focus of Eldrad from the surviving titles of the chapters was less with the building of Novalesa's physical holdings than its intellectual ones.[22] Unfortunately, the activities are lost due to the fragmentary preservation of book 4 of the *Chronicle,* but the titles of the lost chapters indicate correspondence with Florus of Lyon, a prodigious writer working in the

---

20 The *vita rythmica* was partially reconstructed by Bethmann in his edition; see also Cipolla, *Monumenta novaliciensia,* vol. 1, 372–73.

21 Cipolla, *Monumenta novaliciensia,* vol. 1, 375: "Novalici, [in]monasterio. depositio beati Helderadi abbatis. Hic vir egregius ex Gallicana provintia fuit indigena [...]. Ad ultimum vero venit Novalicium, quo vitam ducens celibem, et huius rei gratia factus est monachorum ferme quingentorum optimus pater."

22 CN, 2.30–31.

Lyon scriptorium, evidence of intellectual exchange in the service of the monastery.[23]

One example of this exchange survives in a letter from Florus to Eldrad that addresses Florus's method of textual criticism and aptitude in editing a psalter that he received from and then returned to Eldrad.[24] Although the earlier correspondence does not survive, the text of the letter suggests that Eldrad had obtained the services of Florus in an innovative venture to improve the language of the translations of the liturgically employed psalms. More so than the boastful and uncorroborated gifts and privileges that the monastery could obtain from the Carolingians, this letter alludes to a now-lost intellectual activity and exchange that served as one of the links within the monastery's networks in the ninth century.

The intellectual activities taking place in Novalesa are further confirmed in a section of the *Chronicle* that makes references to the production of Novalesa's own master of the scriptorium, Attepert, who like Florus used a unique hand, and served during the tenure of Frodoin in the generation before Eldrad. The *Chronicle* dedicated an entire chapter to his career:

---

23 On the production of Florus, see S. Tafel, "The Lyons Scriptorium (continued)," in *Palaeographia Latina,* part IV, ed. Wallace M. Lindsay (London: Humphrey Milford, 1925), 40–49. The now-lost letters were included as "4. Epistola sancti Elderadi ad Florum directa; 5. Rescriptum Flori ad beatum Elderadum; 6. Item Florus ad eundem abbatem." CN, 4.

24 The letter appears in Monumenta Germaniae Historica, Epistolae 5, ed. Ernst Dümmler (Berlin: Weidmann, 1899), 340–43. On the letter, see Pierre-Maurice Bogaert, "Florus et le Psautier: La lettre à Eldrade de Novalèse," *Revue bénédictine* 119, no. 2 (2009): 403–19. A partial translation of the letter and a discussion of Florus's position with the Carolingian tradition of textual tradition can be found in Evina Steinová, "Psalmos, notas, cantus: On the Meanings of nota in the Carolingian Period," *Speculum* 90, no. 2 (2015): 439–41. The MGH edition of this letter comes from the "Bible of Ripoll" MS Vat. Lat. 5729, one of a series of illuminated bibles produced in Saint Maria in Ripoll in the 10th and early 11th centuries. Florus also wrote a poem for Eldrad on the occasion of his editing the psalter: *Carmen ad Hylradem,* published in MGH, Poetae Latinae aevi Carolini 2, ed. Ernst Dümmler (Berlin: Weidmann, 1884), 549–50.

This same Attepert was a monk and a priest in this oft-mentioned monastery, namely in the times of the dear Frodoin. He was a servant of this monastery, as greatly imbued with the knowledge of letters as he was an extremely swift scribe of correct writing. As a matter of fact, he himself copied many diverse and very large books at the monastery in his time. Therefore, whenever we find among the other books ones written in his calligraphic hand, we immediately recognize them.[25]

Although no extant manuscripts are known in his hand, this shaped both contemporary understanding of Novalesa's importance and the reflection of the eleventh-century context of the *Chronicle*. Now visible only though its shadows, ninth-century Novalesa's intellectual links to Carolingian Gaul must have been extensive given that a chapter was dedicated in its history to the copying activities in their own scriptorium.

Eldrad's career left no other contemporary trace but for references in two problematic charters. The first is a mid-tenth-century forgery or interpolation that claims to record a royal endowment for 825 (the extant copy dates from the twelfth century), and one from 827 that also appears as a copy, although that has been described as more faithful to the original and was available to the compiler of the *Chronicle*. While Cipolla has discussed both at length, it is worth noting as a final coda to the career of Eldrad that the charters position the abbey within two different contexts, one imperial and one local.[26]

The 825 charter deals with the foundation of an almshouse at Moncenisio (the location of Novalesa) dedicated to Mary in

---

25 CN, 3.21: "Fuit enim hisdem Attepertus monachus et sacerdos in iam sepe dicto monasterio, scilicet in temporibus almi Frodoini. Hic famulus fuit predictae aecclesiae, tam in scientia litterarum valde imbutus, quamque in recta conscriptione scriptor velocissimus. Siquidem ipse multos et varios ac permaximos libros in eadem aecclesiam suis conscripsit temporibus. Ergo ubicumque sua manu antiquaria libros a se conscriptos inter alios invenimus, extimplo recognoscimus." Trans. Clark.

26 Cipolla, *Monumenta novaliciensia,* 71–80.

fulfillment of a vow made by the Carolingian Lothar I (who was king of Italy at the time), and places the monastery of S. Pietro di Pagno under Novalesa's control. In this case, Eldrad was engaged with some of the most powerful secular figures, perhaps those who were responsible for his elevation referred to in the last line of his entry in the *martyrologium* in Berlin mentioned above, with the outcome that the monastery strengthened its local holdings and regional position, as Pagno and Moncenisio are both located in the southwestern area of the Piedmont. Even if fictitious in part or whole, its mid-tenth-century context affirms how the community of Novalesa may have imagined this part of its past while in exile.

The charter from 827 encompassed some of the focus of the 825 charter with its geographic focus on the immediate areas around Novalesa, yet reflected a distinct framework of local elites. Rather than a granting of rights, this document was a notice of a judgment made in the presences of several vassals of Emperor Louis the Pious, and finally under the authority of the Count of Turin, Ratpert. The judgment recapitulates the complete dispute, which began as an accusation made by fourteen named men, described as *commanentes* (that is, *manentes* or *coloni*) of *villa Auciatis,* who claimed that Eldrad as the abbot of Novalesa had unjustly held them in servitude.[27] The advocate for the monastery, Ghiseberto, denied their claim, arguing that they had been included with a gift of land from a certain Hunno; as a counterclaim the *commanentes* said that Dionisio, the father of Hunno, had granted them a *cartola libertatis,* freeing them from servile labor. This claim was refuted and the fourteen admitted that their document had been forged, with the result that they committed to continue to serve the *villa.*

Although there is no evidence that Eldrad took part in the two phases of the dispute, the first in Turin under Count Boso, and the second in Catenasco under Ratpert, the monastery's in-

---

27 Ibid., 77: "commanentes in villa Auciatis, et dicebant quod pars aecclesie sancti Petri, monasterio Novalicio, ubi Elderado abba esse videtur, qui contra legi pigneratos abebat, vel iniuste eos in servitio replegare volebant."

sistence on maintaining control over the peasants who worked its land reflects its economic and strategic priorities at the local level. The use of secular authority to enforce its claims suggests that Novalesa and its abbots had strong links to regional elites, not just the counts of Turin but also landholders like Hunno, although no other documents (copied, forged, or otherwise) help to elucidate the relationships. Yet like the links maintained through exchanged manuscripts to Florus of Lyon, this manifestation of authority via local connections ceased abruptly in 906 when the monks were forced to leave their community, resulting in the loss of the majority of their manuscripts and charters and significant portions of their institutional history.

Gezo

Gezo's career was marked by two related events: his reclaiming the original site of Novalesa and his desire to move the community back. He belonged to the community that had evolved from those who had fled Novalesa and reestablished the monastery in Breme. The historical context of Gezo, who served as abbot from possibly as early as the 980s to after 1002, was radically different from his pre-exile predecessors. In the intervening century, not only had the monastery relocated twice, but the Carolingian dynasty dissolved completely, replaced by the Ottonians in Germany in 919 and the Capetians in Gaul in 987. The late Carolingian kingdom of Italy had suffered far greater instability than those regions, as Frankish claimants contended for the remnants of diminished royal authority, and at times an imperial title, beginning with Berengar I in 887.

During the tenure of Gezo, Italy had become a core holding for the Ottonians, and under the brief reign of Otto III, many monasteries whose fortunes had waned found renewed favor. Despite the establishment of stability in the kingdom following the arrival of the Ottonians in 951, the Novalese community at Breme suffered internal strife. The *Chronicle* presented an ill-defined attempt made by Arduin Glaber (count and later margrave of Turin) to dispossess the monastery of its independence or claim ownership of its territory.[28] Through the intervention of an emperor Otto (likely Otto II), Gezo was able to restore the monastery's privileges and have them reaffirmed.[29] In another set piece in the *Chronicle,* Gezo faced the wrath of the margrave Guido (presumably the grandson of Arduin Glaber); Gezo was forced to leave, but in a vision he saw Saint Peter direct a demon to set upon Guido with sticks. Guido quickly fell into madness.[30]

It was with the tacit support of the Ottonians that Gezo began the project of rebuilding Novalesa, by sending a monk to ascertain the state of the ruins and to build a small chapel dedicated to St. Andrew on the site that had been "destroyed and had been nearly forgotten."[31] This began the process of rebuilding and even moving the community, one that is not clearly described in the *Chronicle,* but seems to have taken place in the decades following the first attempts at restoration. An anecdote in the appendix of the *Chronicle* describes a community of monks from Breme occupying the monastery in Novalesa, but without ecclesiastical support: "Then in modern times, the monks living there, deploring the devastation, beseeched the bishop of Ventimiglia to consecrate the ruined chapels, that is to say, those of Saint Michael and of Holy Mary Mother of God, and of Saint Salvator and of Saint Eldrad."[32]

Beyond the support of the Ottonians, the *Chronicle* underscored the monastery's strained relationships with the lords of Turin and Leo of Vercelli, and described Gezo's career in miracles among the monks and inhabitants of northern Italy. In one instance, a bishop of Alba named Fulcred gave Gezo relics of

---

28 CN, 5.21-22. The *Chronicle* does not describe the event, only that Arduin used a *privata lex* in his unsuccessful attempt; Otto restores order by publicly burning the offending document.

29 CN, 5.22.

30 CN, 5.31.

31 CN, 5.25. A charter that specifically mentions the support of Gezo, in this case a confirmation for the community of Breme, was granted by Otto III in 998 (Monumenta Germaniae Historica, Diplomatica, Könige und Kaiser 2, Otto II & Otto III, ed. Theodor Sickel [Hanover: Hahn, 1893], 707–8), and Cipolla, *Monumenta novaliciensia,* 123–27.

32 CN, App. 44, trans. Clark.

Frontian and Silvester because Fulcred had once been a monk, but other miracles were set in the territory of Pollentia, the passes of Mount Cenis, and the town of Camerletto on the backs of the river Dora, all locations within the immediate area of Turin or Novalesa.[33] These regionally centered episodes are especially fitting given that Gezo himself belonged to this milieu rather than sharing the connections to Gaul that were dominant in the careers of the abbots of pre-exile Novalesa. Both his career and the continued importance of Novalesa within the region demonstrated the position of the monastery and its local links as they were interpreted by the established post-exile community that created the *Chronicle*.

Aldradus

While the accounts of Gezo's career focus on the reestablishment of a community in Novalesa while contesting local authority and seeking the approval of imperial power, the career of Aldradus marks a renewed connection to Gaul. Although we only know small snippets about his career and life, the timing of his monastic career, from Vendôme to Cluny to Novalesa and finally to Chartres, also traces a new pattern for the intellectual position of Novalesa, this time in relation to the ascendant Cluny. In her authoritative study of Aldradus's life, Giuliana Giai argues that he was the son of the Count of Nogent and his career began as a monk in Vendôme, ca. 1033.[34] He is next noted in the extant records as a member of Cluny by 1048. Following a short stint as prior in the monastery of Peterlingen (which had been restored by the abbot Odilo of Cluny), Aldradus was abbot of Breme and Novalesa in 1060.

No record exists of his activities in Novalesa, but given his previous posts and connection to Odilo of Cluny, he likely carried forward not only the initiative of reform from Cluny but

---

33 CN, 5.34, 40, 43, and 45, respectively.
34 The biography presented here is abbreviated from Giuliana Giai, "Tra Novalesa e Chartres: Adraldo e la Renovatio novalicense nell'XI secolo," *Benedictina* 59, no. 2 (2012): 271–96.

also sought to revive Novalesa's own traditions in the post-exile period by memorializing its earlier history. For example, the oldest surviving frescos on the chapel of Eldrad were painted during Aldradus's tenure and include him as a patron. The earliest prose *vita* of Eldrad may have appeared in this period as well, although what later circulated comes in the early twelfth century as the *vita* mentions the fall of Jerusalem to the crusaders.[35] The success of Aldradus was not in the refurbishment of the church in Novalesa, but in his next assignment. According to the report on his career in Peter Damian's biography of Odilo of Cluny, in 1069 Aldradus became the bishop of Chartres, a position he held until his death in 1075.[36]

The connections that Aldradus brought to Novalesa were critical to preserving its historical memory. Through the more substantial network of Cluny's monasteries and reformed houses, Novalesa regained access to the same types of materials that it had lost in its exile and, more importantly, from many of the same institutions or their intellectual successors. The return to face Gaul — not just Burgundy and Provence — also served to help restore the importance of Novalesa's history with the Carolingians, whose hagiography was continually revised.

Networks of the *Novalesa Miscellany*

This single manuscript, made up almost entirely of well-circulated texts and copied in the restored monastery, makes a unique witness to the intellectual connections and possible

---

35 The prose VITA mentions an oratory dedicated to Eldrad at Novalesa, which is most likely the frescoed chapel. The text of the prose *vita* was edited by Cipolla and appears in *Monumenta novaliciensia vetustiora* I, 375–98. There is an earlier *vita* written in meter known as the *Vita Eldradi Abbatis Novaliciensis Rhythmica* and published as *Fragmenta vitae b. Eldradi* in Monumenta Germaniae Historica, Sciptores 7, ed. Georg Heinric Pertz (Hanover: Hahn, 1846), 128–30. Cipolla suggested that it dated to the tenth century (*Monumenta novaliciensia vetustiora* 1, 372–73).

36 This shifting between monastic and ecclesiastic positions had not been unknown for the abbots of Novelesa-Breme; in 845, Joseph, bishop of Ivrea, simultaneously served as abbot.

networks built by Novalesa during this period. Yet the construction of the *Miscellany,* the selection of texts it contains, and, ultimately, its violation of genre, connect it both to the world of the mid-eleventh century and that of the Carolingian age.

This particular manuscript has had an interesting afterlife. It was bound with the short section of the *Historia Langobardorum* in the late Middle Ages, and in this form the manuscript entered private hands following the first suppression of the monastery in 1785. It made its way to England and to the Phillipps collection; at the dissolution of that collection, the Newberry Library purchased the manuscript in 1936.[37]

While still part of the Phillipps collection, it came to the attention of Cipolla, who published the first full account of the manuscript's content while making important observations about the miscellany's formation as part of his studies on the material related to Novalesa's medieval history. It was Cipolla who fully recognized the importance of the interpolations and additions related specifically to Novalesa in the section containing Paul the Deacon's *Historia Longobardorum.*[38] This finding, which connected to the legendary history of the monastery as promoted in the *Chronicle,* greatly overshadowed the various texts contained in the first section of the miscellany.

While Cipolla was able to identify many of the texts contained in the first section (some of which had been described by earlier commentators), what was left unstudied proves to be a unique informant on Novalesa's history in the eleventh century and the types of texts deemed useful to the reestablished house

---

37 Schoolman, "Of Lost Libraries and Monastic Memories," 42–43.

38 For an overview of the manuscript tradition of the *Historia,* see Rosamond McKitterick, "Paul the Deacon and the Franks," *Early Medieval Europe* 8, no. 3 (1999): 319–39, 334–37, repr. Rosamond McKitterick, *History and Memory in the Carolingian World* (Cambridge: Cambridge University Press, 2004), 77–80. For a full discussion, see Waitz's introduction in *Historia Langobardorum,* Monumenta Germaniae Historica, Scriptores Rerum Langobardorum, ed. Ludwig Bathmann and Georg Waitz (Hanover: Hahn, 1878), 28–45. A brief description of the *Novalesa Miscellany* appears on 42, n. 3.

in order to restore, or at the very least begin to rebuild, its once expansive library. In so doing, it connects to manuscripts and monasteries within some of the same transalpine networks to which it belonged during both its Carolingian apex and its later eleventh-century Cluniac restoration.

Its direct connection to Cluny is related to perhaps the least important aspect of the manuscript, what had been described as a "Greek–Latin glossary" but is, in reality, a set of glosses taken from the *Vita sancti Gregorii Magni,* the four-part life of Gregory the Great by John the Deacon of Rome (also known as John Hymmonides), a cleric who worked in the papal administration of John VIII in the late ninth century.[39] Although it was divorced from its original context, modern commentators had assumed that this *glossae collectae* in the *Novalesa Miscellany* was related to Isidore's *De natura rerum* because the first term defined is indeed the description and etymology of *Olympias* from that text. However, the rest of the glossary offers a very different set of definitions, whose only parallel comes from a now-lost manuscript viewed by Jean Mabillon and published in a short note after his death in *Itineratium Burgundicum,* the "Journey into Burgundy," a record of his visit to the monastic houses and other sites in 1682.[40] Mabillon's list is substantially shorter than the *glossae collectae* in the *Novalesa Miscellany.* Both contain terms not found in the other, indicating a shared ancestor, that is, part of a manuscript in Cluny's possession containing John the Deacon's *vita* of Gregory. Due to its form, the glossary in the *Miscellany* served little purpose unless one was reading the *vita,* a text not included in the collection. Yet despite these limitations, it was deemed valuable enough to include, perhaps because of its provenance.

Provenance may have also dictated the inclusion of a number of rarely circulated short treatises, such as Heiricus of Auxerre's *Quid sit ceroma* or Remigius of Auxerre's *Letter on the Hungarians,* neither of which are common, but both share Carolingian

---

39 Bibliotheca Hagiographica Latina, 3641 and 3642.

40 *Ouvrages posthumes de Jean Mabillion et de Thierri Ruinart,* vol. 2. (Paris, 1724), 1–33.

pedigrees.[41] On the other hand, in this eleventh-century context, a letter concerning the Hungarians could have seemed relevant. Although the *Chronicle* was clear on the identity of the raiders who forced the abandonment of the monastery, described uniformly as *saraceni,* Hungarian raids began in Italy in the first years of the tenth century, and remained a threat until their conversion.[42]

A further connection is made through an identification of the contents of the first twelve folios of the *Miscellany,* which begins imperfectly roughly sixteen folios into the *Expositio missae* of Amalarius of Metz and ends with Heiric of Auxerre, as a close parallel is known from Santa Maria in Ripoll (MS 206). Although dating from the twelfth century, the Ripoll manuscript includes the same rubrics and even the forms of initials, but in other ways is different. Ripoll 206 contains almost the entire *eclogae* of Amalarius of Metz, and after an abbreviated conclusion continues with the *Exposito missae,* when the Novalesa manuscript begins. Yet, the Ripoll manuscript ends in the middle of a sentence after ten lines of Heiric of Auxerre's *Quid sit ceroma,* suggesting that the original manuscript may have lost its final page. In this case, like the Greek–Latin glossary,

---

41 Originally attributed to Lupus of Ferrières; published as one of his letters by Ernst Dümmler in Monumenta Germaniae Historica, Epistolae 6 (Berlin: Weidmann, 1899), 114–17. On the new attribution of *Quid sit ceroma,* see Veronika von Büren, "Heiricus [Autissiodorensis] mon.," in *Clavis des auteurs latins du Moyen Âge: Territoire français 735–987,* ed. Marie-Hélène Jullien and Françoise Perelman (Turnhout: Brepols, 2010), vol. 3, 375–98. Charles Beeson originally argued for the authorship of Lupus: Charles H. Beeson, "The Authorship of '*Quid sit ceroma*,'" in *Classical and Mediaeval Studies in Honor of Edward Kennard Rand,* ed. Leslie Webber Jones (New York: Leslie Webber Jones, 1938), 1–7.

42 On both issues, see Aldo A. Settia, "Monasteri subalpini e presenza saracena: una storia da riscivere," in *Dal Piemonte all'Europa: Esperienze monastiche nella società medievale* (Turin: Deputazione Subalpina di Storia Patria, 1988), 79–95, and Aldo A. Settia, "I monasteri italiani e le incursioni Saraceni e Ungare," in *Il monachesimo italiano dall'età longobardia all'età ottoniana (secc. VIII–X),* ed. Giovanni Spinelli (Cesena: Badia di Santa Maria del Monte, 2006), 292–310.

both Ripoll 206 and the *Novalesa Miscellany* are derived from the same family of sources.

Although their direct connection was only speculative, both Ripoll and Novalesa were connected to Cluny. Under the leadership of its abbot, Count Oliba, in the first half of the eleventh century, Santa Maria in Ripoll became a node in a network of monasteries spanning both sides of the Pyrenees, building on a tradition of interconnection, especially in the transmission of texts, between the Carolingian Empire and the region of Catalonia.[43] While Cluny never made direct inroads in Catalonia to establish daughter houses, Cluny's influence was imparted first through the Moissac Abbey in southwestern France (which was a Cluniac foundation), and later through ancillary branches connected to that monastery.[44]

While the first fourteen folios reflect connections to Cluny directly and perhaps through Ripoll, the largest section of the miscellany of Novalesa, ninety-three folios, is devoted to eighteen texts about saints and saintly figures that would have held relevance for the reestablished monastic community. On its surface, the organization may seem haphazard, with shorter epigrams, letters, and sermons mixed together with longer *vitae*. The works were not organized by literary genre, but rather generally by the position and gender of the saint and present internal coherency, according to which the subjects of the hagiographic texts can be divided into three categories: bishops and clerics, female saints, and materials related to the Virgin. The outlier from these may be the ninth-century miracles of Saint Benedict by Adrevald of Fleury, representing both the importance of monastic institutions and of pilgrimage, in this case to the shrine of Benedict in Fleury, reiterating a draw toward Gaul.

---

43 Matthias M. Tischler, "How Carolingian Was Early Medieval Catalonia?," in *Using and Not Using the Past after the Carolingian Empire: c.900–c.1050,* ed. Sarah Greer, Alice Hicklin, and Stefan Esders (London: Routledge, 2019), 111–33.

44 Anscari M. Mundó, "Monastic Movements in the East Pyrenees," in *Cluniac Monasticism in the Central Middle Ages,* ed. Noreen Hunt (London: Palgrave Macmillan, 1971), 98–122.

Together, these tracts represent a varied assortment of hagiographic writings of the ninth century and tenth century, as well as those of early medieval authors; crucial here is that it is not just a local collection, but one with texts commemorating both long-standing cults and those of more recent vintage, with a chronological range from those written by and celebrating figures with connections to ancient Christianity and the early Christian East up to the short poem offered in 970 by Ruotger as a eulogy for Bruno of Cologne, the brother of the Holy Roman Emperor Otto I, a figure whose dynasty was celebrated in the *Chronicle of Novalesa*.[45] The compilation of hagiographic texts in the *Novalesa Miscellany* suggests the placement of the monastery within the context of a wider Christian world, expansive both geographically and chronologically, one that complements its growing proximity to Cluny.

Conclusions

Even in the twilight of the early Middle Ages, the connections between Novalesa and the other monasteries of the Carolingian world remained strong. The well-known Necrology from Reichenau, published in the MGH in the supplement to the Necrologia Germaniae including the confraternities of St. Gall, Reichenau, and Farfa, includes simply the name of the monastery of Novalesa as an effort to include that community and what has been judged to be a list of its abbots and other leaders from before the exile in 906.[46] This includes a number of prominent abbots, including:

---

45 On Ruotger's *Vita Brunonis,* see Henry Mayr-Harting, *Church and Cosmos in Early Ottonian Germany: The View from Cologne* (Oxford: Oxford University Press, 2007), 10–21.

46 MGH Necr. Suppl., 166. The relevant section on Novalesa was also included in Cipolla, *Monumenta novaliciensia,* vol. 1, 279–82.

- Godo abba [Novalesa's first abbot] (726)
- Asinarius abba (ca. 760–770)
- [F]rodoinus abba (ca. 773–814)
- Amblulfus [one of two possible abbots, a successor of Frodoin or one known from the late ninth century] (post 814 or ca. 880)
- Hildradus [likely Eldradus, although not noted as abbot] (ca. 825–27)
- Ioseph episcopus et abba [Joseph, Bishop of Ivrea] (ca. 845)

This list was compiled by various hands, and likely served to signify a continuing relationship through the ninth century between Reichenau and Novalesa.

It is this kind of relationship that is reiterated in the *Miscellany* through the choices of texts it includes, but with those from Cluny rather than Reichenau. In the same ways, the careers of the abbots in the *Chronicle of Novalesa* first emphasize the connection to the Carolingians, often personally, and with the first push toward restoration, a shift to the Ottonians (likely to balance the relationship with the counts and later margraves of Turin). Counter to this, the development of Novalesa's hagiographic corpus is through the addition of primarily local and regional saints.

The texts used to rebuild Novalesa did not recreate the institution, its library, or the political and intellectual networks to which it belonged. But rather, they projected something about its uncertain status at the end of the tenth century, and its new position by the mid-eleventh.

Appendix: Abbreviated Novalesa Timeline

Date	Event
726	Monastery established by the will of Abbo; Godo elected as first abbot
fl. 739	Abbo (not founder) serves as abbot
ca. 773–810/4	Abbacy of Froduin
fl. 825–826–?	Abbacy of St. Eldrad
906	Monastery destroyed by "Saracens"
post-906	Monks flee to Burgundy, Turin
926	Monks establish house in Breme following gift by Adalbert of Turin
ca. 1000	Abbot Gezo reestablishes monastery in Novalesa
1014	Last date recorded in the *Chronicle of Novalesa*
ca. 1060	Aldradus serves as abbot; later becomes bishop of Chartres
1785	Monastery first suppressed; many manuscripts dispersed
1855	Monastery finally suppressed

Bibliography

Manuscripts
Vatican City. Biblioteca Apostolica Vaticana, Vat. Lat. 5729. https://opac.vatlib.it/mss/detail/Vat.lat.5729.

Primary & Reference
Bibliotheca Hagiographica Latina. Brussels, 1898–1901.
Chronicon Novaliciense. In Monumenta Germaniae Historica, Scriptores Rerum Langobardorum, edited by Ludwig Bethmann, 73–133. Hanover: Hahn, 1846.
Chronicon Novaliciense. Edited by Celestino Combetti. Turin: ex Regio Typographeo, 1843.
Cronaca di Novalesa. Edited by Gian Carlo Alessio. Turin: G. Einuadi, 1982.
Florus of Lyon. Monumenta Germaniae Historica, Poetae Latinae 2, edited by Ernst Dümmler. Berlin: Weidmann, 1884.
Historia Langobardorum. In Monumenta Germaniae Historica, Scriptores Rerum Langobardorum, edited by Ludwig Bethmann and Georg Waitz, 12–187. Hanover: Hahn, 1878.
Monumenta Germaniae Historica, Diplomatica Karolinorum 1. Edited by Michael Tangl. Hanover: Hahn, 1906.
Monumenta Germaniae Historica, Diplomatica, Könige und Kaiser 2, Otto II & Otto III. Edited by Theodor Sickel. Hanover: Hahn, 1893.
Monumenta Germaniae Historica, Epistolae 5. Edited by Ernst Dümmler. Berlin: Weidmann, 1899.
Monumenta Germaniae Historica, Epistolae 6. Edited by Ernst Dümmler. Berlin: Weidmann, 1899.
Ouvrages posthumes de Jean Mabillion et de Thierri Ruinart. 2 volumes. Paris, 1724.
Vita Eldradi Abbatis Novaliciensis Rhythmica (Fragmenta vitae b. Eldradi). Monumenta Germaniae Historica, Sciptores 7, edited by Georg Heinric Pertz, 128–30. Hanover: Hahn, 1846.
Vita Walarici. Monumenta Germaniae Historica, Scriptores Rerum Merovingicarum 4, edited by Bruno Krusch, 157–75. Hanover: Hahn, 1902.

Secondary

Beeson, Charles H. "The Authorship of *'Quid sit ceroma'.*" In *Classical and Mediaeval Studies in Honor of Edward Kennard Rand,* edited by Leslie Webber Jones, 1–7. New York: Leslie Webber Jones, 1938.

Bogaert, Pierre-Maurice. "Florus et le Psautier: La lettre à Eldrade de Novalèse." *Revue bénédictine* 109, no. 2 (2009): 403–19. DOI: 10.1484/J.RB.5.100498.

Cipolla, Carlo. *Monumenta novaliciensia vetustiora: Raccolta degli atti e delle chronache riguaardanti l'abbazia della Novalesa.* FSI 32. 2 volumes. Rome: Isituto Storico Italiano, 1898-1901.

———. "Notizia di alcuni codini dell'antica biblioteca novalicense." *Memorie della reale accademia della scienze di Torino* 2, no. 44 (1894): 193–213.

———. *Ricerche sull'antica biblioteca del monastero della Novalesa.* Turin: Carlo Clausen, 1894.

Clark, Elizabeth Artemis. "The Chronicle of Novalese: Translation, Text, and Literary Analysis." PhD diss., UNC–Chapel Hill, 2017.

Constable, Giles. "Cluniac Reform in the Eleventh Century." In *The Abbey of Cluny: A Collection of Essays to Mark the Eleven-Hundredth Anniversary of Its Foundation,* edited by Giles Constable, 81–112. Münster: LIT, 2010.

———. "Cluniac Reform in the Eleventh Century." In *Vom Umbruch zur Erneuerung? Das 11. und beginnende 12. Jahrhundert,* edited by Nicola Karthaus, Jörg Jarnut, and Mattias Wemhoff, 231–46. Munich: Fink Wilhelm GmbH, 2006.

Costambeys, Marios. *Power and Patronage in Early Medieval Italy: Local Society, Italian Politics and the Abbey of Farfa, c.700–900.* Cambridge: Cambridge University Press, 2008. DOI: 10.1017/CBO9780511496271.

Craig, Kate M. "Bringing Out the Saints: Journeys of Relics in Tenth to Twelfth Century Northern France and Flanders." PhD diss., University of California–Los Angeles, 2015.

D'Acunto, Nicolangelo. "Forms of Transmission of Knowledge at Saint Gall (Ninth to Eleventh Century)." In *Horizontal Learning in the High Middle Ages: Peer-to-Peer Knowledge*

Transfer in Religious Communities, edited by Micol Long, Tjamke Snijders, and Steven Vanderputten, 207–15. Knowledge Communities. Amsterdam: Amsterdam University Press, 2019. DOI: 10.2307/j.ctvnb7nbt.13.

Dell'Oro, Ferdinandom, and Gionata Brusa. *Un compendio del "Martyrologium Adonis" proveniente dall'Abbazia di Novalesa.* Rome: Centro Liturgico Vicenziano, 2012.

Dubois, Jacques, and Geneviève Renaud. *Le Martyrologe d'Adon, ses deux familles, ses trois recensions.* Paris: Éditions du Centre National de la Recherche Scientifique, 1984.

Geary, Patrick J. *Aristocracy in Provence: The Rhône Basin at the Dawn of the Carolingian Age.* Middle Ages Series. Philadelphia: University of Pennsylvania Press, 1985.

———. *Phantoms of Remembrance: Memory and Oblivion at the End of the First Millennium.* Princeton: Princeton University Press, 1994.

Giai, Giuliana. "Tra Novalesa e Chartres: Adraldo e la Renovatio novalicense nell'XI secolo." *Benedictina* 59, no. 2 (2012): 271–96.

Hildebrandt, Madge M. *The External School in Carolingian Society.* Boston and Leiden: Brill, 1992.

Iogna-Prat, Dominique. *Agni immaculati: Recherches sur les sources hagiographiques relatives à Saint Maieul de Cluny (954–994).* Paris: Éditions du Cerf, 1988.

Ludwig, Uwe. "Die Gedenklisten des Klosters Novalese — Möglichkeiten einer Kritik des Chronicon Novaliciense." In *Memoria in der Gesellschaft des Mittelalters,* edited by Dieter Geuenich and Otto Gerhard Oexle, 32–55. Göttingen: Vandenhoeck & Ruprecht, 1994.

Mayr-Harting Henry. *Church and Cosmos in Early Ottonian Germany: The View from Cologne.* Oxford: Oxford University Press, 2007. DOI: 10.1093/acprof:oso/9780199210718.001.0001.

McKitterick, Rosamond. *History and Memory in the Carolingian World.* Cambridge: Cambridge University Press, 2004. DOI: 10.1017/CBO9780511617003.

———. "Paul the Deacon and the Franks." *Early Medieval Europe* 8, no. 3 (1999): 319–39. DOI: 10.1111/1468-0254.00051.

Mundó, Anscari M. "Monastic Movements in the East Pyrenees." In *Cluniac Monasticism in the Central Middle Ages,* edited by Noreen Hunt, 98–122. London: Palgrave Macmillan, 1971. DOI: 10.1007/978-1-349-00705-9_7.

Rapp, Claudia. *Brother-Making in Late Antiquity and Byzantium.* Oxford: Oxford University Press, 2016. DOI: 10.1093/ac prof:oso/9780195389333.001.0001.

Schoolman, Edward M. "Of Lost Libraries and Monastic Memories: Creating the Eleventh-Century Novalesa Miscellany." *Haskins Society Journal* 28 (2017): 39–61. DOI: 10.1017/9781787441446.004.

Settia, Aldo A. "I monasteri italiani e le incursioni Saraceni e Ungare." In *Il monachesimo italiano dell'età longobardia all'età ottoniana (secc. VIII–X),* edited by Giovanni Spinelli, 79–95. Cesena: Badia di Santa Maria del Monte, 2006.

———. "Monasteri subalpini e presenza saracena: una storia da riscivere." In *Dal Piemonte all'Europa: Esperienze monastiche nella società medievale,* 292–310. Turin: Deputazione subalpina di storia patria, 1988.

Steinová, Evina. "Psalmos, notas, cantus: On the Meanings of *nota* in the Carolingian Period." *Speculum* 90, no. 2 (2015): 424–57. DOI: 10.1017/S0038713415000275.

Tafel, S. "The Lyons Scriptorium (continued)." In *Palaeographia Latina,* part IV, edited by Wallace M. Lindsay, 40–70. London: Humphrey Milford, 1925.

Tischler, Matthias M. "How Carolingian Was Early Medieval Catalonia?" In *Using and Not Using the Past after the Carolingian Empire: c.900–c.1050,* edited by Sarah Greer, Alice Hicklin, and Stefan Esders, 111–33. London: Routledge, 2019. DOI: 10.4324/9780429400551-7.

Vanderputten, Steven. *Monastic Reform as Process: Realities and Representations in Medieval Flanders, 900–1100.* Ithaca: Cornell University Press, 2013. DOI: 10.7591/cornell/9780801451713.001.0001.

Von Büren, Veronika. "Heiricus [Autissiodorensis] mon." In *Clavis des auteurs latins du Moyen Âge: Territoire français*

735–987, Vol. 3, edited by Marie-Hélène Jullien and Françoise Perelman, 375–98. Turnhout: Brepols, 2010.

6

The Early Reception History of the First Book of Isidore's *Etymologies* as a Mirror of Carolingian Intellectual Networks: A Proposal

Evina Steinová

The *Etymologies* of Isidore of Seville have been called the single most read medieval text after the Bible.[1] While perhaps an exaggeration, this claim is a fitting tribute to the tremendous influence and popularity of Isidore's work in the Middle Ages. The most impressive testimony to the importance of Isidore's *oeuvre majeure* is perhaps August Eduard Anspach's handlist of the manuscripts of the *Etymologies* containing almost 1,100 codices, fragments, and excerpts of this text datable to before the end of the sixteenth century.[2] As the roughly 300 manuscripts

---

1 Ernst Robert Curtius, *European Literature and the Latin Middle Ages,* trans. Willard R. Trask, Bollingen Series 36 (Princeton: Princeton University Press, 1953), 496–97.

2 This number is taken from the unfinished catalogue of the manuscripts of the *Etymologies* prepared by A.E. Anspach before his death in 1942. The catalogue was published as José María Fernández Catón, *Las "Etimologías" en la tradición manuscrita medieval estudiada por el Prof. Dr. Anspach* (León: centro de estudios e investigacion San Isidoro, 1966). Overviews of the man-

of the *Etymologies* in Anspach's handlist predating the eleventh century attest, Isidore was established as a major *auctoritas* already in the early Middle Ages.[3] Most researchers agree that Isidore's knowledge compendium was received eagerly early on, as is indicated by its rapid dissemination into Ireland, Gaul, and Italy, and revealed by the references to the *Etymologies* in many

---

uscripts based on Anspach's handlist can be found in Baudouin Van den Abeele, "La tradition manuscrite des *Étymologies* d'Isidore de Séville," *Cahiers de Recherches Médiévales et Humanistes* 16 (2008): 195–205, and more recently Evina Steinová, "The Oldest Manuscript Tradition of the *Etymologiae* (Eighty Years after A.E. Anspach)," *Visigothic Symposia* 4 (2020): 100–143. The most important studies of the manuscript transmission of the *Etymologies* are (in rough chronological order): Charles Henry Beeson, *Isidor-Studien*, Quellen und Untersuchungen zur lateinischen Philologie des Mittelalters 4, no. 2 (Munich: Beck, 1913); Wallace M. Lindsay, *"Etymologiarum" sive "Originum" libri XX*, 2 vols. (Oxford: Clarendon Press, 1911); Walter Porzig, "Die Rezensionen der *Etymologiae* des Isidorus von Sevilla. Vorbemerkung," *Hermes* 72, no. 2 (1937): 129–70; Bernhard Bischoff, "Die europäische Verbreitung der Werke Isidors von Sevilla," in *Isidoriana: Collección de estudios sobre Isidore de Sevilla*, ed. Manuel C. Díaz y Díaz (León: Centro de estudios San Isidoro, 1961), 317–44; Marc Reydellet, "La diffusion des *Origines* d'Isidore de Séville au Haut Moyen Âge," *Mélanges d'archéologie et d'histoire* 78, no. 2 (1966): 383–437; Manuel C. Díaz y Díaz, *Los capítulos sobre los metales en las "Etimologías" de Isidoro de Sevilla*, La minería hispana a iberoamericana 7 (León: Catedra de San Isidoro, 1970); Ulrich Schindel, "Zur frühen Überlieferungsgeschichte der *Etymologiae* Isidors von Sevilla," *Studi medievali* 29, no. 2 (1988): 587–605; Carmen Codoñer Merino, "Fases en la edición de las *Etymologiae*, con especial referencia al libro X," *Euphrosyne* 22 (1994): 125–46; Carmen Codoñer Merino, "Historia del texto de las *Etimologías* isidorianas," in *Actas del III Congreso Hispánico de Latín Medieval (León, 26–29 de Septiembre de 2002)*, ed. Maurilio Pérez González (León: Universidad de León, 2002), vol. 2, 483–94; and Carmen Codoñer Merino, José Carlos Martin, and Adelaida Andres, "Isidorus Hispalensis ep.," in *La trasmissione dei testi latini del Medioevo/ Medieval Texts and Their Transmission*, ed. Paulo Chiesa and Lucia Castaldi (Florence: SISMEL – Edizioni del Galluzzo, 2005), vol. 2, 274–417.

3 The real number of the surviving pre-1000 manuscripts transmitting the *Etymologies* is closer to 500. On Isidore as an early medieval authority, see Bernice M. Kaczynski, "The Authority of the Fathers: Patristic Texts in Early Medieval Libraries and Scriptoria," *Journal of Medieval Latin* 16 (2006): 1–27, at 25, and Richard M. Pollard and Anne-Gaëlle Weber, "Le canon des Pères à l'époque carolingienne et la place de Flavius Josèphe," *Revue d'Études Augustiniennes et Patristiques* 67, no. 2 (2021): 275–318.

seventh- and eighth-century texts.[4] Yet, it was the Carolingian users who played the decisive role in elevating the *Etymologies* to the status of a universal encyclopedia and the Carolingian *scriptoria,* with their prodigal output, that defined the shape and form the text was to be received by the following generations up to modern times. Walter Porzig captured the centrality of Isidore's encyclopedia to the Carolingian world when he stated that every larger library endeavored to possess several copies of the *Etymologies,* and even the humbler ones must have owned at least one exemplar.[5]

The permeation of the *Etymologies* into the Carolingian world was not a passive process. We should not talk of it as merely a reception but rather as an appropriation, as Carolingian users transformed the *Etymologies* with every stroke of the pen involved in the copying, correcting, and annotation of this work, shaping it in their own image, and often leaving behind a tangible trace of their reshaping. The task was made easier by the fact that the *Etymologies,* being a knowledge compendium with a complex textual history,[6] was from the beginning a malleable

---

4   In particular, Jocelyn N. Hillgarth has argued that the *Etymologies* reached Ireland already around the mid-seventh century. See Jocelyn N. Hillgarth, "The East, Visigothic Spain and the Irish," *Studia Patristica* 4 (1961): 442–56; Jocelyn N. Hillgarth, "Visigothic Spain and Early Christian Ireland," *Proceedings of the Royal Irish Academy* C 62 (1962): 167–94; and Jocelyn N. Hillgarth, "Ireland and Spain in the Seventh Century," *Peritia* 3 (1984): 1–16. All three were reprinted in Jocelyn. N. Hillgarth, *Visigothic Spain, Byzantium, and the Irish* (London: Variorum, 1985). Hillgarth's thesis has recently been revised in Marina Smyth, "Isidorian Texts in Seventh-Century Ireland," in *Isidore of Seville and His Reception in the Early Middle Ages,* ed. Andrew Fear and Jamie Wood (Amsterdam: Amsterdam University Press, 2016), 111–30. See also Bischoff, "Die europäische Verbreitung."

5   Porzig, "Die Rezensionen der *Etymologiae,*" 133.

6   There was, in all likelihood, never a single archetype of the work. Rather, an earlier version, consisting of the first ten books, may have been put into circulation by Isidore around 625. Later, Isidore added ten more books, but never completed this enterprise, dying in 636. The unfinished work was then completed by Isidore's close friend and fellow bishop, Braulio of Zaragoza, who made several notable changes to the text and its arrangement. From Braulio we also learn that the uncorrected version of the *Etymologies* was in circulation before his own revision could have been prepared.

text, open to rewriting and adjustment, addition and omission, reordering and reformatting.[7] Already the oldest well-preserved manuscripts of the encyclopedia, dated to the eighth century, reveal the fingerprints of several generations of users who felt the need to correct, expand, and reorganize Isidore.[8] The process only accelerated in the Carolingian environment. It was in this period, too, that a single *scriptorium* could possess, for the first time, multiple copies of the *Etymologies* descending from distinct textual families and thus be faced with the significant heterogeneity of its textual tradition. At least in several places, scribes responded to this heterogeneity in a typically Carolingian fashion, producing new recensions that harmonized the earlier text versions in line with their own expectations and needs.[9] One of the ninth-century Carolingian redactions produced the family ξ of the *Etymologies,* whose paramount influ-

---

The history of these three earliest text-versions and their relationship to the text in surviving manuscripts are discussed in Reydellet, "La diffusion des *Origines*," 387–88, and Codoñer Merino, Martin, and Andres, "Isidorus Hispalensis ep.," 282–85.

7 Porzig, "Die Rezensionen der *Etymologiae*," 143.

8 The reworking of the *Etymologies* began, as noted in footnote 6, with Braulio. For the overview of interpolations attributed to him, see Michel Huglo, "The *Musica Isidori* Tradition in the Iberian Peninsula," in *Hispania Vetus: Musical-Liturgical Manuscripts from Visigothic Origins to the Franco-Roman Transition (9th–12th Centuries),* ed. Susana Zapke (Bilbao: Fundacion BBVA, 2007), 64–67. Other early recensions include one that contains a reference to the *annus praesens* in the reign of Recceswinth in book V, making it datable to ca. 660, and a recension in which the first ten books were re-divided into three books. A fragment of a seventh-century Irish codex of the *Etymologies* preserved at the Longleat House, one of the oldest witnesses of Isidore's text, clearly descends from a redaction of the *Etymologies* made in Visigothic Spain in 655. See James P. Carley and Ann Dooley, "An Early Irish Fragment of Isidore of Seville's *Etymologiae*," in *The Archaeology and History of Glastonbury Abbey: Essays in Honour of the 90th Birthday of C. A. Ralegh Radford,* ed. Lesley J. Abrams and James Patrick Carley (Woodbridge: Boydell Press, 1991), 135–61.

9 Reydellet, "La diffusion des *Origines*," 388. Two examples of Carolingian redactions of the *Etymologies* attempting to harmonize different text versions are analyzed in Evina Steinová, "Two Carolingian Redactions of the *Etymologiae* from St. Gallen," *Mittellateinisches Jahrbuch* 56, no. 2 (2021): 298–376.

ence is attested by the fact that some of the innovations that originated with this redaction, such as unified tables of contents at the beginning of each book of the *Etymologies,* even found their way into the critical edition of Wallace M. Lindsay.[10]

The family ξ illustrates the phenomenon at the center of this chapter, that of the "Carolingian *Etymologies.*" This name can be applied to manuscripts of the Visigothic encyclopedia that reflect its appropriation in Carolingian contexts and carry specific traces of this intervention. Scholars such as Lindsay or Porzig looked at these interventions as interpolations. Their goal was to edit the text as faithfully to its archetype as possible (Lindsay)[11] or to reconstruct its stemma (Porzig).[12] However, seeing these interventions as neutral and helpful is equally valuable. Once our focus shifts away from seventh-century Spain to the Carolingian period, those manuscripts of the *Etymologies* that had been seen as deviant and unreliable become a treasure trove of unexplored material informing us about the Carolingian intellectual, social, and cultural life.[13] For this reason, I talk below not of Carolin-

---

10 Cf. Lindsay, *Etymologiae,* with Reydellet, "La diffusion des *Origines,*" 399. The credit for the discovery of family ξ belongs to Walter Porzig, who believed that it is a descendant of Braulio's recension. See Porzig, "Die Rezensionen der *Etymologiae,*" 142–50 and 165–67. Marc Reydellet showed that it is not merely an offshoot of the Spanish family, as suggested by Porzig, but a separate Carolingian redaction. See Reydellet, "La diffusion des *Origines,*" 419.

11 Wallace M. Lindsay, "The Editing of Isidore *Etymologiae,*" *The Classical Quarterly* 5 (1911): 42–53.

12 Porzig, "Die Rezensionen der *Etymologiae,*" 131.

13 It needs to be added that the process of appropriation of the *Etymologies* did not cease after the Carolingian period. Scholars have noted many examples of innovations of post-Carolingian origin. See Carmen Codoñer Merino, "Textes médicaux insérés dans les *Etymologiae* isidoriennes," in *La réception d'Isidore de Séville durant le Moyen âge tardif (XIIᵉ–XVᵉ s.),* ed. Jacques Elfassi and Bernard Ribémont, Cahiers de Recherches Médiévales 16 (Orléans: CNRS, 2008), 17–38; Carmen Codoñer Merino, "Transmisión y recepción de las *Etimologías,*" in *Estudios de latín medieval hispánico. Actas del V Congreso Internacional de Latín Medieval Hispánico,* ed. José Martínez Gázquez, Óscar de la Cruz Palma, and Cándida Ferrero Hernández (Florence: SISMEL – Edizioni del Galluzzo, 2011), 5–26; and Carmen Cardelle de Hartmann, "Uso y recepción de las *Etymologiae* de Isidoro," in *Wisigothica:*

gian interpolations but rather of innovations. Furthermore, the purposeful flexibility of this term allows it to include phenomena as varied in character as annotations, separate transmission of individual books of the *Etymologies* or their constituent units, changes in the order and organization of material, and changes in the physical format of the book — all of which are as valuable reflections of early medieval appropriation as are textual additions, which alone can be termed interpolations.

Importantly, the "Carolingian *Etymologies*" tell us not only how Carolingians read the *Etymologies* and what they desired to find in it, but also how new knowledge was produced, disseminated, and received in this period in which Isidore's encyclopedia became one of its most important vessels. This is due to several unique properties of the *Etymologies*: a large number of surviving Carolingian manuscripts, the fact that many of them can be associated with well-known centers, and the degree of dynamicity of the *Etymologies* in a Carolingian environment, which promises a large number of innovations that can be studied. Many innovations did not remain restricted to a single manuscript or community but travelled through the veins of Carolingian intellectual networks, pumped into these veins by the centers that produced them or served as important hubs of their reception and dissemination. By tracking and analyzing the pattern of dissemination of these innovations, we can learn about the properties of the Carolingian intellectual ecosystem and its dynamics. The "Carolingian *Etymologies*" are, in other words, an ideal probe into examining the contours of Carolingian knowledge networks and the dynamics of innovation in this period. Such a study is the objective of the NWO VENI project entitled Innovating Knowledge: Isidore's *Etymologiae* in the Carolingian Period.[14]

After M.C. Díaz y Díaz, ed. Carmen Codoñer Merino and Paulo Farmhouse Alberto, mediEVI 3 (Florence: SISMEL, 2014), 477–502.

14 The project, its objectives, and outputs are described on the project website https://innovatingknowledge.nl/.

In this chapter, I illustrate the aims and methodologies of this project, using three case studies concerning Carolingian innovations in the first book of the *Etymologies*. These three case studies exemplify distinct diffusion patterns of innovations and trace different relationships between centers participating in their exchange. They are compared and contrasted using the following four scalable qualitative descriptors:

– Impact: How many surviving manuscripts transmit the innovation?
  Innovations vary from small-scale ones, including those that appear only in a single manuscript, to large-scale ones, featuring in tens or hundreds of manuscripts.

– Duration: For how long since the presumed point of origin can the innovation be detected in surviving manuscripts?
  Short-term innovations survive in manuscript evidence for a limited amount of time, perhaps several decades. Long-term innovations continue to appear in codices for several hundreds of years. It is also important to consider the chronological pattern in dissemination, e.g., whether an innovation spread fast after its first appearance in the manuscripts (or possibly the moment of introduction prior to the surviving manuscripts) or whether it became successful only after a delay.

– Direction of spreading: What were the main means of transmission of the innovation?
  Textual innovations spread vertically if they were transmitted as a result of book-copying; that is, from an exemplar to its copy. By contrast, innovations could also travel horizontally because of processes other than copying, such as the exchange of books, teachers, and students, or because of ties between centers and people, often along geographical corridors. Vertical and horizontal transmission leave behind distinct traces in manuscript evidence, for in the first case, one will see that a particular innovation appears in genetically related manuscripts, and it may even be a defining trait of a genetic rela-

tionship. In the second case, one will observe that manuscripts that are witnesses of the same innovation are not genetically related. In fact, the same innovation appears in manuscripts that clearly represent different families and branches of manuscript transmission.

– Emergence: How many sources of the innovation can be identified?

A single-source innovation has only one point of origin, being a result of the activity of a single innovator, be it an individual or a group, who, even if they cannot be identified, can be assumed to have worked at a single specific place, at a single specific point in time. A multi-source innovation, on the contrary, does not have a single locus of origin, no single inventor, nor does it reflect a development particular to a single context. Rather, if we can see that the same or a similar innovation occurred many times in multiple places and was realized by multiple agents, especially if it can be shown to have arisen independently, then we are probably looking at a broader societal change that elicited a similar response among those who shared the same culture and schooling.

The First Book of the *Etymologies* in the Transmission History of the Work

It has been widely recognized that the individual books of the *Etymologies* have distinct textual and manuscript histories.[15] The first book of the *Etymologies,* dedicated to grammar and sometimes known as *De grammatica,* holds a special place in this regard.[16] C.H. Beeson observed at the beginning of the twentieth century that this book of the *Etymologies* was the most frequently excerpted and appropriated in the early Middle Ages.[17]

---

15 See especially Porzig, "Die Rezensionen der *Etymologiae*," 134–35.

16 The first book of the *Etymologies* was recently reedited: Olga Spevak, ed. and trans., *Isidore de Séville, "Étymologies." Livre I. La grammaire,* Auteurs latins du Moyen Âge 31 (Paris: Les Belles Lettres, 2020).

17 Beeson, *Isidor-Studien,* 83.

Indeed, the first book was copied, commented on, extracted, quoted from, and blended with comparable texts more often than all but one of the twenty books into which Isidore's encyclopedia was divided by his first editor, Braulio of Zaragoza.[18]

Several decades before Beeson, Hermann Hagen noted that the first book was often transmitted separately as an autonomous work.[19] An attempt at the study of its transmission must, thus, consider not only the manuscripts of the complete text of the encyclopedia, which was standardly transmitted in one or two volumes, but also the codices that transmit only the first book or its parts, not to forget a substantial number of fragments that survive from the early Middle Ages.[20] As will be shown below, the diversity of material contexts in which the first book was embedded, from bulky codices of the entire *Etymologies* with perhaps 400–600 large-format pages, through the somewhat smaller and slimmer compendia, in which the first book was circulated together with other texts, to small-format booklets of as few as two quires that contained only the first book and could be carried out in a pocket, is part of the story of the transmission and transformation of this book in the Carolingian period.[21]

---

18 The most excerpted book of the *Etymologiae* is book VI dealing with the Bible, books and writing instruments, Church Councils, Easter and other holidays, and Church rites, which appear in eighty-nine pre-1000 manuscripts. Excerpts from book I appear in eighty-three pre-1000 manuscripts; see the Innovating Knowledge database at https://db.innovatingknowledge.nl/.

19 Hermann Hagen, "De Isidoro grammatico," in *Grammatici latini. Supplementum,* ed. Heinrich Keil (Leipzig: Teubner, 1870), vol. 8, 255–56.

20 I am aware of at least ten pre-1000 fragments of the first book of the *Etymologies.* See the fragments included in the Innovating Knowledge database.

21 Just to give a few examples of the diversity of material contexts in which the first book was transmitted, the *Codex Karolinus,* Wolfenbüttel, Herzog August Bibliothek, Weiss. 64, consists of 330 folios (660 pages), while the more economically copied St. Gallen, Stiftsbibliothek, MS 237, which likewise contains all twenty books of the *Etymologies,* counts 328 pages. The two-volume copy St. Gallen, Stiftsbibliothek, MSS 231–32, consists of manuscripts with 378 (books I–X) and 331 pages (books XI–XX), respectively. Junius 25, originally a separate codicological unit consisting of only the first book, has 28 folios (56 pages) of similar dimensions as the manuscripts above (204 × 133 mm [8.03 × 5.24 in.]), while the tiny Harley 2713 (148 × 80

To this should be added that the text of the first book is characterized by several major textual variants that differentiate the four main textual families identified by Lindsay, Porzig and Reydellet: the Frankish α, the Italian β, the Spanish γ and the Carolingian ξ, each of which significantly problematized editing of this book.[22] There is, for example, the question of the *capitulum* V, which appears in the overview of the *capitula* attached to the first book in all early medieval manuscripts as *De voce et littera*, but corresponds to no chapter found in the manuscripts. Depending on where one looks, one can find at least seven different solutions to this discrepancy between the structure of the first book and its content in the early manuscript evidence, all of which may be early medieval innovations rather than revealing how the text may have looked on Isidore's working desk or in Braulio's hands.[23] Apart from major textual variants, the text of the first book contains many minor variants that are not captured by Lindsay's critical edition, concealing rather than revealing the textual diversity of the first book in Carolingian manuscripts. Many of these variants provide evidence of crossbreeding and hybridization that does not allow reconstructing

---

mm [5.83 × 3.15 in.]), another manuscript that originally contained only the first book, consists of 34 folios (68 pages). Throughout this chapter, I use abbreviated versions of the shelf marks of the central group of manuscripts. Full references to manuscript shelf marks and information about their dates and places of origin are provided in the appendix to this chapter.

22 See Olga Spevak, "Les additions dans Isid. *Etym.* I: Témoins d'un travail rédactionnel," *Archivum Latinitatis Medii Aevi* 75 (2017): 59–88. Families α, β, and γ were first discerned in Lindsay, *Etymologiae*, vii–xii. The family ξ was identified by Porzig and its place in the transmission history of the *Etymologies* elaborated by Reydellet (see note 10 above). Reydellet's stemma from the 1960s, which represents the current state of examination of textual transmission of the *Etymologies*, has been reprinted in Codoñer Merino, Martin, and Andres, "Isidorus Hispalensis ep.," 279. A different stemmatic relationship between manuscripts was suggested by Veronika von Büren, whose work, however, should be used with caution; Veronika von Büren, "La place du manuscrit Ambr. L 99 sup. dans la transmission des *Étymologies* d'Isidore de Séville," in *Nuove ricerche su codici in scrittura latina dell'Ambrosiana,* ed. Mirella Ferrari and Marco Navoni (Milan: Vita e Pensiero, 2007), 25–44.

23 See Spevak, "Les additions dans Isid. *Etym.* I," 37–40.

the textual tradition of the first book in the ninth century by the traditional methods of textual criticism.[24]

For all these reasons, the early medieval manuscripts of the first book of the *Etymologies* are an excellent corpus for the Innovating Knowledge project, promising a rich harvest of material that could be used to analyze the patterns of dissemination of notable innovations and reconstruct the networks that participated in this dissemination. In this chapter, I have purposefully chosen innovations that reveal the transformation of the encyclopedia on the highest level of its textuality, that is, those affecting the material shape of the *Etymologies* and its properties as a book-object. These macro-level innovations are an expression of early medieval appropriation no less than transformations on lower levels of textuality, such as those of individual books, thematic sections, *capitula,* chapters, sentences, down to individual words and letters, of which a standard *apparatus criticus* typically captures only the last few levels. While textual variants and text-based innovations may have been privileged in our modern study of the transmission history of the *Etymologies* due to its reliance on the methods of textual criticism, any analysis of the transmission of this work needs to start from the macro-level and only then progress to the lower levels if we are seeking purpose-driven innovations rather than innovations that result from mechanical processes and ad hoc low-level decision-making. This is because on the macro-level almost all innovations correspond to a purpose-driven enterprise and because the analysis of the macro-level can provide a basis for discerning micro-level innovations that belong to a larger enterprise from those that reflect mechanical processes (e.g., scribal errors) or ad hoc low-level decision-making (e.g., hypercorrection) — a distinction that may be crucial when engaging in the reception history.

---

24 See especially Porzig, "Die Rezensionen der *Etymologiae*," 133–36, and Spevak, *Étymologies. Livre I,* lxxxviii.

Example 1: The separate transmission of the first book of the *Etymologies*

As mentioned earlier, the first book of the *Etymologies* was frequently copied separately. To this date, I am aware of thirty-three manuscripts transmitting the first book or its significant parts separately (see fig. 1 and the appendix, section a). Twenty-nine of these manuscripts were produced within roughly 100 years between the end of the eighth and the end of the ninth centuries, principally in two regions: France and Germany. This chronological and geographical distribution alone indicates we are looking at a pattern. Indeed, perhaps with the exception of one or two manuscripts, early medieval codices transmitted the first book of the *Etymologies* as a self-standing text form a homogenous cluster. Twenty-one of the manuscripts are grammatical compendia, in which Isidore appears next to Donatus, Servius, Priscian, and other grammatical authors. Five other manuscripts originally transmitted the first book of the *Etymologies* as the only text. In one manuscript, the first book of the *Etymologies* was attached to a florilegium of poetry, a subject of *grammatica*.[25] In another case, a sequence of grammatical texts, including material from the first book, were copied at the end of a manuscript of the entire *Etymologies,* presumably from a grammatical handbook, and in one manuscript, the first book of the *Etymologies* is transmitted together with book II (*De rhetorica et dialectica*) in a collection dedicated to the trivium. Smaller segments of the first book of the *Etymologies* appear in five additional early medieval grammatical compendia.[26] This list makes

---

25 See Bernhard Bischoff, "Libraries and Schools in the Carolingian Revival of Learning," in *Manuscripts and Libraries in the Age of Charlemagne,* ed. and trans. Michael Gorman, Cambridge Studies in Palaeography and Codicology (Cambridge: Cambridge University Press, 1994), 103.

26 It should be perhaps added that there are also five early medieval fragments of the first book that, due to their small dimensions, cannot be considered remnants of the entire encyclopedia. They presumably represent vestiges of manuscripts of the type mentioned here, including grammatical compendia.

Fig. 1. Geographical distribution of the manuscripts separately transmitting the first book of the *Etymologies* (dark: precise localization to a specific center; light: approximate localization by region). Made with Google My Maps.

it clear that the first book of the *Etymologies* circulated separately in the early Middle Ages because it was repurposed as a grammatical handbook.[27] Three of the manuscripts even call it

27 This has been observed already by Hagen (see footnote 18), yet to this date, relatively little has been written on the separate transmission of the first book of the *Etymologies* as an *ars grammatica*. Apart from Hagen, those who were aware of the existence of an Isidorean *ars grammatica* include Max Manitius, *Geschichte der lateinischen Literatur des Mittelalters* (Munich: Beck, 1911), vol. 1, 67; A.E. Anspach, "Das Fortleben Isidors im VII. bis IX. Jahrhundert," in *Miscellanea Isidoriana* (Rome: Universita Gregoriana, 1936), 347–48; Louis Holtz, *Donat et la tradition de l'enseignement grammatical: Étude sur l'Ars Donati et sa diffusion (IV.-IX. siècle) et éd. crit.* (Paris: CNRS, 1981), 256–60; Vivien A. Law, *The Insular Latin Grammarians,* Studies in Celtic History 3 (Woodbridge: Boydell Press, 1987), 24; Malcolm B. Parkes, *Pause and Effect: An Introduction to the History of Punctuation in the West* (Aldershot: Scolar, 1992), 22–23; Louis Holtz, "Le 'De grammatica' des Étymologies d'Isidore de Séville, structure générale et traitement des sources," in *IV Congreso Internacional de latim medieval hispânico,* ed. Pau-

an *Ars Isidori,* suggesting that Isidore was a grammarian comparable to Donatus.[28]

Furthermore, most of the twenty-nine pre-900 manuscripts transmitting the first book of the *Etymologies* separately are relatively small in size and weight compared to a standard manuscript of the entire *Etymologies*.[29] The five manuscripts transmitting the first book of the *Etymologies* as the only text, in particular, can be viewed as a portable version of Isidore suitable for classroom use. Leiden VLO 41 with pages measuring 200 × 150 mm (7.87 × 5.9 in.), Paris lat. 11278 with pages measuring 200 × 140 mm (7.87 × 5.51 in.), and Harley 2713 with pages measuring 180 × 120 mm (7.09 × 4.72 in.) perfectly exemplify how lightweight Isidore could get once separated from the rest of the bulky encyclopedia. The two latter manuscripts and several others from the cluster display another notable trait: they were copied by many hands, among them also unskilled hands of students prone to making mistakes.[30] Fourteen complete manuscripts and two fragments contain glosses, another trait of

---

lo Farmhouse Alberto and Aires Augusto Nascimento (Lisbon: Centro de Estudos Clássicos, 2006), 55–68; and Elizabeth Archibald, "Methods and Meaning of Basic Education in Carolingian Europe" (PhD diss., Yale University, 2010).

28 These manuscripts are Bern 207, Munich Clm 6411, and Leiden VLQ 86.

29 The early medieval manuscripts of the entire encyclopedia have an average taille (height + width) of 537 mm (21.14 in.) roughly corresponding to pages of 30 × 24 cm (11.81 × 9.45 in.). The average taille of the early medieval grammatical compendia transmitting the first book of the *Etymologies* separately is, by contrast, 416 mm (16.38 in.) roughly corresponding to pages of 25 × 17 cm (9.84 × 6.7 in.). See Evina Steinová, "The Materiality of Innovation: Formats and Dimensions of the *Etymologiae* of Isidore of Seville in the Early Middle Ages," in *The Art of Compilation: Manuscripts and Networks in the Early Medieval Latin West,* ed. Anna Dorofeeva and Michael J. Kelly (Earth: punctum books, forthcoming).

30 This seems also to be the case with Vatican Pal. lat. 1746.

schoolbooks.[31] Paris lat. 11278, moreover, features a unique colophon that identifies it as a students' book.[32]

Taken together, the traits characterizing the group of early medieval manuscripts indicate that the first book of the *Etymologies* was transmitted as a self-standing text because Carolingian masters decided to adopt it for teaching grammar in schools. A change in use led to a set of textual innovations — the first book of the *Etymologies* was separated from the rest of the encyclopedia; it shrunk in format and therefore became portable and began to attract a specific type of glosses. In the process of its appropriation, chapters were left out or reshuffled to fit it better into the curriculum or the first book could be combined with other grammatical texts, such as that of Donatus.

The appearance of the *Ars Isidori* follows the broader pattern of copying and transmission of grammatical texts in the Carolingian period observed by Vivien Law. She noticed that a general surge in the copying and compilation of grammatical texts took place in the last decades of the eighth century, peaking around 800 but rarely lasting after 850. This grammatical revival should be credited for the survival of many rare, obscure, and unpractical pre-Carolingian grammars as well as for the compilation of new grammatical texts.[33] It is difficult not to see how this newfound enthusiasm for grammatical studies attested by the copying of grammatical manuscripts responds to

---

31 While not all glosses should be connected with schools, it is one context of their origin. See Markus Schiegg, *Frühmittelalterliche Glossen: Ein Beitrag zur Funktionalität und Kontextualität mittelalterlicher Schriftlichkeit*, Germanistiche Bibliothek 52 (Heidelberg: Universitätsverlag Winter, 2015), 127–53.

32 This colophon reads: "Si sis [*sic!*] me legere, tracta me bene; si vero nescis me legere, trade me sapienti." See Beeson, *Isidor-Studien*, 85.

33 Vivien A. Law, "The Transmission of Early Medieval Elementary Grammars: A Case Study in Explanation," in *Formative Stages of Classical Traditions: Latin Texts from Antiquity to the Renaissance; Proceedings of a Conference Held at Erice, 16–22 October 1993, as the 6th Course of International School for the Study of Written Records,* ed. Oronzo Pecere and Michael D. Reeve, Biblioteca Del Centro per Il Collegamento Degli Studi Medievali e Umanistici in Umbria 15 (Spoleto: Centro Italiano di studi sull'alto medioevo, 1995), 239–61.

the aims of the Carolingian *renovatio*.[34] Importantly, the pattern of the manuscript copying also shows that while some of the rediscovered and newly composed grammars emerged from the critical period of experimentation and innovation as mainstays, many other texts failed to attain popularity and were dropped from teaching, and therefore ceased to be copied after the first half of the ninth century or remained a local peculiarity.

The oldest surviving manuscripts containing the self-standing first book of the *Etymologies* can be dated to the end of the eighth century, that is, to the time of school and education reforms. Among them is a fragmentarily preserved miscellany copied by an Irish scribe in Regensburg,[35] one of only two codices of the separately transmitted first book of the *Etymologies* copied by an insular hand.[36] This manuscript lacks the traits typical for the

---

34 The *grammatica* is explicitly mentioned as one of the subjects of the *scolae puerorum* to be established in every bishopric and monastery in the famous *capitulum* 70 (olim 72) of the *Admonitio Generalis*. See Hubert Mordek, Klaus Zechiel-Eckes, and Michael Glatthaar, eds., *Die Admonitio generalis Karls des Großen,* Monumenta Germaniae Historica, Fontes iuris germanici antiqui in usum scholarum separatim editi 16 (Wiesbaden: Harrassowitz, 2013), 222–24. On the place of the *grammatica* in Carolingian reform thought and practice, see also Bernhard Bischoff, "Libraries and Schools in the Carolingian Revival of Learning," *Manuscripts and Libraries in the Age of Charlemagne,* ed. and trans. Michael Gorman (Cambridge: Cambridge University Press, 1994), 98–103, and John J. Contreni, "The Pursuit of Knowledge in Carolingian Europe," in *The Gentle Voices of Teachers: Aspects of Learning in the Carolingian Age,* ed. Richard Sullivan (Columbus: Ohio State University Press, 1995), 118–22.

35 This manuscript now survives at four different institutions as Munich Clm 29410/2 + Clm 14938, Harvard Typ. 613, New York Plimpton 127, and Regensburg Fragm. 1. The miscellany probably once contained the complete first book of the *Etymologies* and parts or the whole book XI as well as an Irish computistic treatise, exegetical texts, and a sermon of Augustine. With its small pages, which can be reconstructed to have measured roughly 20 × 15 cm (7.88 × 5.9 in.), it ranks among the smallest codices transmitting the first book of the *Etymologies* separately.

36 The other manuscript autonomously transmitting the first book of the *Etymologies* copied by an insular hand is Bern 207, which had been dated to the turn of the eighth century on the basis of a calendar that the manuscript contains, see CLA V 568 and CLA VII **568. However, Bernhard Bischoff seems not to have found this dating satisfactory, as he proposed a

Carolingian codices preserving the first book as a self-standing text; in particular, it is not a grammatical handbook. It may be considered a predecessor of the Carolingian group. The story of the *Ars Isidori* may have begun, it seems, in the "British Isles," even though no remnant of a separately transmitted first book of the *Etymologies* survives from the insular world.[37] It was, nevertheless, only in the Carolingian environment that the trend expanded dramatically.

Twenty of the twenty-nine early medieval manuscripts containing the first book can be dated to the last decades of the eighth or the first half of the ninth centuries, the period that Law connected with an intensification of interest in new grammatical texts. Three codices cannot be dated more precisely than to the ninth century and may have been copied in its first half. Only six manuscripts were certainly copied in the second half of the ninth century, suggesting perhaps a decline in interest. Additionally, in the first half of the ninth century, the *Ars Isidori* can be found both in French and German centers, while only one German manuscript comes from the second half of the ninth century. France emerges as the stronghold of the repurposing of the first book of the *Etymologies* as a grammar, with one French center standing out in particular: Fleury. Fleury,

---

date in the ninth century. See Bernhard Bischoff, *Katalog der festländischen Handschriften des neunten Jahrhunderts (mit Ausnahme der wisigotischen).* I: *Aachen-Lambach,* ed. Birgit Ebersperger, Veröffentlichungen der Kommission für die Herausgabe der mittelalterlichen Bibliothekskataloge Deutschlands und der Schweiz (Wiesbaden: Harrassowitz, 1998), n. 551a. The hand that copied Bern 207 is believed to have belonged to a Breton scribe who also copied a codex of the complete *Etymologies* (now surviving as a fragment, Wolfenbüttel Herzog August Bibliothek, Helmst. 455, fol. 1), and whose hand proves difficult to date due to its peculiarity. See Bernhard Bischoff, *Latin Palaeography: Antiquity and the Middle Ages,* trans. Dáibhí O'Cróinín and David Ganz (Cambridge: Cambridge University Press, 1990), 90.

37 Or perhaps, it began in several different cultural zones independently, as is suggested by other early manuscripts transmitting material from the first book of the *Etymologies* in a grammatical context that may reflect the appropriation of this text for teaching in the Beneventan and the Visigothic areas.

which became particularly important as a center of learning in the tenth century, can be connected with five of the twenty-nine pre-900 manuscripts from the group, including some of the oldest and some of the youngest codices.[38]

Example 2: Glosses to the first book of the *Etymologies*

Another textual innovation particular to the "Carolingian *Etymologies*" is annotations. A survey of the manuscripts transmitting glosses to the *Etymologies* produced by the Innovating Knowledge project has revealed so far thirty-four manuscripts that contain substantial annotations to this text, among them twenty-seven codices that were equipped with at least twenty annotations to the first book of Isidore's encyclopedia.[39] Based on the paleographical and philological traits, the oldest surviving annotations to the first book comes from the eighth century (even though they sometimes appear in pre-Carolingian manuscripts), and the most recent date perhaps to the twelfth century.[40] Most of the annotated manuscripts were glossed by

---

38 These five manuscripts are Bern 207, which was produced at Fleury in the ninth century; Orléans 296, which was kept at Fleury in the early Middle Ages and may have been annotated there; Leiden VLQ 86, which was copied from Bern 207 around the mid-ninth century; Leiden VLO 41, copied in northern France at the end of the ninth century and annotated at Fleury around the same time or at the beginning of the tenth century; and Vatican Reg. lat. 1587, which was produced in the second quarter of the ninth century in western France and owned by Fleury in the tenth century. Bern 207 and Leiden VLQ 86 are treated in detail in Edward K. Rand, "A Vade Mecum of Liberal Culture in a Manuscript of Fleury," *Philological Quarterly* 1 (1922): 258–77.

39 See Evina Steinová, "Annotation of the *Etymologiae* of Isidore of Seville in Its Early Medieval Context," *Archivum Latinitatis Medii Aevi* 78 (2020): 5–81. These annotations have been edited in the context of the Innovating Knowledge project. See Evina Steinová and Peter Boot, *The Glosses to the First Book of the "Etymologiae" of Isidore of Seville: A Digital Scholarly Edition,* hosted by Huygens ING, KNAW, 2021, https://db.innovatingknowledge.nl/edition/#left-intro.

40 The oldest contemporary or near-contemporary annotations seem to be those in Junius 25, Paris lat. 11278, and Pal. lat. 1746. The oldest manuscript containing glosses to book I is Vat. lat. 5763, a copy of the *Etymologies* from

contemporary hands in the ninth century or by slightly more recent hands in the tenth century. The most densely annotated specimens come from the end of the ninth century, identifying the glossing of the first book of the *Etymologies* as a Carolingian trend.[41] Indeed, the survey revealed that as many as one-third of the surviving ninth-century manuscripts containing this text bear at least one annotation. Let me offer a glimpse at the phenomenon of the glossing of Isidore's encyclopedia by exploring the glosses to the *capitulum* on special signs, *De notis* (*Etym.*, I.21–26).[42]

Glosses to *De notis* appear in twelve manuscripts (see fig. 2 and the appendix, section b). Some contain as few as nine annotations to this *capitulum,* while others have seventy or more. Five are manuscripts separately transmitting the first book of the *Etymologies,* in two cases, the glosses were added to an excerpt of *De notis* in miscellanies, and five manuscripts are codices of the entire *Etymologies.* These glosses range in date from the first half of the ninth century to the beginning of the eleventh century. Manuscripts carrying them come from France, Germany, Italy, and England. Unlike in the case of the separate transmission of the first book of the *Etymologies,* there does not seem to be a single region from which the annotated manuscripts stem.

Nevertheless, one can recognize three discernible geographical groups of manuscripts based on their shared glosses. The largest of these is the Frankish group (blue), which includes five manuscripts containing similar classroom glosses serving to enhance the comprehension of the *capitulum De notis* from France

---

Bobbio dated to mid-eighth century, see CLA I 39. The glosses in this manuscript were added by a ninth-century Carolingian hand.

41 Steinová, "Annotation of the *Etymologiae* of Isidore of Seville," 19–29.

42 This preliminary analysis is based on Evina Steinová, "*Notam Superponere Studui*: The Use of Technical Signs in the Early Middle Ages" (PhD diss., Utrecht University, 2016), 160–71. A fuller analysis based on all *capitula* of book I can be found in Steinová, "Annotation of the *Etymologiae* of Isidore of Seville," 5–81, and Evina Steinová, "Parallel Glosses, Shared Glosses, and Gloss Clustering: Can Network-Based Approach Help Us to Understand Organic Corpora of Glosses?," *Journal of Historical Network Research* 7 (forthcoming, 2023).

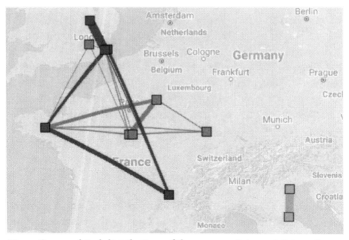

Fig. 2. Geographical distribution of the manuscripts containing glosses to *De notis* (blue: Frankish group; red: Franco-English group; yellow: Italian group). The thickness of the edges connecting manuscripts represents the amount of shared glosses. Made with Google My Maps.

and Germany: one from the area of Murbach, one from Reims, one from Brittany, and two from northern France, which were probably annotated in Fleury. Three of the manuscripts, the two codices associated with Fleury and the only annotated German codex, are manuscripts separately transmitting the first book of the *Etymologies,* as can be expected from annotations stemming from classroom instruction.

The manuscript copied and annotated in Brittany, Harley 3941, serves as an intermediary between the Frankish group and the Franco-English group (red).[43] Besides Harley 3941, the latter includes three other manuscripts — Paris lat. 11278 from southern France or northern Italy; Cotton Caligula A.xv from France, which was, however, annotated in tenth-century England, probably in Canterbury; and Paris lat. 7585, a ninth-century Frankish

---

43 This manuscript and its glosses are discussed in Léon Fleuriot, "Gloses inédites en vieux-Breton," *Études Celtiques* 16 (1979): 197–210.

manuscript that was repaired and annotated in tenth-century Canterbury.[44] To these manuscripts should be added the early eleventh-century *Enchiridion* of Byrhtferth of Ramsey, not a manuscript but a text, in which the same set of glosses is found appended to an excerpt from the *Etymologies*.[45] The chronology of witnesses indicates that the glosses were known in southern France or northern Italy in the first half of the ninth century, in Brittany in the second half of the same century, and across the Channel from the tenth century onward. They, too, may have originated in a teaching context, in particular given that the oldest manuscript preserving them is Paris lat. 11278, discussed earlier as an exemplary students' book. That they were transmitted in a teaching context is evidenced by Byrhtferth's *Enchiridion*. This handbook of *computus* reflects the lessons Byrhtferth received from his master, Abbo of Fleury, who was invited to Ramsey as a teacher in 985–987.[46] Fleury cultivated ties not only with Ramsey but also with Canterbury and Brittany, two other locales where the set of annotations surfaces.[47] Thus, even if none of the several surviving Fleury books contains the Franco-English set of glosses, it may be presumed that the tradition was known there and that Fleury served as an essential hub of their dissemination in the tenth century. It is, nevertheless, unlikely that the tradition originated at Fleury, since the oldest witness of the Franco-English set of glosses, Paris lat. 11278, seems older than the Fleury manuscript containing these glosses. Rather, Fleury, may have served as an accumulator of material from elsewhere due to the influence of its school and *scriptorium* and its connectivity.

---

44 See T.A.M. Bishop, *English Caroline Minuscule,* Oxford Palaeographical Handbooks (Oxford: Clarendon Press, 1971), n. 6.

45 It is edited and translated in Michael Lapidge and Peter Stuart Baker, *Byrhtferth's Enchiridion* (Oxford: Oxford University Press, 1995). The excerpt from the *Etymologies* appears on 176–79.

46 Marco Mostert, "Relations between Fleury and England," in *England and the Continent in the Tenth Century: Studies in Honor of Wilhelm Levison (1876–1947),* ed. David Rollason, Conrad Leyser, and Hannah Williams, Studies in the Early Middle Ages 37 (Turnhout: Brepols, 2010), 190–91.

47 Ibid., 188–90 and 198–99.

A third manuscript group containing a distinct set of glosses to *De notis* consists of two manuscripts of the *Etymologies* from northern Italy (yellow). Cesena S.XXI.5 was copied and annotated in the ninth century.[48] Venice II 46 is an eleventh-century copy of the ninth-century manuscript containing the same set of eleven summarizing annotations to *Etym.*, I.21. The glosses are entirely independent on the two Frankish sets and do not seem to reflect classroom instruction.

The annotations to *De notis* reinforce the impression that we gather from the *Ars Isidori,* namely that the first book of the *Etymologies* was introduced into the Carolingian classroom. However, they also reveal two additional details. First, special signs were not a traditional subject of classroom grammars. They rather represent an unusual addition to the discipline of *grammatica* in Isidore's encyclopedia.[49] Unsurprisingly, some of the earliest grammatical handbooks containing the first book of the *Etymologies* remove the *capitulum De notis,* indicating that it may have been regarded as an obstacle to the appropriation for classroom use. However, in the course of the ninth century, more and more manuscripts of the separately transmitted first book of the *Etymologies* include the *capitulum*. Gradually, this *capitulum* began to attract glosses, indicating that it began to be studied in a classroom setting. It seems that the appropriation of the *Etymologies* was a two-way process, as the Carolingian users not only affected the shape of Isidore's encyclopedia, but the encyclopedia affected their ideas about certain subjects, such as grammar.

Furthermore, while the classroom character of the glosses suggests that they are a result of the appropriation of the first book of the *Etymologies* for teaching grammar, one can note that the glosses appear in the manuscripts with a delay with re-

48 This manuscript, but not the ninth-century glosses, is discussed in Anna Bellettini, "Il codice del sec. IX di Cesena, Malatestiano S. XXI.5: Le *Etymologiae* di Isidoro, testi minori e glosse di età ottoniana," *Italia medioevale e umanistica 45* (2004): 49–114.

49 Jacques Fontaine, *Isidore de Séville et la culture classique dans l'Espagne wisigothique,* 2nd edn. (Paris: Études augustiniennes, 1983), 54.

gard to the inclusion of the first book of the *Etymologies* into grammatical handbooks. The peak of the production of the latter, as noted above, falls into the first half, or perhaps even the first quarter of the ninth century, while most manuscripts seem to have been glossed only in the second half of the ninth century and the densest layers of glosses come from the end of the ninth century. Moreover, while no manuscripts of the separately transmitted first book of the *Etymologies* survive from the tenth century and only one from the eleventh, the classroom-generated glosses continued to live on, transmitted in codices of the complete *Etymologies,* until the twelfth century.[50] Finally, in England in particular, one can observe that glosses begin to trickle in only after the *Ars Isidori* fell out of use on the Continent. While, thus, Carolingian classroom instruction was probably the original stimulus for the generation of glosses, they attained a life of their own in the following centuries.

Example 3: The St. Gallen redaction of the *Etymologies*

A third example of the "Carolingian *Etymologies*" I wish to discuss is a redaction of the *Etymologies* that was undertaken in the ninth-century St. Gall monastery, and I will, therefore, call it the St. Gallen redaction of the *Etymologies*.[51] What we know about this redaction, we owe chiefly to the fact that its prototype survives. This prototype, manuscript Zofingen Pa 32, inserts *De natura rerum,* Isidore's other major scientific work, between books III and IV of the *Etymologies* as if it was an integral part of the encyclopedia.[52] It seems that one of the main objectives of

---

50 The most recent layer of glosses I have been able to uncover so far appears in Oxford, Queen's College, MS 320, which was copied in tenth-century England, but glossed perhaps at the end of the eleventh or the beginning of the twelfth century. These glosses are in many cases identical to those found in earlier manuscripts from England and the Continent.

51 This section is based on an analysis carried out in Steinová, "Two Carolingian Redactions of the *Etymologiae* from St. Gallen."

52 This Zofingen manuscript is described in Charlotte Bretscher-Gisiger and Rudolf Gamper, *Katalog der mittelalterlichen Handschriften des Klosters Wettingen: Katalog der mittelalterlichen Handschriften in Aarau, Laufen-*

the compilers of this redaction was to expand the scope of the *Etymologies,* which do not treat natural phenomena in similar detail as *De natura rerum.*

Another discerning feature of the St. Gallen redaction, which is more relevant for this chapter, is the eccentric order of material in the first book. The unusual order results from an interaction between two scribes of the Zofingen manuscript. The first copied material from the first book up to chapter 33 from an exemplar that seemed to lack certain chapters and transmitted others in a substantially abbreviated form. A second scribe then intervened, using a complete copy of the first book of the *Etymologies,* adding those chapters that were missing at the end of the section copied by the first hand and rearranging the order of folios so as to impose a new order on the chapters of the first book.[53] Given its abbreviated character and peculiar order of material, the first exemplar used for the copying of book I in the Zofingen codex was, in all likelihood, an *Ars Isidori.* It is puzzling that the compilers of the St. Gallen redaction chose an *Ars Isidori* as a basis for the first book of the *Etymologies,* especially since the interventions of the second scribe clearly show that St. Gallen already possessed a good copy of the same text. It could not have been due to the poverty of resources, for St. Gallen possessed at least three complete copies of the *Etymologies,* as is attested by its oldest catalogue.[54] In fact, St. Gallen stands out as

---

burg, Lenzburg, Rheinfelden und Zofingen (Dietikon-Zürich: Urs Graf, 2009), 230–32. Bernhard Bischoff dated the same manuscript to the beginning of the ninth century; see Bischoff, *Katalog* III 7546. However, a production date in the second half of the century seems more plausible. See Steinová, "Two Carolingian Redactions of the *Etymologiae* from St. Gallen," 320.

53 The interaction of the two scribes and the exact order and form of chapters of the first book in the Zofingen codex are analyzed in detail in Steinová, "Two Carolingian Redactions of the *Etymologiae* from St. Gallen."

54 See Paul Lehmann, *Mittelalterliche Bibliothekskataloge Deutschlands und der Schweiz* (Munich: Beck, 1969), vol. 1, 75–81. "Aethimologiarum librum XX et ratio horologii et glosa grecorum verborum in volumine I […] Item de libris Ysidori aethimologiarum, volumina II. corrupta […] Libri ethimologiarum Isidori in sceda I tamen boni." These manuscripts have been variously identified with St. Gallen 237 (after 800), St. Gallen 233 (books

possessing more copies of Isidore's encyclopedia than any other Carolingian center.[55]

The masterminds behind the St. Gallen redaction must have had specific reasons to prefer this type of the first book, perhaps its antiquity, association with notable personage, or perceived suitability for the project. Similarly, the exemplar for the *De natura rerum* integrated into the St. Gallen redaction was Paris, Bibliothèque nationale de France, lat. 10616, a manuscript made at the end of the eighth century for bishop Egino of Verona and later present at Reichenau, even though St. Gallen had possessed an in-house copy of *De natura rerum* since the eight century: St. Gallen, Stiftsbibliothek, MS 238.[56] Since the exemplar of the first book of the *Etymologies* that was used by the first scribe does not resemble any of the text-versions of the *Etymologies* preserved at St. Gallen, it is not unreasonable to assume that it was procured from outside of the monastery, just as the manuscript of *De natura rerum,* showing us the other face of the Carolingian intellectual networks — the one involved in the acquisition of knowledge rather than in its dissemination.

The Zofingen codex is the only ninth-century witness of the St. Gallen redaction of the *Etymologies,* identifying it securely as a Carolingian product, even if most copies of this redaction come from after the ninth century. One line of transmission branched from St. Gallen south to Einsiedeln (Einsiedeln 167, 10th century) and Engelberg (Einsiedeln 360, 12th century). Another branch led to Wissembourg (Wolfenbüttel Weiss. 2, 11th century) and further north into Germany (four 12th-century

---

VI–VIII, XII–XV, 9th century, in.), St. Gallen 235 (books XII–XX, c. 800), and Zofingen Pa 32.

55 Apart from the manuscripts mentioned in the previous footnotes, St. Gallen also produced St. Gallen 231–32 (two-volume *Etymologies,* 880–90) and St. Gallen 236 (books XI–XX, mid-9th century) and may have owned additional manuscripts not produced there, containing the text of families β and γ. See Bischoff, "Die europäische Verbreitung der Werke Isidors von Sevilla," 340.

56 Jacques Fontaine, "La diffusion de l'oeuvre d'Isidore de Séville dans les scriptoria helvétiques du haut Moyen Âge," *Schweizerische Zeitschrift für Geschichte* 12 (1962): 305–22, at 315–16.

Fig. 3. Geographical distribution of the manuscripts of the St. Gallen redaction (star: St. Gallen; pointer: a known place of production; square: the estimated area of origin). Made with Google My Maps.

manuscripts and one 15th-century manuscript). Altogether, I have identified nine witnesses of the Carolingian redaction dating between the ninth and the fifteenth centuries (see fig. 3 and the appendix, section c).[57]

The geographical distribution of its witnesses shows that the redaction spread from St. Gallen in the German area along the corridors of mutual relationships between monastic communities. For example, the Einsiedeln manuscript is a direct copy of Zofingen Pa 32 made shortly after the founding of Einsiedeln Abbey in 934, presumably in the process of stocking the library of the new foundation from the nearby St. Gallen.[58] The

---

57 Another potential candidate is Erlangen, Universitätsbibliothek Erlangen-Nürnberg, MS 186 (12th century, ²⁄₂, Heilsbronn). I could not examine this manuscript combining the *Etymologies* and *De natura rerum* and therefore cannot say whether it is a witness of the St. Gallen redaction.

58 For the relationship of Einsiedeln 167 to Zofingen Pa 32, see Fontaine, "La diffusion de l'oeuvre," 319, and Anton von Euw, "Die Einsiedler Buchmalerei zur Zeit des Abtes Gregor (964–996)," in *Festschrift zum tausendsten Tod-*

Engelberg Abbey, founded in 1120, received its copy in a context similar to that of Einsiedeln and from this abbey.[59] Wissembourg and St. Gallen were tied closely in the ninth century when Grimald of St. Gallen was the abbot of both communities.[60] It is possible that the exemplar of the eleventh-century manuscript arrived here around this time. However, the tempo of the diffusion of the St. Gallen redaction of the *Etymologies* increased dramatically in the twelfth century, perhaps thanks to Cistercian scriptoria. It is unclear what may have attracted the Cistercians to this Carolingian redaction. If the oldest twelfth-century copy of the St. Gallen redaction, which can be dated to 1136, is a Cistercian manuscript, the re-discovery must have happened at a rather early date, as the Cistercians settled in Germany only from 1123.[61] Once the St. Gallen redaction made it into Cistercian hands, its fortunes seem to have been largely secured. The ninth-century redaction, perhaps never intended to be widely distributed, can be found copied in Germany as late as in the fifteenth century.[62] The Augsburg printer Günther Zainer used

---

estag des seligen Abtes Gregor, ed. Odo Lang, Studien und Mitteilungen zur Geschichte des Benediktinerordens und seiner Zweige 107 (Sankt Ottilien: Editions Sankt Ottilien, 1996), 199–202. Von Euw dates Einsiedeln 167 to the time of abbot Gregor (964–996).

59 Einsiedeln 360 was copied during the abbacy of Frowin of Engelberg (1143–1178). See Martin Steinmann, "Abt Frowin von Engelberg (1143–1178) und seine Handschriften," *Der Geschichtsfreund* 146 (1993): 7–36. Engelberg was founded by Benedictines from Muri, a daughter house of Einsiedeln.

60 See Dieter Geuenich, "Beobachtungen zu Grimald von St. Gallen, Erzkapellan und Oberkanzler Ludwigs des Deutschen," in *Litterae medii aevi. Festschrift für Johanne Autenrieth zu ihrem 65. Geburtstag*, ed. Michael Borgolte and Herrad Spilling (Sigmaringen: Thorbecke, 1988), 55–68.

61 This twelfth-century manuscript, Harley 2660, was copied in west Rhineland. This means that it may come from one of the following Cistercian abbeys: Kamp (founded in 1123), Himmerod (founded in 1134/35), or Eberbach (founded in 1136).

62 This fifteenth-century manuscript, Harley 3035, was produced presumably by the canons regular that settled in Eberhardklausen (today Klausen) in the Eifel region only some 22 km (13.67 miles) from the Cistercian abbey of Himmerod.

a manuscript of the St. Gallen redaction as a basis for his *editio princips* of the *De natura rerum* published in 1472.[63]

Conclusion

Let us now compare and contrast the three innovations described above using the four criteria articulated above: the impact, the duration, the emergence, and the direction of spreading. The separate transmission of the first book of the *Etymologies* was the most impactful innovation, leaving behind at least thirty-three witnesses, twenty-nine of them from before the year 900. At the same time, however, it was also the most short-lived of the three, having a main time span of only about one hundred years, as it seems that it may have almost entirely ceased to propagate after the year 900. By contrast, the St. Gallen redaction has only nine known witnesses, but it was copied until the end of the Middle Ages, with most copies produced several centuries after its Carolingian parent was copied. The glosses to *De notis* fall in between these two innovations, with twelve witnesses spanning three centuries. The glossing of *De notis* (and annotation of the first book of the *Etymologies* more broadly) was also the innovation with the most substantial geographical reach, given its spreading into England. The other two innovations discussed here, on the other hand, seem to have been either regional (the St. Gallen redaction) or nearly so (the separately transmitted first book of the *Etymologies*).

The St. Gallen redaction is the only of the three examples that spread exclusively vertically and from a single source: the St. Gallen prototype preserved as Zofingen Pa 32. The separate transmission of the first book of the *Etymologies* represents an opposite extreme of emergence, as it seems that, perhaps with the exception of one or two manuscripts, all pre-900 codices

---

63 Isidorus Hispalensis, *De responsione mundi (De natura rerum)*, Augsburg: Günther Zainer, 7.XII.1472 (H 9302, Klebs 537.1). See Calvin B. Kendall and Faith Wallis, trans., *Isidore of Seville, "On the Nature of Things,"* Translated Texts for Historians 66 (Liverpool: Liverpool University Press, 2016), 100.

containing the separately transmitted first book of the *Etymologies* are independent realizations of the same phenomenon: they represent not only distinct text-versions of the *Etymologies* but also select and order the material from this book differently and combine it with different texts so that individual manuscripts differ in obvious ways one from another.[64] The individual instances of the separately transmitted first book of the *Etymologies* in grammatical handbooks were derived from locally available full copies of the *Etymologies* by rewriting rather than by being copied from one compendium to another. The case of the separate transmission of the first book of the *Etymologies* should make us wary of relying too much on models that presuppose a singular innovator or a central point of dissemination. As is clear from this example, notable innovations can result from uncoordinated emergence at multiple locations by many independent agents triggered by large-scale societal or cultural trends, such as the general revival of grammatical studies.

Regarding the patterns of emergence and dissemination, the annotations to *De notis* fall again in the middle. They probably came into being in response to practical teaching needs at several locations, thus representing a similar pattern of emergence as the separate transmission of the first book of the *Etymologies*. However, rather than each annotated manuscript containing a unique set of annotations, the surviving glosses to *De notis* form three "traditions," two that are evidenced in France and one in northern Italy, suggesting a degree of transmission. Annotations, we may assume, spread mostly horizontally since they are found in manuscripts belonging to distinct textual families and representing different transmission formats (e.g., both in manuscripts transmitting the first book of the *Etymologies* separately and those of the entire *Etymologies*). Teaching, that is, a transmission involving masters and students, as well as masters' and and students' books, surely represented an important channel of the dissemination of annotations in the early stages of their for-

---

64 The two exceptions are Leiden VLQ 86, which is a copy of Bern 207, and the destroyed Chartres 92, which was perhaps a copy of Erfurt Ampl. 2° 10.

mation. Yet, not all annotations found in the manuscripts of the *Etymologies,* especially in those of the entire encyclopedia, can be explained as a vestige of teaching. Other processes, such as copying from an exemplar to a copy, implying a vertical transmission, must have also been at play.

While each textual innovation discussed in this chapter reflects a different pattern of dissemination, it needs to be pointed out in conclusion that they are interconnected. The link between the separate transmission of the first book of the *Etymologies* and the annotations is rather clear: both reflect the appropriation of this text for teaching and, more importantly, it seems that the separation of the first book from the rest of the *Etymologies* proved the precondition for the emergence of glosses in France (but not in Italy). That the makers of the St. Gallen redaction opted for a separately transmitted first book of the *Etymologies* as a basis for the first book of the *Etymologies* in their project is a choice that cannot be easily explained, particularly as their enterprise does not seem to be intended for a classroom. It nevertheless shows a link between the two processes — the repurposing of Isidore's *Etymologies* for teaching grammar at the end of the eighth century and the production of a new redaction of his work in the second half of the following century. It appears that separating the first book from the rest of Isidore's encyclopedia in the services of teaching grammar was a momentous decision for the Carolingian world, not because the Carolingians were necessarily the first to use the first book of the *Etymologies* for teaching grammar (the primacy may belong to the Irish or Anglosaxon masters), but because the impact of this separation over roughly one hundred years stimulated many notable developments, of which glosses and redactions of the *Etymologies* are far from the most important.[65]

---

65 Isidore had a profound influence on Carolingian conceptualizations of grammar and on major Carolingian authors of grammatical texts, such as Alcuin. The Isidorian influence on the latter are discussed in Louis Holtz, "Le dialogue de Franco et de Saxo," *Annales de Bretagne et des Pays de l'Ouest. Anjou. Maine. Poitou-Charente. Touraine* 111, no. 13 (2004): 135–45.

Finally, let me remark that the three innovations discussed above reveal the centrality of two Carolingian centers for the "Carolingian *Etymologies*." Fleury played a role in promoting the *Ars Isidori* and the accumulation and dissemination of glosses. At the same time, St. Gallen was a locus of the production of a notable Carolingian redaction of Isidore's encyclopedia (in fact, not just one, but two of them).[66] The nature of the engagement with the *Etymologies* at these two Carolingian hubs was quite different: in Fleury, innovations seem to have been stimulated by teaching needs and disseminated via school; in St. Gallen, from which we have little evidence of the use of the *Etymologies* for teaching and no annotations to the first book,[67] a large medieval collection of manuscripts containing the *Etymologies* was accumulated in the early Middle Ages, and the agenda was to improve the text of the *Etymologies* and produce a better scholarly version of the essential encyclopedia. It is beyond doubt that St. Gallen acted as a point of origin of the St. Gallen redaction and the central hub for its dissemination. In contrast, many of the glosses transmitted to Britanny and England did not originate in Fleury. Instead, it acted as an accumulator and an amplifier for material that originated elsewhere, perhaps at many different locations, condensing them into rich layers of glosses, which appear for the first time in a Fleury manuscript of the separately transmitted first book of the *Etymologies* in the first half of the ninth century. Herein is another presupposition that should be dispelled, namely that the success of specific innovations should be attributed to those with whom they originated rather than with those who were their later recipients, as

---

The effect of the appropriation of the *Etymologies* on the elementary grammatical teaching is documented in Archibald, "Methods and Meaning."

66 See Steinová, "Two Carolingian Redactions of the *Etymologiae* from St. Gallen," 322–41.

67 As can be gleaned from section a of the appendix, below, St. Gallen owned two grammatical compendia featuring the separately transmitted first book of the *Etymologies* in the ninth century. It is telling that, while otherwise heavily annotated, these two manuscripts feature no glosses in the first book of the *Etymologies*.

the latter provided a given innovation with the necessary momentum or twist. In the end, the separate transmission of the first book of the *Etymologies* may represent the same scenario, as there is reason to believe that it originated in the "British Isles," as many innovations attributed to the Carolingians had, but had to collide headlong with the Carolingian *renovatio* to have the significant impact on early medieval intellectual life that it did. Similarly, the success of the St. Gallen redaction in Germany may be due to twelfth-century Cistercian houses rather than the ninth-century Benedictine institutions). The difference between the number of surviving manuscripts from the "British Isles" transmitting the first book of the *Etymologies* as a stand-alone text (zero) and the number of similar codices surviving from the Carolingian area (twenty-nine) demonstrates the power of Carolingian intellectual networks on the tradition of Isidore's *Etymologies*.

Appendix[68]

a. Manuscripts of the separately transmitted first book of the Etymologies

1. Amiens. Bibliothèque municipale, MS 426 (fols. 1–29) (8th/9th century, Corbie).https://bvmm.irht.cnrs.fr/iiif/18868/canvas/canvas-1632389/view. .

2. Berlin. Staatsbibliothek Preussischer Kulturbesitz, MS Diez. B. Sant. 66 (8th century, northern Italy and northern France). http://resolver.staatsbibliothek-berlin.de/SBB000075E500000000.

3. Munich. Bayerische Staatsbibliothek, Clm 29410/2 + Clm 14938. http://nbn-resolving.de/urn/resolver.pl?urn=urn:nbn:de:bvb:12-bsb00071374-7 + Harvard. Houghton Library, Typ. 613 (olim Phillipps 20688). http://id.lib.harvard.edu/aleph/009889598/catalog + New York. Columbia University Library, Plimpton 127. http://ds.lib.berkeley.edu/PlimptonMS127_20 + Regensburg. Staatliche Bibliothek, Fragm. 1 (8th/9th century, Irish scribe on the Continent, Regensburg?, prov.: Regensburg). https://nbn-resolving.org/urn:nbn:de:bvb:155-sbr000002-1.

4. Vatican City. Biblioteca Apostolica Vaticana, Pal. lat. 1746 (ca. 800, Lorsch). http://bibliotheca-laureshamensis-digital.de/bav/bav_pal_lat_1746.

5. St. Gallen. Stiftsbibliothek, MS 876 (c. 800, St. Gallen). http://www.e-codices.unifr.ch/en/list/one/csg/0876.

6. Paris. Bibliothèque nationale de France, lat. 13025 (fols. 1–74) (9th century, in., Corbie). http://gallica.bnf.fr/ark:/12148/btv1b8423831v.

7. Erfurt. Universitätsbibliothek, Dep. Erf. CA, 2° 10 (9th century, in., western Germany/Austrasia). https://dhb.thulb.uni-jena.de/receive/ufb_cbu_00016434.

---

68 Manuscripts in this appendix are organized chronologically rather than alphabetically.

8. Oxford. Bodleian Library, Junius 25 (fols. 134–51) (9th century, southwestern Germany?, prov. Murbach). https://digital.bodleian.ox.ac.uk/inquire/p/451e88c8-39b6-4cbc-8483-c64b290ea00e.

9. Bern. Burgerbibliothek, Cod. 207 (9th century, Fleury).[69] http://www.e-codices.unifr.ch/en/searchresult/list/one/bbb/0207.

10. Munich. Bayerische Staatsbibliothek, Clm 6411 (9th century, ¼, Passau?).[70] http://daten.digitale-sammlungen.de/bsb00012886/image_1.

11. Orléans. Bibliothèque municipale, MS 296 (pp. 1–32). https://mediatheques.orleans-metropole.fr/ark:/77916/FRCGMBPF-452346101-01A/D18012265.locale=fr, + Paris. BnF, lat. 7520 (fols. 25–45) (9th century, ¼, area of Paris?, prov.: Fleury). https://gallica.bnf.fr/ark:/12148/btv1b84900632.

12. Karlsruhe. Landesbibliothek, Aug. Perg. 112 (9th century, ¼, Reichenau). https://digital.blb-karlsruhe.de/id/20141.

13. Paris. Bibliothèque nationale de France, lat. 11278 (9th century, ½, southeastern France or northern Italy). https://gallica.bnf.fr/ark:/12148/btv1b100358546.

14. Paris. Bibliothèque nationale de France, lat. 7559 (9th century, ½, area of Paris?). http://gallica.bnf.fr/ark:/12148/btv1b90782450.

15. Paris. Bibliothèque nationale de France, lat. 7490 (9th century, ½ and 2/4, probably Paris). https://gallica.bnf.fr/ark:/12148/btv1b9066476b.

16. Trier. Bibliothek des Bischöflichen Priesterseminars, MS 100 (fols. 1–16) (9th century, 2/4, France). http://dfg-viewer.de/show/?tx_dlf%5Bid%5D=http%3A%2F%2Fzimks68.

---

69 Earlier dating (ca. 797) was provided by the *Codices latini antiquiores*. See CLA V 568 and CLA VII **568.

70 However, Katharina Bierbrauer dated this manuscript to 9th century, ⅔. See Katharina Bierbrauer, *Die vorkarolingischen und karolingischen Handschriften der Bayerischen Staatsbibliothek,* Katalog der illuminierten Handschriften der Bayerischen Staatsbibliothek in München 1 (Munich: Reichert, 1990), n. 194.

uni-trier.de%2Fstmatthias%2FS0100%2FS0100-digitalisat.
xml&tx_dlf%5Bpage%5D=3&tx_dlf%5Bdouble%5D=0&cH
ash=110e18e0a3598a9464def45f1fcfd97d#.

17. Vatican City. Biblioteca Apostolica Vaticana, Reg. lat. 1587
    (fols. 1–50) (9th century, ²⁄₄, western France, prov.: Fleury).
    https://digi.vatlib.it/view/MSS_Reg.lat.1587.

18. Vatican City. Biblioteca Apostolica Vaticana, Reg. lat. 1553
    (9th century, ²⁄₄, upper Loire area). https://digi.vatlib.it/
    view/MSS_Reg.lat.1553.

19. Leiden. Universiteitsbibliotheek, Voss. lat. Q 86 (mid-9th
    century, France, perhaps Fleury). https://primarysources.
    brillonline.com/browse/vossiani-latini/vlq-086-arator-
    prosper-sedulius-pstertullianus-cato-avianus-anthologia-
    latina-martialis-avitus-isidorus.

20. Berlin. Staatsbibliothek Preussischer Kulturbesitz, lat. Fol.
    641 (fols. 17–257) (mid-9th century, northern Italy).[71]

21. Paris. Bibliothèque nationale de France, lat. 7671 (mid-
    9th century, northeastern France). https://gallica.bnf.fr/
    ark:/12148/btv1b10037019f.

22. Chartres. Bibliothèque municipale, MS 92 (fols. 1–80) (9th
    century, France).

23. St. Gallen. Stiftsbibliothek, MS 882 (9th century, ¾, St. Gal-
    len). http://www.e-codices.unifr.ch/en/list/one/csg/0882.

24. Oxford. Bodleian Library, Auct. T 2.20 (9th century, ¾,
    Auxerre or perhaps Bourges). https://digital.bodleian.ox.ac.
    uk/inquire/p/24fc7bf8-3dab-4f15-947f-c1ab2756ca50.

25. Bologna. Biblioteca Universitaria, MS 797 (9th century, ¾,
    the area of Reims).

26. Fulda. Hochschul- und Landesbibliothek, MS Aa 2 (10th
    century, Bodensee area). https://fuldig.hs-fulda.de/viewer/
    image/PPN31018939X/245/.

27. London. British Library, Harley 2713 (fols. 1–34) (9th
    century, ⁴⁄₄, northeastern France). http://www.bl.uk/cata-

---

71 Grammatical texts including sections of the first book of the *Etymologies* are
    copied on fols. 214ᵛ–254ʳ.

logues/illuminatedmanuscripts/record.asp?MSID=3870&C
ollID=8&NStart=2713.
28. Leiden. Universiteitsbibliotheek, Voss. lat. O 41 (fols.
2–65) (9th century, ⁴⁄₄, northeastern France). https://pri-
marysources.brillonline.com/browse/vossiani-latini/vlo-
041-eutyches-grammaticalia-isidorus-alphabeta.
29. Leiden. Universiteitsbibliotheek, BPL 122 (9th century, ⁴⁄₄,
Lyons). http://hdl.handle.net/1887.1/item:847608.
30. Oxford. Bodleian Library, Add. C 144 (11th century, in.,
central Italy).
31. Troyes. Bibliothèque municipale, MS 1328 (12th century,
Clairvaux). https://portail.mediatheque.grand-troyes.fr/
iguana/www.main.cls?surl=search&p=*#recordId=2.2119.
32. Douai. Bibliothèque municipale, MS 748 (12th century, ex.,
prov.: Anchin). http://bvmm.irht.cnrs.fr/consult/consult.
php?mode=ecran&panier=false&reproductionId=11236&V
UE_ID=1309173&carouselThere=false&nbVignettes=4x3&
page=1&angle=0&zoom=grand&tailleReelle=.
33. Oxford. Bodleian Library, Laud Bibl. Misc. 8 (13th century).

b. Manuscripts containing glosses to De notis *(Etym., I.21–26)*

Frankish group
1. Oxford. Bodleian Library, Junius 25 (fols. 134–51) (9th
century, southwestern Germany?, prov. Murbach). https://
digital.bodleian.ox.ac.uk/inquire/p/451e88c8-39b6-4cbc-
8483-c64b290ea00e.
2. Reims. Bibliothèque municipale, MS 426 (9th century, ¼,
Reims). https://gallica.bnf.fr/ark:/12148/btv1b8449011r.
3. Orléans. Bibliothèque municipale, MS 296 (pp. 1–32)
(9th century, ¼, area of Paris?, Fleury?). https://medi-
atheques.orleans-metropole.fr/ark:/77916/FRCGMBPF-
452346101-01A/D18012265.locale=fr.
4. London. British Library, Harley 3941 (9th/10th century,
²⁄₂, Brittany). http://www.bl.uk/manuscripts/FullDisplay.
aspx?ref=Harley_MS_3941.

5. Leiden. Universiteitsbibliotheek, Voss. lat. O 41 (9th century, ¼, northeastern France). https://primarysources. brillonline.com/browse/vossiani-latini/vlo-041-eutyches-grammaticalia-isidorus-alphabeta.
6. Oxford. Queen's College, MS 320 (10th century, mid. or ¾, England).

Franco-English group
1. Paris. Bibliothèque nationale de France, lat. 11278 (9th century, ½, southeastern France or northern Italy). https:// gallica.bnf.fr/ark:/12148/btv1b100358546.
2. London. British Library, Cotton Caligula A xv (c. 743, northeastern France). http://www.bl.uk/manuscripts/Full-Display.aspx?ref=Cotton_MS_Caligula_A_XV.
3. Paris. Bibliothèque nationale de France, lat. 7585 (9th century, ²⁄₄, St. Bertin?, and 10th century, ²⁄₂, England). https:// gallica.bnf.fr/ark:/12148/btv1b10542288m.
4. London. British Library, Harley 3941 (9th/10th century, ²⁄₂, Brittany). http://www.bl.uk/manuscripts/FullDisplay. aspx?ref=Harley_MS_3941.

Italian group
1. Cesena. Biblioteca Malatesiana, S.XXI.5 (9th century, ⅓, the Po valley). http://catalogoaperto.malatestiana.it/ ricerca/?oldform=mostra_codice.jsp?CODICE_ID=276.
2. Venice. Biblioteca Nazionale di S. Marco, II 46 (11th/12th century, northeastern Italy).

c. Manuscripts of the St. Gallen redaction

1. Zofingen. Stadtbibliothek, Pa 32 (9th century, ⅔, St. Gallen). https://www.e-codices.unifr.ch/en/zos/pa0032.
2. Einsiedeln. Stiftsbibliothek, MS 167 (970–990, Einsiedeln).
3. Wolfenbüttel. Herzog August Bibliothek, Weiss. 2 (11th century, Wissembourg). http://diglib.hab.de/mss/2-weiss/ start.htm.

4. Einsiedeln. Stiftsbibliothek, MS 360 (1143–1178, Engelberg). https://www.e-codices.unifr.ch/en/searchresult/list/one/ sbe/0360.

5. London. British Library, Harley 2660 (ca. 1136, western Germany). http://www.bl.uk/manuscripts/FullDisplay. aspx?ref=Harley_MS_2660.

6. Leiden. Universiteitsbibliotheek, PER F 2 (12th century, ½, Germany). http://hdl.handle.net/1887.1/item:2708985.

7. Bonn. Universitäts- und Landesbibliothek, S 193 (12th century, ⅓, Altenberg). http://www.manuscripta-mediaevalia. de/dokumente/html/obj31275205.

8. Heidelberg. Universitätsbibliothek, Sal. IX 39 (12th century, ex., Salem). https://digi.ub.uni-heidelberg.de/diglit/sa-lIX39.

9. London. British Library, Harley 3035 (ca. 1496, western Germany, perhaps Eberhardsklausen). https://www.bl.uk/ catalogues/illuminatedmanuscripts/record.asp?MSID=406 2&CollID=8&NStart=3035.

Bibliography

Primary & Reference

Bierbrauer, Katharina. *Die vorkarolingischen und karolingischen Handschriften der Bayerischen Staatsbibliothek. Katalog der illuminierten Handschriften der Bayerischen Staatsbibliothek in München* 1. Munich: Reichert, 1990.

Bischoff, Bernhard. *Katalog der festländischen Handschriften des neunten Jahrhunderts (mit Ausnahme der wisigotischen)*, Vol. 1: *Aachen-Lambach*. Edited by Birgit Ebersperger. Veröffentlichungen der Kommission für die Herausgabe der mittelalterlichen Bibliothekskataloge Deutschlands und der Schweiz. Wiesbaden: Harrassowitz, 1998.

Bretscher-Gisiger, Charlotte, and Rudolf Gamper. *Katalog der mittelalterlichen Handschriften des Klosters Wettingen: Katalog der mittelalterlichen Handschriften in Aarau, Laufenburg, Lenzburg, Rheinfelden und Zofingen*. Zurich: Urs Graf, 2009.

Die Admonitio generalis Karls des Großen. Edited by Hubert Mordek, Klaus Zechiel-Eckes, and Michael Glatthaar. Monumenta Germaniae Historica, Fontes iuris germanici antiqui in usum scholarum separatim editi 16. Wiesbaden: Harrassowitz, 2013.

Fernández Catón, José María. *Las "Etimologías" en la tradición manuscrita medieval estudiada por el Prof. Dr. Anspach*. León: centro de estudios e investigacion San Isidoro, 1966.

Isidore of Seville. *Etymologies*. Edited by Wallace M. Lindsay. *"Etymologiarum" sive "Originum" libri XX*. 2 Volumes. Oxford: Clarendon Press, 1911. Book 1: Edited and translated by Olga Spevak. *Isidore de Séville, "Étymologies." Livre I. La grammaire*. Auteurs latins du Moyen Âge 31. Paris: Les Belles Lettres, 2020.

Isidorus Hispalensis. *De responsione mundi (De natura rerum)*. Augsburg: Günther Zainer, 7.XII.1472 (H 9302, Klebs 537.1).

Kendall, Calvin B., and Faith Wallis, trans. *Isidore of Seville, "On the Nature of Things."* Translated Texts for Historians 66. Liverpool: Liverpool University Press, 2016. DOI: 10.3828/978-1-78138-293-6.

Lehmann, Paul. *Mittelalterliche Bibliothekskataloge Deutsch-lands und der Schweiz.* Vol. 1. Munich: Beck, 1969.

Secondary

Anspach, August Eduard. "Das Fortleben Isidors im VII. bis IX. Jahrhundert." In *Miscellanea Isidoriana,* 322–56. Rome: Universita Gregoriana, 1936.

Archibald, Elizabeth. "Methods and Meaning of Basic Education in Carolingian Europe." PhD diss., Yale University, 2010.

Beeson, Charles Henry. *Isidor-Studien.* Quellen und Untersuchungen zur lateinischen Philologie des Mittelalters 4, no. 2. Munich: Beck, 1913.

Bellettini, Anna. "Il codice del sec. IX di Cesena, Malatestiano S. XXI.5: Le *Etymologiae* di Isidoro, testi minori e glosse di età ottoniana." *Italia medioevale e umanistica* 45 (2004): 49–114.

Bischoff, Bernhard. "Die europäische Verbreitung der Werke Isidors von Sevilla." In *Isidoriana: Collección de estudios sobre Isidore de Sevilla,* edited by Manuel C. Díaz y Díaz, 317–44. León: Centro de estudios San Isidoro, 1961.

———. *Latin Palaeography: Antiquity and the Middle Ages.* Translated by Dáibhí O'Cróinín and David Ganz. Cambridge: Cambridge University Press, 1990. DOI: 10.1017/CBO9780511809927.

———. "Libraries and Schools in the Carolingian Revival of Learning." In *Manuscripts and Libraries in the Age of Charlemagne,* edited and translated by Michael Gorman, 93–114. Cambridge Studies in Palaeography and Codicology. Cambridge: Cambridge University Press, 1994.

Bishop, T.A.M. *English Caroline Minuscule.* Oxford Palaeographical Handbooks. Oxford: Clarendon Press, 1971.

Büren, Veronika von. "La place du manuscrit Ambr. L 99 sup. dans la transmission des *Étymologies* d'Isidore de Séville." In *Nuove ricerche su codici in scrittura latina dell'Ambrosiana,* edited by Mirella Ferrari and Marco Navoni, 25–44. Milan: Vita e Pensiero, 2007.

Cardelle de Hartmann, Carmen. "Uso y recepción de las *Etymologiae* de Isidoro." In *Wisigothica: After M.C. Díaz y Díaz,*

edited by Carmen Codoñer Merino and Paulo Farmhouse
Alberto, 477–502. mediEVI 3. Florence: SISMEL, 2014.

Carley, James P., and Ann Dooley. "An Early Irish Fragment
of Isidore of Seville's *Etymologiae*." In *The Archaeology and
History of Glastonbury Abbey: Essays in Honour of the 90th
Birthday of C.A. Ralegh Radford,* edited by Lesley J. Abrams
and James Patrick Carley, 135–61. Woodbridge: Boydell, 1991.

Codoñer Merino, Carmen. "Fases en la edición de las *Etymologiae,* con especial referencia al libro X." *Euphrosyne* 22 (1994):
125–46.

———. "Historia del texto de las Etimologías isidorianas." In
*Actas del III Congreso Hispánico de Latín Medieval (León, 26–
29 de Septiembre de 2002),* edited by Maurilio Pérez González,
vol. 2, 483–94. León: Universidad de León, 2002.

———. "Textes médicaux insérés dans les *Etymologiae* isidoriennes." In *La réception d'Isidore de Séville durant le Moyen
âge tardif (XIIᵉ–XVᵉ s.),* edited by Jacques Elfassi and Bernard
Ribémont, 17–38. Cahiers de Recherches Médiévales 16. Orléans: CNRS, 2008. DOI: 10.4000/crm.10452.

———. "Transmisión y recepción de las *Etimologías*." In *Estudios de latín medieval hispánico. Actas del V Congreso Internacional de Latín Medieval Hispánico,* edited by José Martínez Gázquez, Óscar de la Cruz Palma, and Cándida Ferrero
Hernández, 5–26. Florence: SISMEL – Edizioni del Galluzzo,
2011.

Codoñer Merino, Carmen, José Carlos Martin, and Adelaida
Andres. "Isidorus Hispalensis ep." In *La trasmissione dei testi
latini del Medioevo/Medieval Texts and Their Transmission,*
edited by Paulo Chiesa and Lucia Castaldi, vol. 2, 274–417.
Florence: SISMEL – Edizioni del Galluzzo, 2005.

Contreni, John J. "The Pursuit of Knowledge in Carolingian Europe." In *The Gentle Voices of Teachers: Aspects of Learning
in the Carolingian Age,* edited by Richard Sullivan, 106–41.
Columbus: Ohio University Press, 1995.

Curtius, Ernst Robert. *European Literature and the Latin Middle
Ages.* Translated by Willard R. Trask. Bollingen Series 36.
Princeton: Princeton University Press, 1953.

Díaz y Díaz, Manuel C. *Los capítulos sobre los metales en las "Etimologías" de Isidoro de Sevilla*. La minería hispana a iberoamericana 7. Léon: Catedra de San Isidoro, 1970.

Euw, Anton von. "Die Einsiedler Buchmalerei zur Zeit des Abtes Gregor (964–996)." In *Festschrift zum tausendsten Todestag des seligen Abtes Gregor,* edited by Odo Lang, 183–241. Studien und Mitteilungen zur Geschichte des Benediktinerordens und seiner Zweige 107. Sankt Ottilien: Editions Sankt Ottilien, 1996.

Fleuriot, Léon. "Gloses inédites en vieux-Breton." *Études Celtiques* 16 (1979): 197–210. DOI: 10.3406/ecelt.1979.1628.

Fontaine, Jacques. *Isidore de Séville et la culture classique dans l'Espagne wisigothique*. 2nd Edition. Paris: Études augustiniennes, 1983.

———. "La diffusion de l'oeuvre d'Isidore de Séville dans les scriptoria helvétiques du haut Moyen Âge." *Schweizerische Zeitschrift für Geschichte* 12 (1962): 305–22.

Geuenich, Dieter. "Beobachtungen zu Grimald von St. Gallen, Erzkapellan und Oberkanzler Ludwigs des Deutschen." In *Litterae medii aevi. Festschrift für Johanne Autenrieth zu ihrem 65. Geburtstag,* edited by Michael Borgolte and Herrad Spilling, 55–68. Sigmaringen: Thorbecke, 1988.

Hagen, Hermann. "De Isidoro grammatico." In *Grammatici latini. Supplementum,* edited by Heinrich Keil. Vol. 8. Leipzig: Teubner, 1870.

Hillgarth, Jocelyn N. "Ireland and Spain in the Seventh Century." *Peritia* 3 (1984): 1–16. DOI: 10.1484/J.Peri.3.54.

———. "The East, Visigothic Spain and the Irish." *Studia Patristica* 4 (1961): 442–56.

———. "Visigothic Spain and Early Christian Ireland." *Proceedings of the Royal Irish Academy C* 62 (1962): 167–94.

———. *Visigothic Spain, Byzantium, and the Irish.* London: Variorum, 1985.

Holtz, Louis. *Donat et la tradition de l'enseignement grammatical: Étude sur l'Ars Donati et sa diffusion (IV.–IX. siècle)* et édition critique. Paris: CNRS, 1981.

————. "Le 'De grammatica' des *Étymologies* d'Isidore de Séville, structure générale et traitement des sources." In *IV Congreso Internacional de latim medieval hispânico,* edited by Paulo Farmhouse Alberto and Aires Augusto Nascimento, 55–68. Lisbon: Centro de Estudos Clássicos, 2006.

————. "Le dialogue de Franco et de Saxo." *Annales de Bretagne et des Pays de l'Ouest. Anjou. Maine. Poitou-Charente. Touraine* 111, no. 13 (2004): 135–45. DOI: 10.4000/abpo.1229.

Huglo, Michel. "The *Musica Isidori* Tradition in the Iberian Peninsula." In *Hispania Vetus: Musical-Liturgical Manuscripts from Visigothic Origins to the Franco-Roman Transition (9th–12th Centuries),* edited by Susana Zapke, 61–92. Bilbao: Fundacion BBVA, 2007.

Kaczynski, Bernice M. "The Authority of the Fathers: Patristic Texts in Early Medieval Libraries and Scriptoria." *Journal of Medieval Latin* 16 (2006): 1–27. DOI: 10.1484/J.JML.2.303227.

Lapidge, Michael, and Peter Stuart Baker. *Byrhtferth's Enchiridion.* Oxford: Oxford University Press, 1995.

Law, Vivien A. *The Insular Latin Grammarians.* Studies in Celtic History 3. Woodbridge: Boydell Press, 1987.

————. "The Transmission of Early Medieval Elementary Grammars: A Case Study in Explanation." In *Formative Stages of Classical Traditions: Latin Texts from Antiquity to the Renaissance; Proceedings of a Conference Held at Erice, 16–22 October 1993, as the 6th Course of International School for the Study of Written Records,* edited by Oronzo Pecere and Michael D. Reeve, 239–61. Biblioteca Del Centro per Il Collegamento Degli Studi Medievali e Umanistici in Umbria 15. Spoleto: Centro Italiano di studi sull'alto medioevo, 1995.

Lindsay, Wallace M. "The Editing of Isidore *Etymologiae*." *The Classical Quarterly* 5 (1911): 42–53. DOI: 10.1017/S0009838800019273.

Manitius, Max. *Geschichte der lateinischen Literatur des Mittelalters.* Vol. 1. Munich: Beck, 1911.

Mostert, Marco. "Relations between Fleury and England." In *England and the Continent in the Tenth Century: Studies in*

Honor of Wilhelm Levison (1876–1947), edited by David Rollason, Conrad Leyser, and Hannah Williams, 185–208. Studies in the Early Middle Ages 37. Turnhout: Brepols, 2010. DOI: 10.1484/M.SEM-EB.3.4698.

Parkes, Malcolm B. *Pause and Effect: An Introduction to the History of Punctuation in the West.* Aldershot: Scolar, 1992.

Pollard, Richard M., and Anne-Gaëlle Weber. "Le canon des Pères à l'époque carolingienne et la place de Flavius Josèphe." *Revue d'Études Augustiniennes et Patristiques* 67, no. 2 (2021): 275–318. DOI: 10.1484/J.REA.5.131239.

Porzig, Walter. "Die Rezensionen der *Etymologiae* des Isidorus von Sevilla. Vorbemerkung." *Hermes* 72, no. 2 (1937): 129–70.

Rand, Edward K. "A Vade Mecum of Liberal Culture in a Manuscript of Fleury." *Philological Quarterly* 1 (1922): 258–77.

Reydellet, Marc. "La diffusion des *Origines* d'Isidore de Séville au Haut Moyen Âge." *Mélanges d'archéologie et d'histoire* 78, no. 2 (1966): 383–437. DOI: 10.3406/mefr.1966.7523.

Schiegg, Markus. *Frühmittelalterliche Glossen: Ein Beitrag zur Funktionalität und Kontextualität mittelalterlicher Schriftlichkeit.* Germanistische Bibliothek 52. Heidelberg: Universitätsverlag Winter, 2015.

Schindel, Ulrich. "Zur frühen Überlieferungsgeschichte der *Etymologiae* Isidors von Sevilla." *Studi medievali* 29, no. 2 (1988): 587–605.

Smyth, Marina. "Isidorian Texts in Seventh-Century Ireland." In *Isidore of Seville and His Reception in the Early Middle Ages,* edited by Andrew Fear and Jamie Wood, 111–30. Amsterdam: Amsterdam University Press, 2016. DOI: 10.1017/9789048526765.007.

Spevak, Olga. "Les additions dans Isid. *Etym.* I: Témoins d'un travail rédactionnel." *Archivum Latinitatis Medii Aevi* 75 (2017): 59–88.

Steinmann, Martin. "Abt Frowin von Engelberg (1143–1178) und seine Handschriften." *Der Geschichtsfreund* 146 (1993): 7–36.

Steinová, Evina. "Annotation of the *Etymologiae* of Isidore of Seville in Its Early Medieval Context." *Archivum Latinitatis Medii Aevi* 78 (2020): 5–81. DOI: 10.17613/m6k5-5622.

———. "*Notam Superponere Studui*: The Use of Technical Signs in the Early Middle Ages." PhD diss., Utrecht University, 2016.

———. "Parallel Glosses, Shared Glosses, and Gloss Clustering: Can Network-Based Approach Help Us to Understand Organic Corpora of Glosses?" *Journal of Historical Network Research* 7 (forthcoming, 2023).

———. "The Materiality of Innovation: Formats and Dimensions of the *Etymologiae* of Isidore of Seville in the Early Middle Ages." In *The Art of Compilation: Manuscripts and Networks in the Early Medieval Latin West,* edited by Anna Dorofeeva and Michael J. Kelly. Earth: punctum books, forthcoming.

———. "The Oldest Manuscript Tradition of the *Etymologiae* (Eighty Years after A.E. Anspach)." *Visigothic Symposia* 4 (2020): 100–143.

———. "Two Carolingian Redactions of the *Etymologiae* from St. Gallen." *Mittellateinisches Jahrbuch* 56, no. 2 (2021): 298–376.

Steinová, Evina, and Peter Boot. *The Glosses to the First Book of the "Etymologiae" of Isidore of Seville: A Digital Scholarly Edition.* Hosted by Huygens ING, KNAW. 2021. https://db.innovatingknowledge.nl/edition/#left-intro.

Van den Abeele, Baudouin. "La tradition manuscrite des Étymologies d'Isidore de Séville." *Cahiers de Recherches Médiévales et Humanistes* 16 (2008): 195–205. DOI: 10.4000/crm.10822.

Contributors

Elizabeth P. Archibald is a lecturer in the Department of History of the University of Pittsburgh. She holds a PhD in History from Yale University, and her research focuses on the history of education and literacy in early medieval Europe. She has published on topics including school texts in the medieval curriculum, women's book ownership, and the use of dialogues in early pedagogy. She is co-editor of *Learning Me Your Language: Latin and Greek as Second Languages from Antiquity to the Present Day* (Cambridge: Cambridge University Press, 2015).

Ksenia Bonch Reeves is Professor of Spanish and Chair of the Department of Modern Languages at Wright State University. She the author of *Visions of Unity after the Visigoths: Early Iberian Latin Chronicles and the Mediterranean World* (Turnhout: Brepols, 2016) and has published semi-paleographic editions of Old Castilian chronicles and legal texts. Her research interests include Medieval Iberian chronicle writing, Iberian Latin culture, law and literature, travel narratives, and the transition from Medieval to Renaissance culture with a particular focus on Spanish mysticism.

K. Patrick Fazioli is an Associate Professor in the Department of Humanities and Co-Director of the Global Honors Program at

Mercy College (NY). An anthropological archaeologist focusing on the late antique and early medieval eastern Alpine region, he is the author of *The Mirror of the Medieval: An Anthropology of the Western Historical Imagination* (New York: Berghahn Books, 2017).

Yitzhak Hen is Professor of Late Antique and Early Medieval History at The Hebrew University of Jerusalem, and the Director of the Israel Institute for Advanced Studies.

Michael J. Kelly lectures history, critical theory, and the philosophy of history at Binghamton University (SUNY) and is Director of Networks and Neighbours. His publications include *Isidore of Seville and the "Liber Iudiciorum": The Struggle for the Past in the Visigothic Kingdom,* The Medieval and Early Modern Iberian World 80 (Boston and Leiden: Brill, 2021), and the co-edited volume *Theories of History: History Read across the Humanities* (London: Bloomsbury, 2018). He is currently preparing a monograph on the concept of in/humanity in early medieval theology.

Sven Meeder is lecturer in Medieval History at the Radboud University. He currently leads the project "A Living Law: Minor Canonical Collections in the Carolingian Period" (funded by the Gerda Henkel Foundation) and was project leader of "Networks of Knowledge: The Spread of Scholarship in the Carolingian Era" (2013–2017, funded by the Dutch Research Council).

Edward M. Schoolman teaches at the University of Nevada, Reno, where he focuses on the late antique and early medieval Mediterranean. He published a monograph, *Rediscovering Sainthood in Italy: Hagiography and the Late Antique Past in Medieval Ravenna* (New York: Palgrave Macmillan, 2016), and is currently working on new book project on Greek identity; as part of an interdisciplinary team, his research extends into the interconnections between history and ecology in Italy.

Evina Steinová is a postdoctoral researcher at the Huygens Institute in Amsterdam. Her research centers on early medieval intellectual life, early medieval manuscripts and written culture, and on the diffusion of innovations during the Carolingian period. She is keenly interested in applying digital and statistical methods to traditional humanities subjects. Evina received her PhD in Medieval Studies from Utrecht University. Her most recent book, *Notam superponere studui: The Use of Annotation Symbols in the Early Middle Ages* (Turnhout: Brepols, 2019), maps the landscape of annotation symbols used in the early medieval Latin West.

Index

Made in the USA
Middletown, DE
28 May 2023

31609063R00139